NEVER LOST

Mary Keenan

Copyright © 2026 **Mary's Testimony, LLC**. All rights reserved.
First Edition, 2026

NIV: Scripture quotations taken from the Holy Bible, New International Version® NIV®. Copyright © 1973, 1978, 1984, 2011 by Biblica, Inc.™ Used by permission. All rights reserved worldwide.

NLT: Scripture quotations are taken from the Holy Bible, New Living Translation, copyright ©1996, 2004, 2015 by Tyndale House Foundation. Used by permission of Tyndale House Publishers, Carol Stream, Illinois 60188. All rights reserved.

AMPC: Scripture taken from the Amplified Bible, Classic Edition (AMPC), Copyright © 1954, 1958, 1962, 1964, 1965, 1987 by The Lockman Foundation. Used by permission. www.Lockman.org

NKJV: Scripture taken from the New King James Version®. Copyright © 1982 by Thomas Nelson. Used by permission. All rights reserved.

AMP: Scripture quotations taken from the Amplified® Bible (AMP), Copyright © 2015 by The Lockman Foundation. Used by permission. www.Lockman.org

TLB: Scripture quotations marked (TLB) are taken from The Living Bible copyright © 1971. Used by permission of Tyndale House Publishers, Carol Stream, Illinois 60188. All rights reserved.

ESV: Scripture quotations are from the ESV® Bible (The Holy Bible, English Standard Version®), copyright © 2001 by Crossway, a publishing ministry of Good News Publishers. Used by permission. All rights reserved.

NASB: Scripture taken from the NEW AMERICAN STANDARD BIBLE®, Copyright © 1960,1962,1963,1968,1971,1972,1973,1975,1977,1995 by The Lockman Foundation. Used by permission.

ISBN 979-8-9944294-1-9 (Hardcover)
ISBN 979-8-9944294-0-2 (Paperback)
ISBN 979-8-9944294-3-3 (Paperback)
ISBN 979-8-9944294-2-6 (E-Book)

For updates and future releases, visit MarysTestimony.com

To my sons.

I love you and thank God for you.

From the Author

It is my understanding that the U.S. government is unable to assist women and children who are trying to escape an Islamic (Sharia) law country—but God.

There are no words to adequately describe how grateful I am to the Lord for everything he's done. I'll never know what the back story was, or just how he managed it. All I know is that he did. He has proven to me many times over that he is truly the God who comes through for anyone who calls on his name, cries out for mercy, and holds fast to his promises.

This book is a true account. However, out of respect for and protection of those involved, the names of individuals and certain locations have been changed.

The writing of this testimony would not have been possible without the aid of the Holy Spirit who was faithful to help me every day when I asked. The pain that a parent experiences from the abduction, separation, or alienation of a child is profound. Reliving it was difficult, but God was with me throughout and provided healing in the process.

To those who prayed for us, made phone calls to public officials and international attorneys on our behalf, provided a hot meal, a much-needed hug, or even a chair for me to work in your salon—I am eternally grateful. Your kindness was a great comfort to me and surely did not go unnoticed by the Lord. And to my English professor clients who encouraged me in the years-long writing process: you brought new meaning to divine appointments.

This is a story I knew needed to be told. However, I often felt that I was late in telling it. Some say it is too controversial for the tumultuous times we now find ourselves in. But I believe God's timing is perfect. Jesus, himself, reprimanded the people for not knowing the season they were in:

He replied, "When evening comes, you say, 'It will be fair weather, for the sky is red,' and in the morning, 'Today it will be stormy, for the sky is red and overcast.' You know how to interpret the appearance of the sky, but you cannot interpret the signs of the times. Matthew 16:2-3 NIV

It is my conviction that if I had waited for a more convenient time to tell this story, I would have missed the mark. I believe we are in a season when it is imperative that as believers we answer the call of God on our lives to fearlessly "demolish arguments and every pretension that sets itself up against the knowledge of God" (2 Corinthians 10:5 NIV). And the word assures us:

" ...they overcame and conquered him because of the blood of the Lamb and because of the word of their testimony, for they did not love their life and renounce their faith even when faced with death." Rev. 12:11 AMP

What does all this have to do with my memoir? Read on.

But first, to my dear friend Gina: your husband Jev said it best, "When these two women come together to accomplish a mission, they are a force to be reckoned with." You and I had no idea what God was getting ready to do when we called on his name in desperation to bring Lilah home more than twenty years ago. And to this day, we are both still in awe.

Now to him who is able to do *IMMEASURABLY MORE* than all we ask or (even) imagine... to him be all the glory. (Adapted from Ephesians 3:20-21)

CONTENTS

1. A Season's Change 1
2. The Things We Leave Behind 19
3. Red Sky at Morn 27
4. Stop Overthinking 37
5. Just another Day 43
6. Plan A 55
7. All True 61
8. Clarity 69
9. Jerusalem Bound 73
10. The Holy Land 79
11. Hummus and Falafel 85
12. Damascus Gate 95
13. Promises, Promises... 105
14. Into Jordan 111
15. Stage One - Act Two 121
16. Maybe Next Time 135
17. Judgment at Work 143
18. Christmas in the Middle East 151

1. Custom-Made Cages 161
2. September 11, 2001 173
3. A Reprieve 189
4. Engagement 201
5. Ashes on the Alter - A Poetic Affirmation 211
6. A Dark Proposal 215
7. Show Me the Way I Should Go 223
8. And a Little Child Will Lead Them 233
9. Don't Forget to Breathe 243
10. Narrow is the Gate 255
11. Break of Day 269
12. Nice Try 279
13. The Hills Are Alive - Jabal Linum 291
14. Word 303
15. High-Level Talks 313
16. The God of Promise 323
17. The Trees of the Field 335
18. Who Is This Coming Up From the Wilderness? 341

Based on Qur'an 33:33,
Sharia law gives husbands legal authority
to confine their wives to their homes.

"And abide in your houses and do not display yourselves as (was) the display of the former times of ignorance."
Qur'an 33:33 Sahih International

Chapter 1

A SEASON'S CHANGE

Nahaven, South Givenia was experiencing a false spring. The unseasonably mild temperatures were the kind that lured us into believing winter was finally over. The hardwood trees stood firmly set and largely unnoticed in the background, patiently biding their time. Their unwavering resolve to see each winter through drove their roots deeper and made them more resilient. Brown and still bare of any visible new growth, their unadorned branches testified that true spring was still weeks away. Unassuming, they silently watched as we were fooled once again by another warm-weather tease.

As I ran to my car, the adage "fool me once, shame on you; fool me twice, shame on me" played as a reminder in my mind, so I ran back into the house and grabbed my blazer. It would be dark and chilly by the time I left the salon that night, and the idea of a cold ride home from work did not appeal to me. Under normal conditions, I may have felt clever for thinking of it. But clever was the last thing I was feeling.

On the drive to work, my mind went back to the day when I made the decision to marry Kashan. It had been months since I'd seen him.

Realizing the complications that a marriage to Kashan would bring. I told him time and time again to stay away. One of the major obstacles between us was our polar opposite ideologies.

He had tried to convince me that Christianity and Islam were similar. But I believed they were different to the very core. Not that he was a practicing Muslim. Not that I could tell, anyway.

So I had willed myself to stay away from him. And although I had purposely refrained from seeing him, I was in love with him and had been for years. Not a day went by that I didn't miss seeing him. But I consoled myself with the thought that he was close by, loving me, and wanting to be with me.

> The human heart is the most deceitful of all things…
> Jeremiah 17:9 NLT

Then one afternoon, there he was at my door telling me goodbye, that he was leaving the States forever. He had to return to the Middle East and wouldn't come back to the States since his student visa had expired.

I realized right then that I was utterly incapable of letting Kashan go. I had been fooling myself to imagine I could ever be apart from him. My heart shattered at the thought of never seeing him again—it was more than I could bear. And at that moment in time, I was willing to do anything to rectify the situation.

"Okay, okay, I'll marry you!" I cried.

He came close and looked into my eyes, as if unsure he had heard correctly. "I thought... I thought you..."

"Kashan, I'll marry you. Please don't leave me!"

"You tell me this now?" He grabbed onto my shoulders firmly, almost shaking me. "Mary, I've tried to convince you for years to marry me. I've dreamed of you belonging to me and me alone. I asked you so many times and you always said no to me! But now you are saying yes? When I have to leave, you tell me yes?" He shook his head. "What can I do? Now it's too late."

"I'm sorry. I'm so sorry. Please don't leave me, Kashan." "I love you—I have always loved you," I sobbed.

He wiped my tears gently with his hands. "How can I leave you, ya hayati [my life]?" Then, kissing my flushed cheeks, he promised he would figure out how we could be married so we would never be apart from each other again.

"Really?" I asked, wanting desperately to believe him. "So, you're not leaving me?"

"Of course, I'm not leaving you. Are you crazy?" He pulled me into his arms. "I love you!"

Then, after some thought, he said, "Listen Sweetheart, you will come to Jordan with me."

"What?" I could barely believe what I was hearing. "I will? You want me to go to Jordan with you?"

"Yes, Mary. It's the only way we can get married. That way, I can be completely sure we will be able to remain together. We will get married in Jordan and then get my papers processed at the U.S. Embassy there in Amman... to satisfy immigration requirements, I mean. Then we will return to the States together."

"So... I'm going to Jordan with you?" I asked, still unsure.

He took hold of my hands and looked in my eyes. "Yes, habibti [my love]. This is the only way. But my parents will not agree to our marriage." "So, we have to keep it a secret until it's done," he added.

At the time, I failed to realize the full impact that reckless decision would have on our lives, the loss it would cause, and the devastation it would bring. Seven years had passed since that summer day in '93. They were difficult ones, but they had grounded me and made me stronger. God had been faithful to see me through.

Tears of gratefulness welled up in my eyes. I grabbed some napkins from the glove compartment and quickly caught the tears before they ran down my face and ruined my makeup. It didn't take much for me to cry whenever I thought about God. Turns out it was his love I was looking for all along.

☙◊❧◊

Gina Weatherington was in the salon receiving her seven-week highlight touch-up. I meticulously weaved out small sections of Gina's dark blonde hair and carefully held a foil strip in place underneath. Once bleach lightener was applied to the strands, I folded the foil neatly, then moved on to the next section. It was something I had done thousands of times over the last fifteen years.

Fortunately, the exactitude of the process kept me focused and ensured I was never bored. A beautiful result was my goal and, if achieved, a satisfied client my reward. Even though my earnings fluctuated along with the economy, I could not imagine having a more fulfilling career.

Gina and I first met over three years prior when my daughter began attending the childcare center where Gina was director. I had only been living in Nahaven for one year at the time. A single mother then, I had recently separated from my husband, Kashan. Lilah was just eighteen months old and I was anxious about leaving her to return to work. But I found Gina's professionalism and concern for the well-being of children reassuring during that season of new beginnings.

Lilah, now five years old, sat on one of the styling chairs in the salon. She was so busy playing with her Powerpuff Girl dolls that she didn't notice who my client was. When she finally realized it was Gina, she lit up.

"Ms. Gina!" Lilah ran over for a hug.

Gina's eyebrows shot up in surprise. "Hey, Lilah. It's so good to see you, hun." Gina reached out to embrace her.

After Lilah returned to her dolls, Gina asked, "Why is Lilah here at the salon, Mary?" "Isn't her daddy keeping her at home while you're working?"

"Well, not anymore," I stated flatly. "He can't wake up in the morning to take care of her because he stays up all night."

"What is he doing all night?" she asked.

"You don't want to know," I whispered into her ear.

"What?" She turned the styling chair around to face me as she grasped the seriousness of the situation.

Realizing with some regret that I had already said too much, I paused for a moment before giving a response. Up to this point, I had not fully disclosed to anyone just how bad my predicament was.

It had only been a year since I suffered the heartbreak of my mom passing away unexpectedly. Shortly after that, the small church I was attending dissolved. In the meantime, I was working hard to build my salon business while bearing up under an absolute mockery of a marriage. When I compared my marriage to Kashan with my parents' loving 49 years together, it felt like just another layer of heartache and disappointment.

The embarrassment of the reprehensible circumstances I was living in being brought to light was something I wanted to avoid. Besides, I didn't want to disappoint my church friends who were still hoping for a happily-ever-after outcome for Kashan and me. But with Gina, it felt different somehow. Interaction between Gina and Kashan had been limited up to that point. That meant she had not been taken in by his charm the way some of the others had. And I found Gina to be a woman of integrity: one who adhered to Godly beliefs and acknowledged the sanctity of marriage. She never came across as judgmental, though, so I felt comfortable confiding in her.

"Mary, tell me," she said as she looked directly in my eyes with concern, "is your marriage in trouble?"

Before answering Gina's question, I glanced over at the styling station where Lilah sat. She was still busy playing and oblivious to anything else.

"Lilah, honey, why don't you take your dolls to the front desk?" I suggested, "You can sit there and let me know when the phone rings."

Excited to play receptionist, Lilah scurried to the front desk while Gina continued to look at me expectantly. Once I saw Lilah was settled, I began to explain to Gina what was going on at home.

"Things are bad, Gina. Sometimes Kashan doesn't come home until two or three o'clock in the morning."

With an incredulous expression, I tilted my head toward her, then paused, allowing my statement to sink in. Gina gasped in disbelief.

"He nonchalantly walks in the door offering no explanation at all," I continued with indignation.

"Oh my goodness, that's terrible," her face showed genuine concern.

"He never says a civil word to me, either. He just mumbles obscenities in Arabic like he's miserable all the time—as if I'm the one responsible for his misery. It's horrible." "And…" I continued with a sigh, "he's cheating on me again."

"Again? Wow." Gina paused for a moment as if in thought. Then eventually, it occurred to her. "This is your second time around with him, though, isn't it?"

I confirmed with a nod.

"Gosh, Mary, I am so sorry." Gina looked down and shook her head. Then, attempting to find a glimmer of hope, she looked back up at me. "Are you sure he's cheating?" she asked.

"Fairly sure," I said, rolling my eyes. "I've found women's names and phone numbers in his pants pockets—it's not the first time, Gina. And when I confront him about it, he claims they are just people interested in buying cars."

"Buying cars?" she asked.

"Yes. That's Kashan's so-called job. It's his way of 'working smart and not hard,' as he puts it. He purchases vehicles, drives them around for a while, then resells them."

"Oh, does he?" Gina drew her brows together. "Where does his money to invest in vehicles come from?"

"It comes from his father. Evidently, his father's business in Kuwait was fairly profitable."

"Kuwait? I thought Kashan was Palestinian." Gina's eyes widened.

"Yes, he is Palestinian. But Kashan and his siblings were actually born in Kuwait. His parents' families were displaced as a result of the first Arab-Israeli War, so they relocated to Kuwait."

"Oh. I see." "So…" Gina said, returning to our original topic, "Kashan moved from Prominence to Nahaven to reconcile your marriage, right? Then he opened Salon Amani for you to work in. But unlike you, he's busy working smart instead of hard, besides doing God-knows-what behind your back. And he's not even helping to take care of his daughter. Does that about sum it up?"

"Yes, unfortunately." I nodded while keeping my eyes on the foil I was applying. "And listen to this," I added. "I decided to call one of the phone numbers I found in his pocket and a woman answered. When I asked which vehicle she was interested in purchasing, she said, 'I'm not interested in buying a vehicle—who is this?'"

Gina raised her head and made eye contact with me through the mirror. "Oh, my gosh! Did you tell her who you were?"

"No. I was too embarrassed, so I quickly hung up," I admitted. "He's cheating on me again, Gina—I know he is."

"It sounds like that's exactly what he's doing," she concurred. "And right now he's at home sleeping while you're at the salon working hard all day?"

"Yeah. It's pretty bad," I agreed sullenly. "And on more than one occasion when I called to check on them, Lilah herself would answer the phone. When I asked what Daddy was doing, she would tell me he was sleeping. I'd have to leave the salon, go pick her up, and bring her back here so I could finish my workday."

"And not even willing to look after his own daughter," she interjected while shaking her head.

"Exactly," I said, feeling relieved to finally tell someone how awful things were at home. "Tragically," I divulged, "one day when her father was sleeping in, Lilah wandered outside to the back yard." "Kashan had been burning a fire the night before and the embers were still smoldering. Lilah lost her balance and fell forward, burning her little hands on the hot coals."

Hearing this, Gina gripped the armrests of the styling chair and leaned forward in disbelief.

"Fortunately, her screams woke Kashan and he took her to the emergency room." "I was furious with him," I said angrily. "Since then, I bring her to work with me every day."

"Wow," Gina shook her head, her face turning redder by the minute.

Neither of us said anything as I folded the final foils in place and set a timer for 20 minutes. Finally, Gina broke the silence.

"Mary, why don't you leave him? Do you think the Lord expects you to stay in a relationship with a man who is running around on you?"

"Well..." I paused, carefully considering my choice of words. "The men in the church counseled me to give Kashan another chance since he still wanted to be with me," I said, feeling defeated.

"And you have given him another chance, Mary," she insisted. "And look what he's done with it."

She wasn't telling me anything I didn't already know. I sighed as a sense of hopelessness began to overwhelm me.

"I'm so sorry to hear this, Mary," she said tenderly. "I thought everything was fine. I'd even heard from a parent of one of our daycare children that Kashan gave his life to the Lord."

"Nooo," I said, shaking my head vehemently. "That was just a card he played so I would drop the charges I filed against him for hitting me."

"Hitting you?" Her jaw dropped. "Mary, he hit you?"

"Well, he threw the phone at me, actually," I stated flatly, not wanting to relive it.

"A phone?" she asked.

"Yes. He got mad and threw the phone across the room and hit me. So I pressed charges. I didn't have a choice. That's abuse, Gina."

"That is abuse," she agreed, looking more somber as she spoke. "So, what happened then? Did you drop the charges after he… supposedly gave his life to Christ?"

"No. I didn't fall for it. And I figured if he really did give his life to Christ, then he would at least have the Lord with him if he went to jail."

Hearing this, Gina placed her hand over her face and shook her head. She let her hand slip back down onto her lap and asked, "Mary, what are you waiting for?" "Why are you still in this marriage?"

"Whew," I sighed and looked up toward the ceiling.

"Listen to me," Gina urged. "Think about everything God's done for you since you've come to this town—all the doors he's opened for you. Consider how hard you've worked to establish a new life here for you and your daughter. You don't need a loser like Kashan. He's pulling you right back down into the situation you were in before. And you don't belong there. That's not you. You left that lifestyle behind when you left him before."

I nodded as I considered everything Gina was saying. She was right; that's not who I was anymore. God had changed my life when I cried out to him five years earlier. Kashan was cheating on me then—but even worse. He would insist that I not leave the house without him and instructed me not to answer the door when he wasn't home, regardless of who it was. I promised God I would fully commit my life to him if he would help me escape that horrible situation. And he did just that. He got us out of Prominence.

Starting over in an unfamiliar town with a six-month-old baby girl had not been easy. We arrived with nothing. However, God was faithful and provided all our needs. And since then my relationship with the Lord has been fully restored. More than that—it was better than ever. It was more meaningful and more intimate. The Lord had fully captured my heart. I grew to cherish the time I spent with him in prayer. And in those moments spent with him, I was changed. God had restored me. Everything was different now. And yes, Gina was right. I was different now.

"Everything you're saying is true," I admitted. "God has done amazing things for me. It's not like I haven't considered leaving him, Gina. It's just that... I know what Kashan will do. He'll try to take Lilah from me. He'll try to take her to the Middle East. He's told me many times that I should never think he would allow his daughter to be raised in this country apart from him."

"Mary, listen to me." Gina looked me square in the eyes. "You can't keep yourself in a horrendous situation like this due to fear. Do you really think that's what God expects you to do?"

I tidied up my work area and didn't answer immediately. Then I responded.

"I know this isn't God's best for me, Gina, but Kashan tried to take Lilah from me before. He tried when I left him back in '95 when Lilah was just a baby. That's why I'm afraid to divorce him. I'm afraid he'll try to take her. I wouldn't put it past him. He would take her to the Middle East, and I'd never see her again!" I insisted

At the mention of it, my mind was immediately inundated with memories of how Kashan tried to take Lilah from me when she was only six months old and still breastfeeding. With guidance from the Prominence Women's Shelter, I had made plans to leave Kashan. But on the day I was leaving, he came home unexpectedly and caught me in the process. He snatched Lilah away from me and took off with her. I called the police, but they informed me they could do nothing since Kashan was her father and we had no court-ordered custody arrangement. But because he had struck me in the face the day before I tried to leave, I was able to go to the magistrate's office and press assault charges against him. The police picked him up at the convenience store he owned in downtown Prominence, and I was able to get Lilah back.

Once that happened, the shelter deemed it too dangerous to house us locally. They suggested we relocate to another town and insisted on providing us with a police escort to the Greyhound Bus Station. So, I reached out to my friend, Terri, in Shandee Island. I asked if we could stay with her until I got on my feet. Already aware of my situation, Terri quickly agreed. However, the shelter informed me that Terri's tiny town did not have a shelter they could transfer us to. The closest shelter to Terri's town was in Nahaven.

After we arrived at the shelter in Nahaven, Terri's husband decided we could not stay at their house in Shandee Island after all, for fear of getting blown up by my "terrorist A-rab husband," as he so eloquently put it. But Janis, a friend of Terri's whom I had met only once before, was sympathetic to my situation and offered us a place to stay with her and her two young children, Stone and River.

"Mary, listen to what you just said. Kashan tried to take Lilah. But he didn't succeed, did he?" "God was with you then, and he's with you now," Gina reassured me. "You have to believe that God would not allow Kashan to take Lilah to the Middle East. And even if it did happen, you have to trust that God would bring her back. You simply cannot allow yourself to be paralyzed by fear like this.

"How in the world did you end up with this guy, anyway?" Gina placed her hands on her cheeks as she tried to make sense of it. "Did he cast some kind of spell on you or something? I mean, he is gorgeous, but Mary, he's a monster!"

"He was different before we got married. "And I was so in love with him," I confessed. "His parents were dead set against our marriage for... multiple reasons. But I wasn't going to let them tell this American woman what to do. So, we got married in Jordan without their approval. Once we were married, I left Amman and came back to the States. Then Kashan arrived in America six months later. And when he did, I became pregnant with Lilah.

"Kashan moved us to a suburb outside of Richmond, and immediately after, became abusive. I was pregnant, severely nauseous, and, as you can imagine, very depressed at that point. It wasn't until we moved back to Prominence, where Lilah was born, that I was able to regain my strength… along with the will to live again. That's when I cried out to God for help. That's when we came to Nahaven. And, well… you know the rest of the story."

Gina nodded. A soft melody played in the background while I gave Gina's foils a quick check. They were in no hurry to lighten, but that was okay because I needed time to think about what Gina had said to me. The words she spoke were true. They spoke deeply to my spirit and lingered there. I knew she was right. As a child of God, I was never meant to be controlled or held back by fear.

> For you have not received the spirit of
> bondage again to fear…
> Romans 8:15 NKJV

After checking her highlights one final time, I led her to the shampoo area. Once all the foils were removed, I did two shampoos, towel dried, then applied a cool-toned demi-color that complemented her delicate skin tone. It had been a long process, but much had been accomplished.

"Let me take Lilah home with me when you finish with my hair," Gina offered. "She can play with Breanna and you can come by the house to pick her up later. You can even stay for dinner if you want."

"No, Gina, that's too much to ask," I pulled my brows together and shook my head.

Gina continued speaking as if she didn't hear me. "And just bring her to the daycare on your way to work every day from now on."

"Gina, I can't afford that!" I protested.

"It's okay, just bring her," she insisted, holding her hand up to shush me up. "Precious Gifts Childcare Center isn't just a business; it's a ministry. Believe me, you're not the first parent the daycare has helped, and you won't be the last either. Not as long as I'm the director."

I was struck by Gina's compassion and her willingness to encourage me. Knowing someone cared enough to not only offer good advice but also lend a girl a hand meant so much. I felt a rush of relief and automatically teared up in response.

"Oh, don't do that. C'mon, now." "It's all going to work out," she assured me.

The friendship between Gina and me had developed gradually over the last couple years. I suppose it caught me off guard a little when I realized just how close we had become. Now I knew I had an ally by my side—a person in my corner cheering me on. And she was someone who, I sensed, could handle the magnitude of my unusual situation.

I believed Gina was the kind of person who would help anyone in need, regardless of the circumstances. And that made her even more special to me. It also meant that she definitely had my ear. From there on out, I was receptive to anything she had to say, and I was grateful to God for placing her in my life.

"Lilah," Gina called, pulling me out of my thoughts. "Come here, honey."

Lilah came running toward us from the reception area.

"Would you like to go see your friend, Breanna, after your momma gets finished with my hair?" Gina asked.

"I'm going to see Breanna?" Lilah's eyes widened in excitement as she looked up at me for confirmation.

"Yes, you are," I answered. "But you need to behave and not be running around too much and giving Ms. Gina a hard time."

"Okay, Mommy." "I promise!" Lilah agreed enthusiastically. She was all smiles.

"I get off at 7:00 tonight," I told Gina, talking over the sound of the blow-dryer. "I'll clean up the salon and be right over."

"Take as long as you need," she smiled. "I'll bet Jev is home cooking as we speak, so don't you worry about dinner. I'll go ahead and get the girls bathed too. I'm sure I can find an outfit of Breanna's that will fit Little Miss Lilah."

Lilah hopped up on a styling chair and spun back and forth in half-circles as I finished up with Gina's hair. After applying a touch of hairspray, I emulsified some detailing paste by rubbing it between my palms. Then I moved my hands through Gina's hair so it would look a bit undone. I handed her a small mirror and turned the chair around so she could see it from all sides. Her eyes brightened.

"Thanks so much, Mary."

"Thank you, Gina." "I really appreciate you," I said with moist eyes.

I hugged them both goodbye and they left the salon. I watched Lilah through the glass door as she skipped her way to Ms. Gina's car. While wiping down my station in preparation for my next client, I found myself wondering what it must be like to have a husband who cooks.

Kashan had been the love of my life, the one I couldn't live without, the one I traveled across the world and broke through all sorts of barriers to be with.

And this is where I've landed.

It's all about the choices you made, Mary.

Yes. It's the choices I made that landed me here.

I once believed Kashan loved me. He certainly pursued me more aggressively than any other man ever had. However, time revealed that what I perceived to be love was merely an animalistic attraction and a desire to dominate me. I had been so foolish. Kashan's urge to control me was still in place, but since I no longer allowed him to tyrannize me, his affection for me had turned from attraction to disdain.

From time to time, I still struggled with regrets over my past mistakes. The consequences I faced as a result of my transgressions served as a constant reminder. I had been forgiven much, and I loved God very much because of it.

> "I tell you, her sins-and there are many-have been forgiven, so she has shown me much love. But a person who has forgiven little shows only little love."
> Luke 7:47 NLT

Am I free to go then, Lord? Or do I remain in this adulterous marriage? Do I continue to punish myself? To what end? I could never sufficiently make amends for my sin—and neither is it my job to do so. That price has already been paid for me on the cross. You have forgiven and forgotten my mistakes. And so should I.

As I drove from the salon heading toward Gina's house, her words sounded over and over in my head. I couldn't unhear the truth she had spoken. She had declared that no matter what, I must trust God. Her statements not only spoke to me, but they seemed to awaken something deep within—something that caused my spirit to rise up and take notice.

They resonated first in my mind, and then continued sounding like an echo permeating throughout my being. Gina's words compelled me to make a choice. They called on me to step forward and give a response. They persisted like a question that would not go away until I answered, or more tragically, might go away, closing the door of opportunity forever if not acted on. That was a risk I was not willing to take.

I knew beyond a shadow of a doubt that the only answer within me was a resounding yes! Yes, I was going to break away from Kashan. Yes, I was going to go for it, regardless of my apprehensions. Despite how seemingly legitimate my fears were, I decided that those fears had held me captive for far too long.

And it was as if my response marked that place in time as the beginning. It was like my decision to trust God, no matter what, was the catalyst that would cause subsequent events to manifest—to spring into motion in the spiritual realm and into action in the physical realm. Just as a massive cloud in the heavenlies billows forth preceding a formidable storm, it began.

I looked ahead, imagining life apart from Kashan, and felt a discernible shift in my mindset. And I realized that there was no going back. Although I was still quite unaware that at the very moment I accepted Gina's challenge to trust God, an immense spiritual whirlwind began to pull everything in my world up into it. Our lives would never be the same.

Chapter 2

THE THINGS WE LEAVE BEHIND

Kashan uttered a scoff of disapproval that evening when Lilah mentioned she had gone to Ms. Gina's house to play with Breanna. But I felt no obligation to get his approval. The way I looked at it, he had forfeited his right to have a say in the matter by failing each and every day to wake up and take care of his daughter.

His negativity and sour disposition no longer had the same effect on me. No longer would I take on the weight that Kashan's condescending attitude put forth. Once I made the decision to leave him, I was ready to move on, although I knew I had to be strategic with my tactics to get away from him.

A well-thought-out plan of exit was called for, and the finality of our parting was more than enough incentive for me to implement one. So the following day, I placed a call to U.S. Immigration inquiring about Kashan's ability to take Lilah from the States without my consent.

"No, ma'am," the Immigration Services Officer assured me, "your husband will not be able to obtain a passport for her without your consent." "It requires the consent of both parents.

And he will not be able to take her out of the country if she does not possess a passport."

"Are you sure?" I asked earnestly.

"Yes, ma'am," he stated. "He will not be able to do it."

That was good news to me. Apparently, I had been worrying for no reason. I couldn't wait to tell Gina.

The next thing I had to consider was the salon. Kashan had insisted I open my own shop and had invested the money for me to do so. Upon our divorce, I knew he would want every single dime back, with a profit. Salon Amani would have to be sold for him to recover his investment. And I could not see him sharing any portion of that with me.

I thought about my salon and all the work I had put into planning, designing, painting, and even laying some of its floors. Not to mention how hard I had worked in the salon to bring in the brunt of the money which supported us during those past couple of years. It wasn't fair that I should get nothing. But then I remembered how good God had been to me, and I reconsidered.

It's just stuff. And it isn't worth staying in a bad marriage for. God will provide for us. He always has.

The words of the Michael Card song, "Things We Leave Behind," came to mind. I loved that song and had sung it often. I think it was attached to my spirit at that point. God had been preparing me for this moment for a long time. And I was ready to let everything go and be liberated from the bondage I had been subjected to since giving my heart to Kashan.

I was not even the same person anymore. The evil trickery of blind passion for this man had twisted my heart in knots and wreaked havoc on my mind. But that passion was no longer there. The love I previously felt for Kashan had been systematically destroyed with each lie he told, each foul word he spoke, each controlling action he took, each blow he struck, and each random female he slept with. I was unable to conjure up any respect for him whatsoever. It was over between us.

And now that I was no longer under the influence of fear, there was no reason to put off letting Kashan know our marriage was coming to an end. I decided to tell him later that evening when he returned from meeting a potential car customer. But 12:00 a.m. came and went, and still, no Kashan. Eventually, I gave up and drifted off to sleep. Then the sound of the front door opening at 1:32 a.m. woke me.

Who stays out that late talking with someone about a car? Further confirmation that I'm making the right decision.

I shook my head in disgust as I made my way to the kitchen. There I found *Prince Charming* casually pouring himself a glass of water.

"Where have you been, Kashan?" I asked, not really expecting an answer, or at least not an honest one.

"Who do you think you are, asking me where I've been?"
"You go and do as you please every day," he said angrily.

"Yes, I do," I agreed. "I go to work to support us."

Kashan's eyes widened, daring me to continue addressing him in that manner. I shook my head, indicating that I was no longer affected or intimidated by him. In response, he pulled his lip up in a snarl and murmured a stream of obscenities in Arabic.

I had heard them all before. But this time was different. It could have been that the malevolent fangs embedded in each of his hateful words had simply been worn down from overuse. Or perhaps, over time, I had learned to filter them out as a way of self-preservation. But no, I sensed there was more to it than that.

I wasn't sure exactly what it was, but something inside me had changed. And this I knew: I would never again receive or ingest Kashan's verbal abuse. Realizing that his evil words simply did not apply to me caused me to become indifferent to them, and in doing so, I had rendered them powerless. His words no longer possessed the ability to tear me down as they had in the past.

In the years I had spent with God during my separation from Kashan, I learned who God said I was. God said I was both valued and cherished.

> Every single moment you are thinking of me! How precious and wonderful to consider that you cherish me constantly in every thought! O God, your desires toward me are more than the grains of sand on every shore! When I awake each morning, you're still with me.
> Psalm 139:17-18 TPT

And now, with fear removed from the equation, I no longer felt it necessary to sustain ongoing abuse. I no longer felt it necessary to be in Kashan's presence either.

"Anything else?" I asked in a cool, calm voice.

"Ya shar moo ta!" [B**ch!] Kashan slammed his hand down on the countertop.

"That's it," I said firmly. "We're done!"

"You…" he opened his mouth to utter a word.

"Officially!" I interjected with a wave of my hand. "This—" I pointed my finger toward his face, "—is not a marriage." "I'm divorcing you, Kashan. You can sell the salon. I don't care! But I'm not living like this anymore." "It's over!" my voice rose with resolve.

No longer willing to give him a platform, I turned and walked away. He didn't go after me. Moments later, I heard the front door slam shut. Immediately, the air seemed lighter somehow. It was exhilarating. I could breathe again. I had not felt that good in years.

Keeping my feelings pent up inside whenever Kashan was around had become second nature to me. So getting my intentions out in the open that way felt so liberating. I was instantly relieved and unburdened. I no longer felt scared or stuck. And because I was convinced I had given him more than enough chances, I felt no guilt whatsoever. Especially after everything he had put me through.

It may have taken me a while to figure it out, but my time of suffering at the hands of this fiend is finally over. Thank you, Jesus!

The prospect of change kept me awake for a while. Ever since I had first fallen in love with Kashan, I had never been completely free from his control and influence. Still imagining what the following days would look like, I eventually fell asleep.

When morning came, I woke up feeling excited and energized. Seeing that Kashan had not returned home during the night kept that momentum going. After putting coffee on to brew, I reached for the phone to give Janis a call. I asked her if Lilah and I could stay with her until Kashan moved back to Prominence out of concern that he would follow me to the new place. Thankfully, she agreed, so I secured a temporary storage unit for my furniture and household goods.

Kashan and I barely spoke to each other in the weeks leading up to me moving out. He made no attempts to change my mind. I took that to mean he accepted the outcome. If so, it confirmed that I was taking steps in the right direction and that

I had nothing to worry about. I imagined, perhaps, he too felt a sense of relief that we were finally done.

But one night while I slept, fear showed up and challenged my newfound confidence. I dreamed of an evil person, a devil of sorts. This entity had an air of demise and destruction about him as if hell-bent on causing as much pain as possible. The demon was driving a car at breakneck speed. I suddenly realized that Kashan and Lilah were riding in the back seat of the vehicle. The car turned a curve and started to spin out of control. Flames shot out from the muffler, and dark smoke rose from the tires.

When I abruptly woke from the bad dream, Kashan was in the bedroom going through his pile of messy papers—the papers he always forbade me to touch. When he noticed I was awake, he faked a cough as he was in the habit of doing whenever he felt nervous or wanted to come across as nonchalant and inconspicuous.

"What are you doing going through papers at this time of night?" I asked, suspiciously.

"Just looking for some business documents." "It has nothing to do with you," he said curtly.

"I had a bad dream," I rubbed my eyes and confided sleepily. "I dreamed that some devil was driving Lilah and you in a car." "You would never try to take her away from me, would you?" I asked, still feeling unsettled.

He froze for a moment. Then, without turning his head toward me, he said, "Of course not, don't be silly." "Go back to sleep, Mary."

To console myself, I played the conversation I'd had with the immigration officer back through my mind. The man had clearly said that Kashan could not take Lilah out of the U.S.

without my consent. Reassured, I turned my back to Kashan, placed my head under the pillow to muffle out the sound of rustling papers, and fell back to sleep.

In the days that followed, things moved along at a satisfactory pace. The salon was sold within a month to a former coworker of mine. I had advised her on what price she should offer Kashan, hoping that the transaction would be settled quickly. And I negotiated for terms allowing me to remain at the salon without paying booth rent for a year after the sale.

It seemed only fair, since I would most likely receive nothing from the transaction. I knew Kashan's thought process; in his mind, he deserved to have the entire sum for himself. But I had already come to terms with that. I figured no one could steal something from me that I had already let go of. As far as I was concerned, it was a small price to pay for the peaceful and promising future I dreamed of. And, as expected, I received nothing from the sale of my salon. Everyone seemed satisfied though—or so I thought.

As planned, Lilah and I temporarily moved in with Janis and her two children. Kashan went back to Prominence and became roommates with a friend. His roommate was an Arab guy who owned a convenience store close to campus. I hoped it worked out for them.

Chapter 3

RED SKY AT MORN

The ground was still covered with dew, and the aroma of fresh green foliage filled the air with the promise of a beautiful day. The Altima was packed up with everything we needed for our weekend in Prominence. Lilah sat waiting in her booster seat while I ran back into Janis' house to grab my purse.

Kashan and I agreed that I would drive Lilah to Prominence every other weekend so he could see her. I didn't mind. It was an opportunity for me to get out of Nahaven and spend some time in my hometown. Prominence was a much larger city than Nahaven. The shopping there, not to mention the energy level, was more to my liking and what I was accustomed to. And my sister Sharon didn't mind me staying with her while I was in town.

Lilah was five years old and growing fast. As I drove down the road, I thought about her birthday celebration back in January at Diego's Mexican Restaurant. I had arranged for three men dressed as The Three Amigos—sombreros and all—to sing happy birthday to her. Although it wasn't received as well as I'd hoped. I laughed quietly to myself, remembering Lilah's question to me as we left the restaurant that day.

"Mommy, do we have to have my party at Diego's next year?" she had asked.

The Three Amigos turned out to be no competition for Meowy the Cat, whom we celebrated with at the Cat Café every year since Lilah's second birthday. I had to admit, Meowy was a hard act to follow.

Lilah and I were traveling down Cherry Creek Road heading Northwest toward Prominence, a route I had taken many times since moving to the South Givenia Lowcountry. As we were approaching the highway, I noticed something furry in the opposite lane. I thought I saw it move. When I slowed down, I realized it was a cat that had been hit. Obviously, a driver had struck the poor animal and didn't even bother to stop. I pulled off to the right side of the road, put my flashers on, and approached the kitty.

She was badly injured and there was blood everywhere, but she still showed signs of life. I wanted to move her out of the road before another car came along. As I bent down on the pavement to pick her up, I heard a woman's voice behind me.

"What happened?" she asked.

I was crying by then and got choked up as I tried to speak.

"Someone… hit this poor cat and… they didn't even stop."

"Don't touch her," the woman said. "I'll pick her up and take her to the vet's office where I work. I'm not sure if the doctor will be able to do anything for her, though." "Let me grab a towel from my car to wrap her in," she added, as she ran back to her vehicle.

"Thanks for stopping," she said, as she carefully picked up the wounded feline. "So many people wouldn't have."

"It's just horrible," I said, wiping tears from my face.

"What happened, Mommy?" Lilah asked when I got back into the car.

"Someone ran over a poor kitty with their car, honey," I answered in a shaky voice. I fastened my seat belt and put the car into drive.

"Is the kitty hurt, Mommy?" Lilah asked with concern in her voice.

"Yes, sweetheart, the kitty is hurt." "Let's pray for the kitty," I said, still sniffing back tears. "Jesus, please help the kitty not be in any more pain. Take the kitty up to heaven to be with you. Amen."

"Amen!" Lilah said, sounding as if she was sure everything would be okay now.

It wasn't a great start to our weekend. Ready to put some distance between us and the disturbing scene, I pulled onto the highway and popped a cassette into the stereo.

Listening to the song, "Give Thanks," took me back to our first years in Nahaven at Lowcountry Covenant Church. My friends Janis and Terri were both members of the close-knit nondenominational congregation. Lilah and I were immediately welcomed into the fold.

It was September of 1995 when Lilah and I first attended service there. The small wooden chapel built in the early 1900's had a quaint, narrow steeple. It was located on Highway 21 South heading toward the coast. It was halfway between Terri's home in Shandee Island and Janis' home in Nahaven. They claimed it was well worth the 40-minute drive it took them to get there.

The sandy parking lot was riddled with broken pieces of seashells. The shells intermittently caught the morning sun's rays, calling attention to themselves and reminding me that I wasn't in Prominence anymore. Directly in the center of the unmarked parking area was a huge live oak tree draped in grayish-green Spanish moss. Children played around its full trunk, often stumbling on protruding roots, only to get up again, undeterred.

Upon our arrival, we were introduced to several parishioners before even entering the church. Once inside, I saw there weren't many more than 50 people in attendance. There were enough people to comfortably fill up the sanctuary, yet not so many that you couldn't recall everyone's first name.

The congregation was a good mix of male and female, both young and old alike. With more than a couple people of color in attendance, I ventured to guess they may even consider themselves culturally diverse, especially for that area of Givenia. I couldn't help but notice how kindly they treated one another.

Once everyone was settled in their seats, and not a moment before, worship finally began. I was relieved that I knew most of the songs they sang that morning. It made me feel a little more at ease, despite the tough circumstances I was in.

When the singing was over, my friend Terri wasted no time walking up to the pulpit. Initially, I was impressed, assuming she performed an essential role in the service. But then she extended her hand, pointing toward the only stranger in the room, and proceeded to make a public announcement on my behalf.

"This is my friend, Mary, from Prominence." Her expression conveyed the importance of her communication. "She had to move here to get away from her abusive, Middle Eastern, Arab husband," she proclaimed in an overachieving southern accent.

I wasn't sure where to look, so I just kept my gaze fixed on Terri. One side of my mouth twitched nervously of its own volition.

Janis, seated on the pew beside me, whispered, "Oh my," as our friend continued speaking.

Terri told everyone within earshot that Lilah and I currently resided at the Women's Shelter in Nahaven, and that, unfortunately, we could not receive visitors since the exact location of the shelter was to remain strictly confidential.

My face turned beet red at hearing my story being told out loud in real time—to total strangers, no less. It did sound rather incredible, though, I had to admit. But then I began to wonder just how far back in my history Terri planned to go.

Thankfully, she stopped short of exposing everything. I already had a difficult enough time comprehending the grace of God; the last thing I needed was a public reminder of just how badly I had messed up to get myself in those dire circumstances. Janis noticed my fingers tapping the top of my Bible. She reached out, took hold of my hand and squeezed it.

"Are you okay?" she asked.

I took a breath and nodded that I was.

"Now, this is a secret," Terri continued from her platform, "so please do not tell anyone she's here."

Upon hearing Terri's firm instructions to keep everything secret, Janis and I looked at each other, eyes widened in dismay.

"Oh, well," I said quietly. "So much for keeping it secret."

We both stifled the urge to laugh, but it was pretty funny. Embarrassed, but at the same time relieved that Terri was finally finished giving her version of my testimony, I smiled and nodded a thank you to my well-meaning friend as she left the podium.

After service, nearly everyone in the church came up to Lilah and me to let us know they would keep us in their prayers. And even though I had only just met them, I felt confident they would.

Whenever the church doors were open, we were there: Sunday morning, Sunday evening, and then back again on Wednesday night. Janis and I would load Lilah, Stone, and River into Janis' station wagon to attend every service without fail.

Those were precious memories. I'd never been with a group of believers quite like them. I didn't have much in common with any of them outside of the love of Christ. Yet, that was more than enough to knit us all together. God had placed us well.

> How good and pleasant it is when God's people live together in unity! It is like precious oil poured on the head, running down on the beard, running down on Aaron's beard, down on the collar of his robe. It is as if the dew of Hermon were falling on Mount Zion. For there the Lord bestows his blessing, even life forevermore.
> Psalm 133:1-3 NIV

Gradually, I began to think about the weekend ahead and how to pass the time while Lilah was with her dad. A visit to T.J. Maxx was on my list. Easter was coming up, and I still hadn't gotten anything for Lilah.

Approaching the Tuscaloosa Rd. exit, I noticed smoke coming from the engine of an old car that was pulling off the road. I said a prayer for the guy as we passed him.

My thoughts drifted to Kashan and Lilah's weekend together. It felt weird to be taking her to Prominence to visit him. But it was a much better set of circumstances than living with him and seeing him every day. Thankfully, Kashan was no longer insisting we be together. He had stopped constantly asking me where I had been and if any man had spoken to me while I was out. It appeared he had finally given up and let go of me. Or at least, I hoped he had. I continued to go over things in my mind as I drove.

Why I gave so many years of my life to Kashan.... I hate to even think about it. I gave him chance after chance to prove he had changed... but he proved otherwise. And yet, I stayed with him for fear of losing Lilah. But now there's no stopping me from moving on.

The thought was exhilarating. A new chapter in my life was beginning—a chapter which would no longer include Kashan Shehadeh as my husband. He would always be Lilah's dad, of course, and he would continue to be a part of her life. But he was out of my life. Lilah's and my future was fully in God's hands. And from the way things appeared, that future would be full of promise and good things. We had been living with Janis for more than a couple months now. I planned to stay just long enough to ensure that Kashan was firmly planted far away from us.

My musings were abruptly interrupted by what appeared to be a bright light on the shoulder of the highway ahead of me. But as we got closer, I could see that it wasn't a light at all. It was a small compact car engulfed in huge flames. After shifting over into the left lane to give them more space, I slowed down to better assess the situation. Two men stood nearby, looking on hopelessly. They didn't appear to be in extreme distress, though. I hoped that meant everyone managed to exit the vehicle safely.

"Oh my gosh," I said in a low voice as I passed by.

"What's wrong, Mommy? Why are those men having a fire?"

"Well, Lilah, I don't think they planned on it, honey."

"Oh Lord, please don't let that car blow up on those men," I prayed.

Then I accelerated, purposely putting some distance between us and the fiery vehicle. The way our morning had gone so far was unnerving, to say the least. Trying to make sense of it all, I wondered if the two burning vehicles had been traveling together. I thought maybe the cars had been sitting around unused for a while and shouldn't have been driven in that condition. Or perhaps they put the wrong type of fuel in both vehicles, causing them to catch fire.

What is the connection here? Surely there's a connection.

I was on edge at that point. For the next thirty minutes of our drive, my thoughts constantly went back to the two vehicles. A feeling of dread began to creep over me.

As we were approaching the exit to get on Hwy 26, I asked Lilah, "Are you excited to see your daddy today?"

"Yes, Mommy," Lilah answered from the back seat. "Is Daddy going to take me to get ice cream?"

"I don't know, honey, but I bet he will if you ask..." My voice trailed off as I looked ahead in disbelief.

There was another vehicle on fire! The only difference this time was that it was a truck. It sat just ahead of us on the left, fully engulfed in flames. I couldn't believe it. A separate vehicle had pulled over, apparently wanting to assist. Three people stood watching in a grassy area beside the road. With eyes widened and hands covering their mouths, they watched as the tragic event transpired. Sirens blared with increasing loudness and emergency vehicles approached. After witnessing the latest incident, I was officially in full panic mode. My hands shook as I gripped the steering wheel.

"Oh Lord, what is going on?" I asked in despair.

My breathing became rapid and somewhat staggered. I grabbed my phone and looked back at Lilah, who had somehow managed to fall asleep.

"Hey," my big sister Sharon answered casually. "How far away are you?"

"Sharon, something's wrong," I said frantically. "I-I... I don't know what's happening."

"What are you talking about?" she asked, sounding slightly annoyed at my theatrics.

"I don't know," I answered. "Something just isn't right!" I insisted.

"Okay, calm down and tell me what you're talking about," she said, still unconvinced.

"Well... first it was the cat this morning," I said, deliberately speaking at a slower pace, hoping she would take me more seriously.

"What cat?" she asked flatly, seemingly unimpressed.

"Someone hit a cat this morning and just left it in the road to die. It was suffering and all bloody." "It was terrible!" I insisted.

"Oh, that *is* terrible," she acknowledged.

"Yes. And then I saw an old car smoking on the highway like it was going to catch on fire."

"Okay...," she said, waiting for me to continue.

"Then, not too far down the road, I passed by another car that was actually on fire!"

"Wow, people sure do seem to be havin' car troubles today," she said, trying to make light of it.

"But listen to this, Sharon. I just passed yet another vehicle fully engulfed in flames."

"What? Oh my God." "That's crazy," she admitted.

"It was an inferno!" I said, now sobbing. "I'm telling you, something is just not right. I don't know what it is, but I feel like something terrible is going to happen."

"Why do you feel like something terrible is going to happen?" Sharon asked. "It sounds like something terrible already did happen. But it didn't happen to you. You just happened to see it."

"Whew," I said, trying to calm myself down. "I don't know, Sharon. I just have a really bad feeling."

"Well, try not to worry. Concentrate on driving and getting here safely." "How's Lilah doing?" she asked.

"She's asleep in the back seat, oblivious."

"Good," Sharon said. "Now, just calm down and get here. Are you almost here?"

"Yes, I'm almost to the beltline," I told her.

"Okay." "Well, I made some banana bread," she said, changing the subject. "I'll heat a piece up for you when you get here."

"Okay," I said, my voice still a little shaky. "I'll see you in a few."

Chapter 4

STOP OVERTHINKING

Relieved to finally get there, I looked for a parking space close to Sharon's apartment, thinking I would have to carry Lilah in. It was nearly impossible to wake her up once she had fallen asleep. But she surprised me this time and woke up as soon as she heard me open the back car door.

"Are we at Aunt Sharon's now, Mommy?" Lilah asked sleepily.

"Yes, we are, honey." "Come on, let's go get some banana bread," I said, coaxing her to move a little faster.

I was anxious to get inside the apartment. Sharon had already unlocked the apartment door for us, so we walked right in.

"I'm back here," she called out. "Will you lock the door, please?"

We walked into the bedroom to find Sharon watching TV. She still had her pajamas on.

"Come on, guys, get in bed. I'll heat us up some banana bread." She wasted no time going to the kitchen to make that happen.

I took off Lilah's sandals, then slipped mine off. We hopped into the bed and got under the covers, safe and sound. I heard the microwave go off, and soon after, the sweet smell of banana bread drifted back into the bedroom.

"Mmmm," I said to Lilah with a look of expectancy.

"Mmmm," she mimicked my expression. "Are we going to eat in bed, Mommy?" she asked, surprised.

"Well, we are if Aunt Sharon says we are," I answered. "It's her house—her rules."

Lilah's face lit up with excitement. Once we were all settled with our warm, buttered banana bread, Sharon rewound the movie so we could watch it from the beginning.

"What are we watching?" I asked.

"*The Sound of Music*," Sharon furrowed her brows, as if I should have already known.

The movie had been one of my mother's favorite musicals, and we still enjoyed watching it. When we were children, all six of us often sang the songs together with my mom. Anytime was the right time for a sing-along once my mom got us started.

By the time the nuns in the movie were singing (How do you solve a problem like) "Maria," my nerves were more settled. Lilah sang along even though she didn't know the words. She did a pretty good job of faking it, much like my sister Suzie did when she didn't know the lyrics to a song.

When Sharon and I realized what Lilah was doing, we looked at each other and simultaneously said, "Suzie!"

Lilah asked if Aunt Suzie was there, to which I answered, "Well… in spirit she is."

That made Sharon crack up laughing. It wasn't too difficult to make Sharon laugh, though. It wasn't difficult to make any of the Kennedy siblings laugh when we got together. On that day, I found our laughter especially healing because it hadn't been very long since we had lost our mom.

When the movie was over, Sharon suggested, "We can just stay in bed all day and watch movies, if you want."

"Well, I still need to drop Lilah off at Kashan's apartment, and after that, I thought I'd go to T.J. Maxx and get some Easter stuff."

"Mommy, is the Easter Bunny coming to my house?" Lilah asked with a smile.

"The Easter Bunny?" I asked teasingly. "Well, if the Easter Bunny is coming to your house, why would I need to go to T.J. Maxx? I could just stay here and hang out with Aunt Sharon and eat banana bread."

Lilah sighed and shrugged. "Well, you could still go to T.J. Maxx if you wanted to."

"Hmm," I answered as if considering. "Lilah, you know we aren't celebrating an Easter Bunny on Easter. Who is it that we are celebrating?"

"Jesus!" Lilah answered, excited that she knew the answer.

"That's right. So don't you worry about whether some Easter Bunny is coming to your house. And I'll just take myself to T.J. Maxx while you are spending time with your daddy."

"Okay," Lilah said enthusiastically.

Sharon whispered something in Lilah's ear that made her giggle. Just then, my phone rang. It was Kashan asking if I was in town yet. I let him know I'd be at his apartment with Lilah shortly.

"So Kashan has his own apartment now?" Sharon asked, wrinkling her nose.

"Well, it's not really his. I mean… he moved in with someone—an Arab guy." "The guy owns a convenience store," I added.

"Of course he does," Sharon said sarcastically.

I sighed, partly in response to Sharon's remark and partly at the thought of having to see Kashan.

"Okay, well… come back right after you finish shopping and we can watch another movie," Sharon instructed.

"Okay, sounds good," I agreed. "Come on Lilah, let's get you to your daddy's house," I said reluctantly. "Get your shoes on, sweetie."

Lilah gave Sharon a hug and a buttery kiss, then hopped off the bed. She obediently put her shoes on and followed me out of the room. Moments later, we were back in the car and on our way toward West Prominence.

When we got to Kashan's apartment, Lilah reached up to open the door. I pulled her hand back and told her we needed to knock. She looked at me, somewhat confused, as I proceeded to knock firmly on the door.

"Did you put everything she needs in her bag?" Kashan asked without even saying hello.

"Yes, of course," I said, slightly annoyed that he would even question that.

"Okay, good," he said, smiling.

There was a time when his smile took my breath away. We were way past that now.

"Okay. Tell Mommy bye. Give her a kiss." He seemed anxious to get rid of me.

Oh, Lord, please don't let him have a woman inside his apartment while he's with our daughter.

I knew it would happen sooner or later. Lilah turned around and reached her arms up to me. I bent down and gave her a squeeze and a peck on the lips.

"Okay. See you tomorrow, honey. Have fun with Daddy."

"Oh, she will," Kashan assured me with a grin.

As I walked down the sidewalk toward my car, I turned and looked back for a moment. It wasn't easy leaving Lilah with her dad. Even though we'd already done this a couple of times, it still felt odd. And it didn't help that Kashan seemed somewhat fake and rather anxious for me to leave. Then I recalled the odor coming from inside Kashan's apartment as he stood in the open doorway.

What was that smell? If I had to guess, I would say it was a combination of soiled men's clothing, stale coffee, cumin, greasy dishes, and... oh yeah, cigarette smoke.

I hated the thought of Lilah spending time in that environment, but Kashan assured me he would be moving out soon. I got in my car and tried to shake off the worry.

Once I was on the road again, my mind became occupied with the busy Prominence traffic. The traffic didn't bother me, though. I considered it a small price to pay for all the other things Prominence had to offer.

T.J. Maxx was crowded by the time I got there. The energy of the season was prevalent throughout the store. Spring merchandise was brightly displayed everywhere. An adorable stuffed duck caught my eye. After claiming the duck and depositing it safely into my shopping cart, I strolled over to a display table laden with children's books. There in the mix was an adorably illustrated children's Bible. The price was right, so I placed it in my cart beside the yellow duckie.

Thinking I had finished shopping, I pushed my cart over toward the cash register. On my way there, I spotted a cute, flowery dress. Once I found one in Lilah's size, I quickly added it to my other finds. Next to the dresses was a display rack with rows of little sandals and frilly socks. It took me a few minutes to decide which color socks to get, but once I did, I was quite satisfied with Lilah's new Easter ensemble.

The only items I still needed to purchase were jellybeans, the pastel-colored malted milk eggs *I liked* so much, and, last but not least, a chocolate bunny. I figured if I got the solid kind, Lilah would inevitably need some help eating it. But all those could be picked up later when we were back in Nahaven.

After I got back to Sharon's house, I stayed put for the rest of the day. Being the youngest of the four girls in our family, I always valued the time I got to spend with any of my big sisters. And seeing Kashan again when I returned to pick up Lilah the following day would happen soon enough.

In the meantime, she and I found plenty to talk and laugh about. The traumatic series of unfortunate events that happened on my way to Prominence was no longer on my mind. Finally, I was able to relax and stop overthinking things.

Chapter 5

JUST ANOTHER DAY

On Sunday afternoon, Kashan called asking to keep Lilah for one more day. He told me his aunt was in town and wanted to spend more time with Lilah. Since I was off on Monday, I didn't see how that would be a problem.

"Okay," I agreed. "But let me speak to Lilah."

"Hi, Mommy," she said excitedly. "Daddy bought me some clothes!"

"Oh wow, really?" I said, finding his generosity and willingness to spend a dollar surprising. "That's wonderful, honey. Now you have a good time with Daddy and tell his aunt Mommy said hi, okay?"

"Okay, Mommy, I will," Lilah promised sweetly.

"Okay, honey. I'll see you tomorrow, sweetheart." "I love you," I told her.

"Love you, Mommy," Lilah exclaimed.

Kashan got back on the phone and said, "Okay, well… see you later."

"Wait!" "So… you bought her some new clothes?" I asked.

"Yeah, I wanted to take her to the swimming pool here, so we went to the Children's Place in the mall to get her a bathing suit." "I also bought some other things for her while we were there," he said casually, as if it were an everyday occurrence.

"Okay, good. Well, you guys have a good time and tell your aunt hi. And please, watch her around the water."

"Yes, I will. See you later."

"Oh, wait." "What time do you want me to pick her up tomorrow?" I asked.

"Oh, don't worry about it. I'll bring her to you at Sharon's house. I'll have her back there by… 9:00 tomorrow night."

"That's pretty late, Kashan."

"Well, I want her to spend time with my family too, Mary. She never gets to see them." "And don't forget, she is half Palestinian," he said arrogantly, as if that meant she was half royalty.

"Okay, fine. But don't be late, please. Sharon goes to sleep early. She has to work in the morning, and I don't want her to be disturbed."

"Oh, I promise you," Kashan said curtly, "she won't be disturbed."

"Okay, bye," I said, hanging up the phone abruptly.

Who does he think he's fooling? He's late for everything.

My first appointment on Tuesday wasn't until three o'clock, which meant we could spend another night at Sharon's and leave for Nahaven the next morning. Gina was flexible about what time I dropped Lilah off at the daycare, so getting her there around lunchtime would not be a problem.

It was hard for me to believe how quickly the last year had passed. Big-girl school was right around the corner. I'd already decided our final summer before kindergarten started should be relaxed and filled with fun. Living a life relatively free of Kashan's presence was finally within my reach. I wholeheartedly believed that our lives would be better once we were spared the negativity and uncertainty of everyday life with Kashan.

When Sharon left for work the next morning, I had the house to myself. It was so peaceful and quiet that I took time to savor a second cup of coffee. Then I remembered the banana bread. I heated up the last piece and watched as the butter I spread on it melted and disappeared.

While taking a quick shower, I considered what I should do with my extra day in Prominence. SRH Shoe Outlet seemed like a good idea, especially since we didn't have stores like that in Nahaven. My mind automatically went to why I left Prominence in the first place. I shook off those thoughts, though, realizing it wasn't always productive to think about the past.

Everything is fine now. Everything is different. Everything is good.

> And now, dear brothers and sisters, one final thing. Fix your thoughts on what is true, and honorable, and right, and pure, and lovely, and admirable. Think about things that are excellent and worthy of praise.
> Philippians 4:8 NLT

It was true, I did miss Prominence. But I knew Nahaven was where God had planted me. And besides, Prominence wasn't so far away.

SRH Shoe Outlet had a great selection as usual. Within an hour and a half, I finished shopping. And I did not leave empty-handed. My favorite purchase was a pair of metallic platform sandals. They added nearly two inches to my height and would go quite well with the tan I was planning to get that summer. Definitely a win-win.

Quite certain my better-than-average shopping skills called for proper accolades, I left North Prominence and took the back roads that cut across town to New World Deli. There, I picked up some stuffed grape leaves, tabbouleh, and hummus. Before leaving the deli, I grabbed some pieces of baklava as well. I figured Sharon might appreciate it, especially since I had consumed the rest of her banana bread.

Later, Sharon came home with a chicken dinner she purchased from Boston Market. When she saw the Middle Eastern spread I had already placed on the table, she laughed.

"Well... good thing hummus goes with everything," I joked.

"Yeah, and so does baklava," she agreed.

After dinner, we decided to put our pajamas on and get into bed early. At around 8:30, Sharon fell asleep while we were watching Magnum P.I. reruns. I gently slid the TV remote out of her hand and turned the volume down so I would be sure to hear Kashan at the door when he arrived with Lilah.

At 5:00 a.m., Sharon's alarm sounded. It took a moment for me to realize it was already morning. I gasped and sat upright in bed.

"What is it?" Sharon asked, slightly annoyed that I was being dramatic so early in the morning.

"Kashan never brought Lilah back!" I screamed.

"Kashan's never does anything when he's supposed to." "Don't worry," Sharon tried to reassure me, "they probably just fell asleep like we did." "I'm sure everything is okay."

"I don't think so, Sharon." "Something's wrong," I insisted. "I know it!"

Sharon shook her head and walked to the kitchen to start the coffee. I called Kashan's phone, but he didn't answer.

"You know nothing wakes him up," Sharon said. "Calm down. I'm sure they're just sleeping. It is only five in the morning, you know."

Ignoring my sister's attempts to calm me down, I threw on my jeans and shirt and ran out without saying goodbye. I prayed as I quickly drove to Kashan's place.

"Oh God, please let everything be okay!" I cried.

When I got there, I ran out of the car, not even bothering to close the car door. I pounded on Kashan's door and shouted his name.

"Kashan! Kashan, open this door!" "Open this door NOW!" I screamed.

There was no response.

Where could they be at this time of the morning? This can't be happening. Please God, no!

I continued to beat on the door, yelling, "Kashan, answer the door!"

Thoughts ran at hyper speed through my mind. My instincts told me that every second counted.

"Please, God, please don't let it be too late," I pleaded.

Why wouldn't his roommate answer the door? What are the odds they would both be away from their apartment at this hour?

I called Kashan's number again and put my ear to the door, hoping to hear his phone ringing or someone moving around inside. But there was only silence—horrible silence.

Afraid to waste any more time beating on the door, I ran back to my car. I drove to his roommate's convenience store, desperate for any information that could help me find Lilah. It was close by the apartment complex, so I got there within minutes. I parked on the street right in front of the store and turned my blinkers on. When I got to the doors, I pulled on them frantically. They were locked.

Of course, they're locked. It's still too early for them to be open.

There was a dim light on inside, but I could not make out any human forms through the dirty glass. If anyone was inside, they weren't letting me in.

Kashan's roommate must have been inside the apartment when I was pounding on the door. He must be in on this. He was deliberately not answering the door. The scumbag!

I quickly rushed back to Kashan's apartment. Now sobbing, I banged on the door, repeatedly begging for someone to open up. Hearing the commotion, some of Kashan's neighbors began coming out of their apartments to see what was going on.

"Have you seen a little girl... a five-year-old girl with brown hair and big brown eyes…she was with her dad." "Have you seen them?" I asked, in a desperate frenzy.

One after another gave the same answer: "No, I haven't seen them."

Then, finally, a girl spoke up. "Maybe," she said. "I think I may have seen them going into that apartment sometime yesterday or the day before." "Why, what's wrong?" she asked.

All I could do was shake my head while tears flowed down my cheeks. I couldn't say it. I wouldn't say it.

Back in my car, I grabbed a small notebook from the glove compartment and wrote: Missing five-year-old girl, brown hair, brown eyes, visiting her father at apt 1C. Please call this number with any information.

I made several of the notes and attached them to various apartment doors with Lilah's Power Puff Girl Band-Aids. Then my phone rang. I answered immediately, hoping it was Kashan. It was Sharon.

"They're gone, Sharon!" "They aren't here!" was all I said before hanging up.

Then I got into my car and drove back to the convenience store. It was still closed. I wrote a special note for Kashan's roommate and attached it to the door with the last three Band-Aids: Call me about Lilah. DO THE RIGHT THING! I included both my phone number and Sharon's.

By the time I returned to Sharon's place, my sister Suzie was there. She embraced me as I entered the apartment. Sobbing, I collapsed and fell to the floor. Someone called the police. If it was me who called, I don't remember having that conversation. But the next conversation, I will never forget.

My phone began to ring. The screen showed an unfamiliar number from outside the area. I knew it was the call I was waiting for. I knew it was Kashan.

"It's him!" I said to my sisters before answering.

"Hello," I answered, bracing myself.

"Mary!" Kashan said harshly, as if reprimanding a disobedient child.

"Kashan—what have you done!" I shrieked.

"It's not what I have done." "It's what *you* have done, Mary," he said cruelly. "You made me do this. This is your fault because you decided to divorce me. And I am not willing to have my daughter raised apart from me, as an American."

"No... please, please, Kashan!" "Where are you?" I asked in desperation.

"It's too late. We are already in Paris. There's nothing you can do now."

"No, Kashan! No!" "It's not too late!" I cried.

"I didn't even have to call you. I have to go. We're getting on the plane now. And remember, Mary, this is all your fault. This is because of your selfishness."

Click. Then they were gone, and there was only silence—agonizing silence.

"No, no, no, please, God, nooooo!" I collapsed on the floor again.

Shaking my head back and forth, I continued saying, "No, no, no, no, no," as if I had a say in the matter. But I knew I didn't have a say. And I knew my cries fell on deaf ears. I was writhing in pain and numb at the same time. I was dying.

Then the police were there and I was providing them with the pertinent information. Somehow, words came out of my mouth. But they seemed to be coming from elsewhere. My physical body was there, but I was not present. I could not be present. I simply could not be there to live that. It was as if I had disconnected from my body and was observing all of it from afar. Faintly aware of what was happening, I could hear my sisters answer for me when I could not. The officers continued with the questioning at a slow pace, as if there was no urgency.

What's wrong with them? Why aren't they taking immediate action? They're acting as if time is not of the essence—as if there's really nothing they can do to get Lilah back.

There was mention of federal kidnapping charges. They informed us that the FBI would be in contact. I thought I heard them saying how sorry they were, and then Sharon thanking them as they left.

The pain was more than I could bear. The dark pit I was in was evil and so, so twisted. I never imagined there was a place like that in existence. But there it was, and I was in it. And there was no way out. There was no getting away from the agony of my child being taken. I was required to remain there, cruelly anchored in place.

At some point, the FBI showed up. The two agents introduced themselves and proceeded to explain how they had missed Kashan in Paris. The aircraft with Kashan and my little girl on it was already airborne by the time the FBI were informed, so it was too late for them to stop him. Kashan had gotten away with her. There was nothing they could do.

"When he called you, did he say exactly where in Jordan he was taking your daughter?" they inquired while taking notes.

"His parents live in Amman," I answered. "I have the street address and the home phone number. I've been there before."

I turned to Sharon and asked, "Where's my purse?"

Sharon handed it to me. With nervous jerky movements, I fumbled inside and managed to pull out a small, zippered wallet. Tucked into a slide pocket was a tiny piece of paper. I handed it to one of the agents. He looked at it and copied down the information.

"Can you have the police in Amman arrest him? We know where she is. Can we go get her?" I searched his eyes for any sign of hope.

He shook his head, then answered with a somber look. "It doesn't work like that," he explained. "Once he makes it into Jordan with her, there's nothing we can do since Jordan is not part of the Hague Convention."

Not fully understanding what he was saying, I was unwilling to simply take his word for it.

There has to be something they can do.

"The Hague Convention," he continued to explain, "is an agreement between countries which mandates the speedy return of a child in the case of an international child abduction, among other things." "Jordan is not party to the Hague Convention."

I couldn't believe that. I wasn't ready to accept what he was telling me. I shook my head.

There's no way that could possibly be true!

Next, the agents showed me how to use earpieces devised to record phone conversations. They said I should wear them whenever Kashan called—if he called, that is. I was told not to let Kashan know the FBI was involved or that he had federal kidnapping charges against him. They instructed me to talk with him for as long as possible and get him to admit what he had done. It wasn't clear to me how this would help to get my daughter back. But in my dazed condition, I mechanically agreed.

"Does your husband still want to be with you?" I heard one of the agents ask.

"Yes," I answered, staring into nothingness. "That's why he took her. This is my punishment for leaving him."

At that moment, a willingness to do whatever it took to get my daughter back saturated every cell of my being. I would have done anything to have Lilah there with me again. But it was too late. I began to sob with a regret so deep it could not be consoled. My sister Suzie wrapped her arms around me again while the agents waited. Finally, one of them spoke up.

"Mrs. Shehadeh," he stated seriously, "most parents of abducted children don't have these… circumstances." "In most cases, the abductor never calls the other parent, much less still wants to have a relationship with them."

That got my attention. I looked directly into his eyes.

"What exactly are you saying?" I demanded.

"What I'm saying is, we are not advising you on what to do, but… since he's still interested in being with you," he continued, "perhaps you can use that to your advantage." "Maybe you can convince him to come back to the States with your daughter."

Before he even finished his statement, I began wiping tears from my face and nodding my head in agreement.

Now they're finally making sense. That is EXACTLY what I'll do. I will convince Kashan that I'm still in love with him!

I didn't know how capable these men were in performing their job duties. They had already been clear about the limitations on their ability to bring my daughter back home. But I knew what *I* could do. And I was quite confident in my abilities. My mind raced as I realized the opportunity in front of me and the chance it provided for getting Lilah back.

Yes! I'll convince Kashan beyond a shadow of a doubt that I still love him. I'll tell him that I now realize what a huge mistake I made by leaving him. I'll make him believe I want to reconcile our marriage and, in doing so, I could possibly have Lilah back in my arms. Are you kidding me? Of course I can do this. Yes, sir, I can easily carry out this mission. Just watch me! Just let that phone ring. Oh Lord, please, just let that phone ring.

What the FBI didn't tell me on that day was that only a small percentage of women and children who travel to Sharia law countries and are held against their will ever make it out.

Chapter 6

PLAN A

It wasn't long before Kashan called again. And this time, he let me speak to Lilah. She was in good spirits because she believed they were in Jordan for just a visit, not forever. She had no idea that she had been kidnapped by her father, and I was surely not going to tell her. I felt that withholding the truth from her would protect her psyche until she was returned to the States.

Not knowing if I would ever see her again was killing me. I was in constant anguish. The days came and went, despite my inability to endure them. The sun rose and set each day, even though Lilah was no longer with me. It seemed cruel. Each moment that passed without her was more painful than the one before.

But at least Kashan kept calling. At first, he called every other day, but then he started calling every day. After the first week passed, I had him convinced that I still loved him and deeply regretted leaving the marriage. At that point, he ended each conversation by telling me he loved me, too. He also voiced his frustration over how things functioned in Jordan. I wasn't exactly sure what he meant by that, but it gave me hope he would ultimately decide to return to the States. And I gave him hope he had something to return to.

Each time Kashan called, I placed the recording device in my ear and spoke to him for as long as he wanted to talk. Continuously pressing the earpiece into my ear to make sure it was picking up the conversation caused my ears to be bruised and develop sores. But it did not compare with the pain I was feeling inside.

Even so, I forced myself to sound happy every time Kashan called. In hopes of getting Lilah back, I put my all into being everything he had always wanted me to be: an affectionate, submissive, passionate, and obedient wife who could not bear to live without him.

My stomach was constantly tied up in knots. My nervous system had taken a direct hit. With Lilah gone, I could not eat or sleep. My life had been reduced to a mere brokenhearted existence of sorts marked by continuous, agonizing conversations with Kashan.

How a parent might survive the death of their child, I could not in any way comprehend. How I would survive this was yet to be seen. Although the pain was excruciating, my focus was on surviving so I could do whatever was needed to bring my child back home.

Once I returned to Nahaven, both Janis and Gina tried to comfort me the best they could. Although I was quite inconsolable. I felt utterly alone in my anguish. Other friends, clients from the salon, and even some strangers graciously extended their condolences. I appreciated the sentiment, but it did nothing to ease my suffering. It was just too great.

At times, I managed to fall asleep, but sleep would not keep me. Each morning, without fail, I was greeted with the harrowing reality of my tragic circumstance. It was my first conscious thought of the day. Morning after morning, my earliest function was to come face to face with the formidable dark wall that had become my grim existence.

It presented itself prodigiously as it towered over me. It stood before me, blocking my path. It was seemingly immovable. It fastened itself to me, just in case I had any thoughts of tearing myself loose. It was ugly, cold, and forbidding. It came across as being massive and mighty, terminally final, and entirely void of hope. The pain it caused had sealed my mouth. I couldn't even utter a prayer. Nothing made sense anymore. Logic became futile. Thoughts became hurtful and useless.

My efforts to convince Kashan to come home seemed to be yielding some favorable results, though. Every time he complained about Amman, I encouraged him to come back home to the States. I told him we could live wherever he wanted since he also complained about living in Nahaven. I thought I had him convinced until one night when our conversation took a tragic turn. I was at Janis' house pouring orange juice while talking to Kashan on the phone when he cut me off.

"Listen, Mary, you need to understand that I'm never returning to the States," he said firmly.

I returned the Tropicana container to the shelf and closed the refrigerator door.

"What—what do you mean?" I asked as I froze in place. "What are you saying, Kashan?"

"I'm not coming back to live in the States," he reiterated.

"But... you hate it there," I reminded him in desperation.

"Well, I still don't see myself coming back to the States and raising my daughter there. She's much better off here in Amman." His delivery was cold.

"No, no, please!" I began to scream. "Don't say that!"

"Remember, Mary, your decision to split up our family is the reason I brought Lilah here in the first place. I can't trust that you wouldn't do the same thing again if I returned." His tone left no room for me to argue my point.

"But I promise I won't." "I love you, and I promise to never leave you again!" I pleaded.

At that point, Janis and her boyfriend, Melvin, came to the kitchen to see why I was raising my voice. I barely noticed them, though; I was too distraught.

"Sorry, Mary, you're just going to have to accept the fact that we're not coming back," Kashan stated without compassion.

"No, no, no!" I screamed. "Nooooo!"

The phone went silent. I fell to the floor in hysterics.

"Mary, hold on to your faith, my friend," Janis encouraged me. "You have to trust God to bring Lilah home!"

I got up, grabbed my purse and car keys, and ran out of the house. My intention was to get behind the wheel, pull out onto the street, and accelerate until I could no longer feel… anything. Melvin ran after me while Janis stayed in the house. He reached me before I was able to put my keys into the ignition.

"You don't want to do this, Mary," he said as he grabbed my arm. "You want to be here for Lilah when she comes home."

At hearing her name, I began sobbing and slumped over the steering wheel.

"Come on," he said with compassion. "Get out of the car. You can't go anywhere in this condition."

Realizing he was right, I slowly got out of the car. For Lilah's sake, I had to remain living. He took the keys from my hand and walked with me back into the house.

"Here... sit at the table and have a glass of water." Melvin set the glass in front of me. "Take some deep, slow breaths," he instructed. Then he sat with me at the table until he was sure I wasn't going anywhere.

For a while, I sat there sipping water in silence. Hurting too badly to be embarrassed over my dramatics, I shrugged it off. And I couldn't really blame Janis for not understanding. No one could understand the excruciating pain I was in. I knew that.

"How are you holding up?" Gina asked the following day when she stopped by the salon to check on me.

"Ask Janis," I replied sarcastically. Then I looked away, not really wanting to relive it.

"What do you mean?" her eyes narrowed.

"What I mean is," I turned to face her again, "I fell apart at her house last night when Kashan told me he wasn't coming back with Lilah."

"Oh gosh. I'm sorry, Mary. That had to be so disappointing."

"Yeah. I'm pretty devastated," I started to tear up. "I realize it's a lot for... everyone to deal with." My monotone voice conveyed my lack of desire to discuss it further.

Gina sighed and fell silent for a moment. Then she spoke. "Just go get your things after work and come stay with Jev and me," Gina suggested.

I looked at her, wondering if I had heard correctly.

"Are you serious?"

"Sure," she smiled warmly.

"Will Jev be okay with that?" I asked.

"Well... he will be when I let him know."

I looked at her, still unsure.

"Of course he will, Mary," she shook her head, dismissing my scrutiny.

"Thank you, Gina!" I put my hands up to my head and sighed in relief. "I just—I don't know what to say," I admitted.

"Just say, 'See you tonight,'" Gina answered jokingly.

"Okay, then," I replied. "See you tonight!"

"Thanks so much for everything," I told Janis when I went to her house that evening to collect my things. "I think it might be best if I go stay with Gina now. With everything that's happened… me being here and… well… it's been a lot for you and the kids to handle. But I really appreciate you letting me stay."

Janis wrinkled her brows. Then, after considering, she began to nod in agreement. "Of course, Mary," she answered. "You're my friend, and I love you. And I love Lilah."

"I know you do, Janis. We love you too."

Chapter 7

ALL TRUE

Every day while at work, I felt hollow as if I was an empty shell of a being robotically performing my duties. I wanted desperately to be void of the knowledge that my child was really gone. Much of the time, I managed to move myself into a state of nothingness where thought and emotion were kept at a distance. But without fail, the reality of heartbreak, devastation, and despair showed up uninvited.

This has happened. My child is gone. This nightmare is real, and I'm living it.

How could God let this happen to you, Mary?

Yes, how could he let this happen?

I thought the plans he had for you were for good and not for evil, to give you a future and a hope.

> For I know the plans I have for you, declares the Lord,
> plans for welfare (good) and not for evil,
> to give you a future and a hope.
> Jeremiah 29:11 ESV

Exactly. But this is not good, it's evil. So evil!

Yet God allowed it to happen.

I swept hair up off the salon floor and emptied the contents of the dustpan into the wastebasket mechanically. Again, the thought came:

How could God let this happen? Isn't he sovereign over ALL THINGS? Or… is he?

It was the end of the day. I stood there alone in the empty salon; those questions repeatedly came to mind. They were reasonable, legitimate questions. They deserved to be answered.

Suddenly, my mind was inundated with faith-draining speculation. Loud and indignant thoughts of confusion frantically swirled around in my mind, hoping to find a place to land and take root. One particular thought vied for dominance:

Didn't God say that he would never give you more than you could bear?

Yes, didn't he say that?

"Well… I beg to differ, Lord," I declared defiantly, looking up into the heavens. "This is more, so much more than I can bear. And you have let this happen!"

So… have I been believing lies all this time? Oh, please say it isn't so! Have I been a fool to believe all the promises in your word, only to be abandoned and taken down like this?

I gripped the broom in my hands firmly and determined that everything between God and me would be settled right then and there. Either God's word was all true, or it was a lie. But it could not be both.

I considered all the times the Lord had come through for me in the past—all the times I had taken him at his word and believed the promises he had given me in scripture.

Hadn't he been there for me over and over again when I needed him, though? Hadn't he been faithful to his word and to his promises? Yes, he had.

I could not deny that. He had been loving, faithful, and comforting. He had shown his power and strength as well. He had fought for me and caused me to always come out victorious. He had proven his love for me and even caused me to love him.

But now, this. He allowed THIS to happen. I'm not feeling his love now. I'm feeling abandoned!

Where is your God now? You are all alone.

I feel so utterly alone. And Lilah, my small helpless child… a world away. This is more than I can handle. This pain is more than I can endure.

And then, again, the recurring thought:

Just end it then. Just take your life, and all this pain will instantly go away. It's perfectly within reason. Everyone will surely understand.

I envisioned myself putting a gun to the side of my head, pulling the trigger, and in one second, ending the pain. Immediately, love-filled words came to my mind. With pure-light clarity, they broke through my pain, and with supernatural power, they shattered the darkness.

> "I have told you these things, so that in me you may have peace. In this world you will have trouble. But take heart! I have overcome the world."
> John 16:33 NLT

Yes! Jesus had warned us that in this world we would have trouble. But he told us to be encouraged when it happens because he has overcome the world.

That reminder of the truth made me know I was not alone. Relief from anguish and the weight of hopelessness immediately lifted. I took a breath in and exhaled slowly. Realizing it was a lifeline to me, I latched onto that scripture. Peace and clarity of mind came over me.

Then I began to recall Billy from church giving a testimony. He shared a scripture the Lord had given him during a difficult time in his life. The words he spoke rang clear and true.

> "No temptation has overtaken you except what is common to mankind. And God is faithful; He will not let you be tempted beyond what you can bear. But when you are tempted, he will also provide a way out so that you can endure it."
> 1 Corinthians 10:13 NIV

That's right! God never said he wouldn't put on us more than we could bear. He promised we wouldn't be TEMPTED more than we could bear and that he would always provide us a way out.

I recalled when I had first come to Nahaven. Lilah was just a baby then. I had returned to the Lord as a prodigal, broken and empty-handed. But God had welcomed me back with love and open arms.

Suddenly, a stream of vivid playbacks filled my consciousness. Precious memories came rushing to my mind. Vital recollections of immeasurable worth showed up like the truest of friends in a time of need. They reminded me of the numerous mornings I had spent sitting at the Lord's feet. I recalled the countless hours I put into learning about him, discovering his truth, and memorizing the promises in his word. He had restored me and transformed me. He had strengthened me and built up my faith. I had become firmly rooted in his love.

They had been tough times, yes, but truly the best days of my life. I wouldn't trade them for the world.

Those were the days when I really began to know God as my loving Father, my best friend, my Lord and Savior. His words to me were full of passion and unfathomable love.

> But then I will win her back once again. I will lead her
> into the desert and speak tenderly to her there. I will
> return her vineyards to her and transform the
> Valley of Trouble into a gateway of hope.
> Hosea 2:14-15 NLT

During that time, God had lovingly guided me by his Spirit in the word. He spoke to me on a personal level. In those intimate moments with him, I began to take him at his word. I took his promises to heart. There, in my time spent with him, I found comfort, reassurance, and hope for my life. As the Lord spoke his truth to me, previous misconceptions I had about myself were dispelled. They simply fell away.

Depending on God rather than flesh and blood was new to me then, and a bit scary at times. It was the first time in my adult life that I had been without a man by my side. But God came through time and time again without fail. He provided every answer, every need, and every opportunity. He brought clarity in confusion, stood beside me in conflict, and led me safely in the way I should go.

When I felt alone, he assured me:

> ... for the Lord your God goes with you; He will
> never leave you nor forsake you.
> Deuteronomy 31:6 NIV

When I was unsure of my worth, he revealed how much he paid for me:

> For you know that God paid a ransom to save you from the empty way of life you inherited from your ancestors. And it was not paid with mere gold or silver, which lose their value. It was the precious blood of Christ, the sinless spotless Lamb of God.
> 1 Peter 1:18-19 NLT

Whenever the enemy brought up my past, he reminded me I was redeemed:

> Fear not; you will no longer live in shame. Don't be afraid; there is no more disgrace for you. You will no longer remember the shame of your youth… for your Creator will be your husband; the Lord of Heaven's Armies is his name! He is your Redeemer, the Holy One of Israel, the God of all the earth.
> Isaiah 54:4-5 NLT

When I was afraid, he showed me that he had my back:

> "You will be firmly established in righteousness: You will be far from [even the thought of] oppression, for you will not fear, and from terror, for it will not come near you.
> Isaiah 54:14 AMP

When I worried about having everything I needed, he promised to provide:

> He will always give you all you need from day to day if you will make the Kingdom of God your primary concern.
> Luke 12:31 TLB

When I was impatient for my situation to improve, he showed me how to wait:

> Humble yourselves, therefore, under God's mighty hand, that he may lift you up in due time.
> 1 Peter 5:6 NIV

When medical tests threatened that death was at my doorstep, he spoke life to my flesh and allowed me more time:

> -the God who gives life to the dead and calls
> things into being that were not.
> Romans 4:17 NIV

God's word is true. It's ALL true! We will have trouble in this world, but Jesus has overcome the world! And that means that Jesus is the answer for this—the only answer. God has not abandoned me!

The enemy had tried to convince me that I was all alone. But I was not alone! The Lord was with me. And the battle—it wasn't mine. It was the Lord's.

> This is what the Lord says: do not be afraid! Don't be discouraged…, for the battle is not yours but God's.
> 2 Chronicles 20:15 NLT

When I fully acknowledged the truths already engraved upon my heart, God comforted me with his undeniable presence. A flood of tears came gushing from within me.

This battle is already over, and God has already won. The Lord is worthy of my trust. I will not be deceived into believing otherwise—not after all he's already done for me.

Knowing he was right there with me, I lifted my head toward heaven again.

"Okay, Lord," I said in full determination. "I guess we are doing this!"

Chapter 8

CLARITY

Considering the dire circumstances I was in, God could not have provided a better place for me to rest my head than with Gina. The severity of the assault I endured had partially paralyzed my soul. It would have been easy for me to turn on autopilot and cruise mechanically through daily functions, but that wouldn't have been productive. Gina's ability to remain focused and speak clarity into my situation was a blessing. She was a faithful friend, constantly coaching me out of a barely cognitive, survival-mode state of mind.

At the time, neither of us recognized the magnitude of our connection. Gina was simply helping out a friend in need. But the way God deliberately brought the two of us together would ultimately provide evidence of his sovereign hand in the two of us joining forces.

Gina's championing attitude towards me was just what I needed. She not only could handle all my tears, but she also helped me to discount my fears by continuously reminding me of God's promises. That helped me to see above the bleak details of my situation and put my mind to work. And that was when she and I began to talk about strategy.

For hours, we rocked on her porch and discussed possible scenarios of how I might get Lilah out of Jordan and back home where she belonged. Gina was clever. She was a quick study in understanding Kashan's ways and learning his culture as I explained it to her.

Our initial ideas were quickly discarded as being unrealistic for one reason or another. But at least we felt we were moving forward simply by the process of elimination. I was encouraged as, over time, the two of us became fairly resourceful at coming up with a game plan.

Eventually, we put together a short list of ways to lure Kashan out of Jordan and into a country that recognized The Hague Convention. The ideas that had real potential were based on facts rather than wishful thinking. A compilation of any and all assets already in place that worked in my favor was recognized. We made a note of any tactic that seemed at all plausible. Realistic strategies began to take shape.

We discussed convincing Kashan to meet with me in Spain since it was one of the Hague countries that would acknowledge the U.S. federal kidnapping charges against him. If Kashan agreed to meet me there, I would simply flee to the U.S. Embassy with Lilah. We contacted a private detective in Spain who was willing to assist for a fee. Unfortunately, when I discussed with Kashan the possibility of meeting up in Spain, he shut me down, making it clear he was not interested.

Then, during one of our front-porch discussions, I sat forward in my chair as an idea began to form. With eyes wide, I turned toward Gina.

"Wait a minute. I could convince Kashan to meet me in Israel!"

"Israel?" Gina asked. "Would that even be safe? It *is* in the Middle East, Mary."

"I know that. I've been in Jerusalem before. I was there with Kashan the year we got married. He has family who lives right outside of Jerusalem in Al-Azariya—the town we know as Bethany." "And Gina... Israel is part of the Hague Convention!" I added excitedly. "All I have to do is get Lilah away from him and run to the U.S. Embassy in Tel Aviv."

"You make it sound easy," Gina looked skeptical. "But isn't Israel surrounded by countries that are not part of the Hague Convention? Wouldn't it be too dangerous?"

"Gina, I'm sure I could convince him to meet me there," I explained. "It's a place he's very familiar with. He spent his childhood summers visiting relatives both in Jerusalem and the West Bank. We met up there back when his parents tried to make me return to the States."

"His parents tried to make you return to the States?" Gina's jaw dropped.

"Yes. They didn't want us to get married for… well… multiple reasons." I casually brushed off the impertinent details with a wave of my hand. "That's a whole other story for... another time. I wasn't even the same person then."

"We all have a past," she reminded me with a nod.

"We don't all have a past like mine," I insisted.

"Well, is that who you are today?" Gina asked.

"No—it's not," my brows lifted as I shook my head.

"What's that scripture?" "There is therefore—" she began reciting.

"—no condemnation for those who are in Christ Jesus," I said, finishing her sentence. "I know," I added.

> Therefore, there is now no condemnation for those who are in Christ Jesus, because through Christ Jesus the law of the spirit who gives life has set you free from the law of sin and death.
> Romans 8:1 NIV

"Okay, well... just be sure that you do know," Gina insisted. "That's nothin' but the devil trying to hit you when you're down. Bring that determination and tenacity you had in the past, but leave the guilt behind. It will work against you. You have to know who you are in Christ to be able to pull this off, Mary."

I nodded, acknowledging the truth in her statement.

"It is a good thing that you've been there before, though," Gina added.

"That's right," I agreed. "My past experience in the Middle East provides the knowledge and familiarity with the Palestinian culture that I would not have otherwise. I consider that to be a great asset under the circumstances."

"I agree. It's just scary for me to think about." "But you've actually stayed in his parents' home in Jordan, correct?" she asked.

"Yes, for nearly a month. That's how I was able to tell the FBI where he took Lilah. I know the exact neighborhood in Amman where they live." "I've kept that scrap of paper with their street address and phone number tucked in my purse since 1993," I said with a wink.

Chapter 9

JERUSALEM BOUND

After a couple more agonizing months of convincing Kashan I couldn't possibly live without him, he finally agreed to meet me in Jerusalem in late July. And he promised to bring Lilah with him. With the money I saved from working and the donations Gina collected from the community, I had enough funds to cover my flight into Tel Aviv plus return tickets for both Lilah and me.

I envisioned what it would be like to see my little girl for the first time in nearly four months. Our time apart had been extremely excruciating for me. I imagined how horrible it must be for five-year-old Lilah, who, on most nights, ended up sleeping in the same bed with her mommy.

Is she wondering why Mommy never told her she'd be going away with Daddy all by herself? Does she feel abandoned by me? So many days have gone by, and still, no Mommy. She was unexpectedly plunged into a totally different culture with no comprehension of the language. This must be so scary for her.

To ease Lilah's fears, each time I spoke with her, I made sure to emphasize how wonderful it was that she was able to travel to the Middle East. I kept up the facade that everything was good and I would be joining them soon. It was vital that Lilah remain oblivious to the fact that she had been kidnapped, not only to protect her mental and emotional state of well-being, but also to make sure my plan to get her back was not compromised. Kashan and his family would, no doubt, ask Lilah what her mommy said after every phone conversation between us. The story had to remain consistent: she was there visiting, and Mommy would join them soon.

The upcoming trip to Jerusalem became my sole focus. Finally, I would be able to see Lilah and bring her back home with me. After my plan to lure Kashan back into the States failed, I refused to entertain the thought that the Jerusalem mission would not be successful.

My father, Seán Kennedy, on the other hand, wasn't so optimistic. Imagining the worst, he made it quite clear he didn't think I should travel to Israel to meet Kashan. He doubted the success of my mission and feared for my safety.

"You can't go over there," he said during one of our phone conversations. "You won't make it back alive. You may as well stand in the middle of Hwy 95. That's how good your chances of surviving are if you go!"

"But I have to go, Dad," I insisted. "It's the only way I can get Lilah back. Kashan isn't coming back to the States. He probably suspects that he has federal kidnapping charges against him. He won't risk going to jail. I have to go get Lilah. If Mom was still alive, she would tell you that you would do the very same thing under the circumstances. You would never have left one of us by ourselves in a foreign land. I'm not leaving her there, Dad."

He knew I was right. He would have done the same thing, no matter how dangerous it was. And my mother would have reminded him of that if she were still with us. But I was thankful Mom wasn't there to witness what Kashan had done. It would have been too much for her.

"Well," my dad said, "just promise me that once you get to Israel, you will not, under any circumstances, go into Jordan with him."

"Okay, Dad." "I promise," I assured him.

There was no reason for me to go into Jordan. So, I totally meant it when I said it. I had no desire to see Kashan's parents ever again, and I was quite sure the feeling was mutual. The idea of going back into a country where I had far fewer rights simply because I was female was not appealing to me whatsoever.

And it wasn't like Kashan could knock me unconscious and smuggle me across the border. Israeli security at the borders was no joke. But my father had not been to the Middle East before, so he wouldn't have known. The unknown is always scarier than reality, so I completely understood why my father was afraid for me.

Once my plane ticket was purchased, I could barely contain my excitement over seeing Lilah. I applied for a passport for Lilah using the most recent picture I had of her. I prayed it would come in before I left for Israel. But even if it didn't, I figured it would be easier to obtain a replacement passport abroad than a first issue.

I was concerned that Kashan might listen in on my phone conversations once I arrived in Israel, so I thought it wise to avoid all correspondence with Gina. But I needed to know if

Lilah's passport came in after I already left for the Middle East. So Gina and I came up with a plan.

Our plan involved a Christian woman who currently lived in Israel. Her name was Tal. She had lived with Janis for a few years prior to my arrival in Nahaven. I'd met her briefly when she came back to Nahaven for a visit. I didn't know Tal very well, but I trusted her because she was a good friend of Janis'. And since she lived in Israel, I asked Gina to communicate with Tal, rather than me, to let her know the status of Lilah's passport.

I would meet up with Tal in Jerusalem at the Damascus Gate. It was a location I was familiar with, having been there with Kashan back in 1993. It was also within walking distance from the hotel where I would be staying. Tal would discreetly communicate to me the updated status on Lilah's passport in code.

If the passport had arrived, the code would be: "Breanna slept in her own bed last night." If it had not arrived, the code would be: "Breanna did not sleep in her own bed last night." It was imperative that Tal and I make it appear as if we did not know each other, just in case Kashan was watching me. It seemed like a good plan.

The day of my departure came, but unfortunately, Lilah's passport had not arrived. My first flight left out of Prominence International Airport and went directly to JFK. From there, I would fly El Al Israel Airlines all the way to Ben Gurion Airport in Tel Aviv. While I waited to board my flight at JFK, I heard my name called out over the loudspeaker.

"Mary Shehadeh, please report to the information counter in Terminal 4. Mary Shehadeh, please report to the Terminal 4 information counter."

My mind began to race as I tried to imagine why I was being paged. I hadn't even boarded my flight to see Lilah and already something unexpected was happening.

Oh, please, Lord, don't let anything stop me from boarding this plane. Please let this be good news and not bad.

"Hi... I'm Mary Shehadeh," I said as I approached the counter.

"May I see your identification, please?" the customer service representative asked. Once he verified my identity, he handed me the phone and said, "You have a call."

I put the phone to my ear and said, "Hello," with a shaky voice.

"Hey," Gina's voice sounded. "Guess what came in the mail right after you left?"

"You're kidding me!" I said, relieved that nothing was wrong.

"That's right," Gina answered, "Lilah's passport."

"Well, at least when we get to the Embassy, I can say she already has one, even if I don't have it with me. Hopefully, that will make the whole process a bit easier."

"Exactly," Gina agreed. "How are you holding up?"

"I'm okay." "Just... wired nerves," I admitted. "I freaked out a bit when I heard my name being called throughout the terminal."

"Well, just remember that you have a lot of people praying for you." "And greater is he—" she began to say.

"Yes, I know. Greater is he that is in me. Thanks, Gina." "Love you," I added.

"Love you too, Mary."

As I walked back to my gate, I prayed that the next time I spoke with Gina, I would be telling her we were safely away from Kashan and on our way back home.

The flight was long and exhausting, and the plane was packed. My nose was constantly assaulted by other people's body odor. Cold, artificial air continuously recirculated the musty smell throughout the cabin. But knowing I was on my way to see Lilah, I was more than happy to suffer through it. During the ten-hour flight, I constantly went over the timeline of events ahead of me:

- Exchange some of my cash for Israeli currency.
- Catch a cab to Jerusalem.
- Check into my hotel.
- Freshen up.
- Grab something to eat.
- Meet with Tal later in the evening.
- Meet with Kashan and finally see Lilah tomorrow.

(As if putting them to memory by order would mean the success of my mission.)

Chapter 10

THE HOLY LAND

Holding tightly onto hope (and the armrest of my seat), I finally arrived in Israel. My stress level had maintained high altitude for the duration of the flight. By the time we landed, my nerves were frayed—pushed well beyond healthy limits. But I had made it there! The enthusiastic applause from my fellow passengers upon our safe arrival confirmed it.

Those seated closer to the front began to deplane. I took deep breaths and hoped my legs would support me when it was my turn to stand. My feet hadn't touched Middle Eastern soil since October of 1993. I was so much in love with Kashan then. Much had changed. Yet one thing remained the same; there was something so exceptional, even transcendent, about the Holy Land. These circumstances, as agonizing as they were, could never change that.

It was as if the atmosphere were alive, possessing its own unique expression in space and time. The Holy Land seemed predestined to be the world's platform for major events: past, present, and future. The land struck me as being of another world, one not subject to my limited understanding or my concept of such wondrous things. I wondered if other travelers to the region felt the same way upon their arrival.

Israel, in the expanse of time, had experienced both immeasurable blessing and unfathomable loss. I admired the ability of its people to survive the past and to thrive in the perilous present. I also respected their resolve and fortitude as they tenaciously held onto the long-foretold promises of God.

God had graciously bestowed on this favored soil the privilege of hosting the most miraculous world-changing events of all time. It was the destination for the birth, the life, the death, and the resurrection of the Messiah. It was both the promised land and the land of many promises. And, in Christ, those promises would benefit all mankind for eternity.

> But the land you are crossing the Jordan to take
> possession of is a land of mountains and valleys that drinks
> rain from heaven. It is a land the Lord your God cares for;
> the eyes of the Lord your God are continually on it from the
> beginning of the year to its end.
> Deuteronomy 11:11-12 NLT

> And now that you belong to
> Christ, you are the true children of Abraham.
> You are his heirs, and God's promise to Abraham
> belongs to you.
> Galatians 3:29 NLT

After going through customs at Ben Gurion Airport, I followed a sign directing me to the taxi area. I exited Terminal 3 and stood at the curb long enough to get my bearings. The semi-arid air enveloped me with a warm and dusty embrace.

In my brokenhearted condition, the only salutation I was able to extend was brief but friendly, "Yes... I remember you. How could I forget?"

Then, interrupting my thoughts, an attendant courteously asked which city I was going to. Gesturing with his hand, he directed me to a line of taxis.

"King David Street 26, Jerusalem International YMCA," I instructed the driver as I hopped into the back seat.

I hadn't come that far for a sentimental reunion with the Middle East. I wasn't there to connect with my spiritual forefathers or even to retrace the steps of my beloved Savior. But I knew Jesus was right there with me as the taxi moved swiftly toward the Old City area of Jerusalem, where I would finally be reunited with Lilah.

The telltale rhythms that came from the car speakers, along with the Arabic lettered rearview mirror ornament, indicated to me that the driver was most likely Palestinian.

"Shukran [Thank you]," I said in Arabic as I exited the vehicle. Once the driver removed my bags from the trunk, I paid him in Israeli shekels and thanked him again.

In front of the hotel were huge Italian cypress trees. I stood there for a while looking up at them. Their branches reached elegantly toward the sky. I got the impression they'd been there for a hundred, maybe even a thousand years. The statement they made was one of enduring strength, causing me to feel temporal and insignificant in comparison.

Strategically positioned to serve as beautiful adornments, these organic, living spectators had a towering bird's-eye view. They had been involuntarily subjected to witnessing the countless endeavors and many zealous plights of the flawed humanity that had planted them there.

> For the creation was subjected to frustration, not by its own choice, but by the will of the one who subjected it, in hope that the creation itself will be liberated from its bondage to decay and brought into the freedom and glory of the children of God. We know that the whole creation has been groaning as in the pains of childbirth right up to the present time.
> Romans 8:20-22 NIV

What will they observe from my endeavors here? Whatever the outcome, whether it's failure or success, these trees will, no doubt, remain stoically unmoved and relatively unaffected.

Yearning for the solace I often found in the presence of nature, I lingered a bit longer. I searched for any sign of encouragement from within their massive limbs and dense dark foliage. But I found none.

As I continued looking up, I began to get lightheaded. The earth under my feet seemed to shift as if burdened by the weight of my devastating reality. I felt sure it sank a degree or two as though it were dropping me firmly into the regional time zone. A marked impression of inevitable failure hovered in the Levantine air around me. Unsteady, I sat down on a nearby bench.

I became flooded with notions of hopelessness and lowered my head to my hands. Waves teeming with pessimistic seeds of despair began to wash over my mind. Like tiny ravenous crustaceans that burrow under sand looking for food, disparaging thoughts scoured the shallows of my soul for any bits of fear or particles of doubt to feed on.

You aren't going to pull this off. You won't be successful.

The thought rumbled formidably through my mind. My hands began to tremble in response. If I was going to succeed in my mission to rescue Lilah, I had to get it together. Failing was not an option.

If I can just shift my focus from the surge of despondency that just washed over me to God's faithfulness and power…

> When the enemy comes in like a flood, the Spirit of
> the Lord will lift up a standard against him.
> Isaiah 59:19 NKJV

"Oh Lord, please make my attempts successful," I whispered so only he would hear. "I need you, Lord. How I need you. It is in you that I place my confidence, not in myself. And I know you will never leave me or forsake me."

> Do not be afraid or discouraged, for the Lord will
> personally go ahead of you. He will be with you; he will
> never fail you nor abandon you.
> Deuteronomy 31:8 NLT

Immediately, hopelessness vanished, and I began to feel grounded again. The reminder of whose ability I was relying on was all I needed to settle my nerves and clear my mind. And if my mind wasn't clear, I could easily make a mistake. One wrong word, one wrong expression, one wrong action… even the slightest delay in responding correctly could make Kashan doubt me.

He needed to be convinced of my devotion. All the affection and passion for this man, which had once been so deeply embedded in my heart, had to be re-enacted to perfection. I had been there before. It wasn't unknown territory. Therefore, I was certain I could do it again.

It was cruel for Kashan to separate me from my child and bring her to the Middle East the way he did. So I was determined to take the advice of the FBI and fool him to get her back. I believed I was doing nothing more than any other mother would do to get their child back, and I was confident God was on my side.

> What, then, shall we say in response to these things?
> If God is for us, who can be against us?
> Romans 8:31 NIV

My heart had led me astray, and I had paid a high price for it. I had suffered substantially due to the adultery, verbal and physical abuse, alienation of friends and family, and rigid control Kashan had subjected me to. My indoctrination into his beliefs that dictated everything I did as a woman was degrading, demeaning, and demoralizing. It had caused me great damage. Yet, I had recovered and remained resolute. The man wreaked havoc over the past eleven years of my life. The way I saw it, what was a couple more days for the sake of my daughter?

"Thank you, Lord, for giving me the victory," I declared as I stood up and walked toward the entrance of the hotel. "And thank you that good will surely triumph over evil," I said, intentionally leaving behind any thoughts of hopelessness and defeat.

Chapter 11

HUMMUS AND FALAFEL

As I entered the building, I couldn't help but pause for a moment to take it all in. It was much nicer than I expected. The reception area was grand with beautifully painted arched ceilings. There were arched hallways as well. The carved, solid wood doors down the corridors looked like they were straight out of the first century. The sound of my sandals tapping against the marble floors echoed loudly, announcing my arrival. I pulled out my American passport as I approached the front desk.

"Mary Shehadeh." "I have a reservation," I handed the front desk receptionist the printout showing the details of my confirmation.

As he looked over my documents, his eyebrows raised in what I perceived to be a seasoned effort to convey class and sophistication. I was neither intimidated nor impressed. I would have appreciated a warmer welcome, though. But I was not put off. After all, his position at that lovely hotel was more than likely the envy of his peers. I gave him that.

His posture toward me remained austere with an air of suspicion as he turned to retrieve the key to my room. I suppose he was skeptical of a single woman—especially one bearing a Palestinian last name—checking into a hotel without a husband. Regardless, I remained confident. I knew I was completely within my rights to reserve a hotel room with or without a man, even if it was frowned upon by some of the locals.

Of course, the last thing I wanted to do was draw attention to myself or cause any unnecessary drama. But I was already familiar with Palestinian culture. I knew well enough how to conduct myself with the modesty and reserve that was expected of females. So, I wasn't bothered. And I didn't consider one nosy hotel clerk to be a problem. My focus remained on bringing Lilah back home.

As I followed the bellhop around the corner and down the hallway to my room, I began to reflect on the last time I had been to the Holy Land. It was a different time then, and I was a different person. In defiance of Kashan's parents' attempts to send me back to the U.S., I had come to Jerusalem from Amman to meet up with Kashan. And there I was again, roughly a mile from the Damascus Gate. Back then, young Israeli Police Officers had invited me to stand on top of the wall with them while I waited for Kashan.

I was so in love with him then. Those feelings no longer existed. But even so, it was imperative that I have total recall of how it felt to be in love with Kashan. My daughter's life depended on it. I had to reenact all of it, as if it were simply a continuation of a play, as if I were so blinded by love for him that I could easily forgive and forget anything he had ever done to me.

He had to believe that I still wanted to be with him—that I could not bear to live without him. And thus far, over the phone at least, I had done a pretty good job of convincing him. Being there with him was merely an extension of that performance.

There isn't much else I can do to get Lilah back. But I can do THIS!

I assumed no shame in this dissimulated act. I knew I was totally justified. Everything was at risk. So, I determined to give the performance of a lifetime.

Kashan will be convinced that I want to be with him forever. He will drop his guard and then, somehow, I'll get Lilah away from him and flee to the U.S. Embassy in Tel Aviv. I'll take back what the enemy stole from me. And in the name of everything that is just and right, I will do it with a clear conscience!

Once inside my hotel room, the porter placed my suitcase on the luggage rack without making eye contact. I fumbled around in my purse and quickly pulled out some shekels, guessing what an appropriate amount for his tip should be.

"Shukran," I said to the lanky young man.

He made a slight bowing gesture as he graciously accepted the money, then backed away and promptly disappeared into the hallway. I let the bags I'd been carrying on my shoulders slip down my arms and onto the bed. It felt great to be finally unburdened of what felt like a tremendous amount of weight.

"Whew," I sighed in relief.

The room was meticulously clean and quite nice. It possessed a soft, comfy version of Middle Eastern décor. Creamy white linens beautifully contrasted the dark wood furniture. It wasn't over the top by any means. It was very tastefully done.

I pulled back the sheer window curtains and looked down onto the courtyard below. Large pots of palms and summer flowers were strategically placed among small, round dining tables. Unfortunately, the stone wall surrounding the Old City of Jerusalem was not visible from my window. But I knew exactly where I was. I was just miles away from Lilah, and just hours away from holding her in my arms again.

My stomach tensed up as I searched for the long-distance calling card I had purchased at the Speedy Fresh convenience store before leaving Nahaven. I promised Kashan I would call as soon as I checked into the hotel.

"Hello, sweetheart. How was your flight?" "Are you looking forward to seeing me?" he asked before I had a chance to respond.

Chills ran down my spine at the sound of his voice. I shuddered knowing he was in such close proximity to me. Then I collected myself and answered, matching his enthusiasm.

"You know I'm looking forward to seeing you. I can't believe I'm finally here! My flight was so long, though." "I'm exhausted, but I'm so eager to see you," I professed. "Where are you?"

"I'm still in Jordan, but I'll come first thing in the morning," he promised.

I pretended to believe him. But I knew Kashan did *nothing* first thing in the morning.

"How's Lilah?" "Is she excited to see her mommy?" I asked.

"Listen, sweetheart," he said, cutting me off, "I'll let you get some rest." "I have to get some things done now so I'll be able to come see you tomorrow." "Have you missed me, habibti [my love]?" he asked in pursuit of having his ego stroked.

"Of course I have." "Have you missed me?" I asked in feigned interest.

"I can't wait to show you how much I've missed you," he responded.

The very thought of being close to him made me cringe. But being close to him meant I was going to be with Lilah. And that is what made the whole thing doable.

"Well, just think, we are within only hours of seeing each other now," I reminded him. "Tomorrow can't come soon enough. What time will you guys get here?"

"Well, I'm not sure exactly what time it will be because I don't know how much BS I have to put up with when I go through Israeli security," he grumbled.

For a moment I was silent. Then, remembering my role, I asked sweetly, "Will you call when you're on the way, please?"

"Sure," he answered.

I didn't put much stock in it, though. His sarcastic tone made me feel as if he thought I was trying to call the shots. So, I left it alone.

"Okay, sweetheart, you get some rest now," Kashan said, taking back control of the conversation. "We love you. We will be seeing you soon."

"Okay. I love you. Can't wait to see you!"

"Love you too," he said hurriedly. "Bye!" He hung up abruptly.

Since early spring, I had played the lover's role over the phone with Kashan. Now I would have to act it out in person. If I wasn't convincing enough, I could ruin my chances of saving my daughter. Every time I closed my eyes, her sweet face was all I could see.

I unpacked my toiletries in anticipation of taking a shower to remove the dusty film of travel that had attached itself to me. Continuously going over the role I had to play the next day left me mentally exhausted. I lingered in the shower, allowing the warm, flowing water to provide a therapeutic reprieve from my nonstop mental activity.

The soft white towel from the rack beside the shower felt healing to my skin as I dried off. I grabbed a second towel, wrapped it around my wet curls, and secured it with a tuck at the nape like a turban. Feeling clean and refreshed, I picked out an outfit based on what I would not be wearing the next day when I saw Kashan. Every decision I made was strategic.

My challenge was to appear put together yet totally relaxed, all without straying from the game plan. Kashan was already going to be suspicious—that's just how he was. The slightest change in my composure or appearance could possibly be seen as a red flag to him. And I knew what he was capable of when he became suspicious.

A flashback suddenly came to my mind as I was getting dressed. It was the memory of being physically held down by Kashan and interrogated for hours to the point that I gave false confessions just to satisfy his sick imagination and get him off me. My body froze in place when I recounted the horrible experience.

Just then, a beam of sunlight caught something in my peripheral vision. It twinkled, pulling me away from my dark thoughts. On the bathroom countertop sat a drinking glass beautifully etched with the Greek key design.

"Oh, yes!" I exclaimed, realizing how perfect the glass would be for holding my makeup brushes.

Applying my makeup was always a stress-reliever for me. I took a deep breath in, then exhaled and began applying my foundation. Once I was done with my makeup and hair, I made my way to the dining area. The tables outside were beginning to fill up, but there were still a couple of good options. I claimed a table close to an exterior wall that was adorned with a flowering vine. There was also a beautiful multi-tiered fountain nearby. The sound of trickling water falling into the ceramic basins was a lovely embellishment.

A waiter came immediately with a glass of fresh water. I looked over the bi-fold menu and recognized every item listed. Normally, I would have chosen tabbouleh, stuffed grape leaves, and baba ghanoush, but I didn't feel up to it. Instead, I placed a simple order of hummus and falafel. And hot tea with mint, of course.

The wonder of the Holy Land was all around me. I was younger when I had been there before. Back then, I did not grasp the full significance of the land. But having established an actual relationship with the Lord, the Holy Land had become much more relevant to me on a personal level. It was no longer simply a distant place I had wandered to in pursuit of love.

> All of us, like sheep, have strayed away. We have
> left God's paths to follow our own.
> Isaiah 53:6 NLT

And I am no longer the person I used to be. Since then, the foolish woman I was has been sufficiently schooled by the errors of her past. She has received practical, hands-on education in domestic dysfunction, thus qualifying her, I suppose, for these... continuing studies. Because now, here she is, in the process of earning a master's degree in this lamentable field of study, this abhorrent discipline, this... present-day living hell!

But those kinds of thoughts were defeatist in nature. So I shook them off. This visit to the Holy Land was different. I was there on a more worthy mission this time. And unlike before, I had not arrived disarmed by my own ignorance and naivety. This time was different because the Lord was there with me. I was there in his power, not my own strength. And he had equipped me with everything I needed to succeed. Wisdom was there to guide me, and discernment was ever-present to help me detect any underlying motives Kashan might have.

In my time walking with God, I had come to know the benefits of long-suffering. And long-suffering had produced an endurance in me which, I believed, would serve me well on this mission. God had done a work deep within me, preparing me for what was ahead. He had given me the insight necessary to make wise choices. And I was fully aware that each decision I made while there in the Middle East would impact my chances of success.

"Please, Lord, protect my life and help me bring Lilah back home," I whispered.

"Can I bring you anything else?" the waiter asked, startling me from my thoughts. He placed the requested items on the table and waited for my response.

"No," I replied. "Shukran."

He gave me a quick nod and smile, then retreated. As I watched the steam rise from the cup of hot tea, my mind promptly returned to rehearsing the role I had to play.

I can't let it look like I only care about seeing Lilah. But I will, of course, often convey to Kashan my intention that the three of us will be together forever as a family—never to be separated again. Though... it must appear as if my main focus is to enjoy every moment spent in his presence. This should not be too difficult, really.

It's not like Kashan wouldn't be willing to help a girl out with this kind of performance. I mean, his well-developed ego will be an enthusiastic participant in my conjured-up show of affection toward him. My declaration of love should come into perfect agreement with how highly Kashan thinks of himself. It'll make sense to him that I finally arrived at the conclusion that he is just too wonderful for me to part with.

Going over things constantly in my head was exhausting but necessary. I had to stay on track. Unconsciously nodding my head in determination, I wiped my mouth with a napkin, then placed the napkin firmly on the table.

I knew it was a good plan. It had to be. It was the only plan I had.

Chapter 12

DAMASCUS GATE

There was little movement in the air on that warm summer night. As I made my way to the Damascus Gate to meet up with Tal, I constantly glanced down at my watch, gauging my progress. I had left the hotel ten minutes early, just to make sure I wouldn't be late. Thankfully, I had remembered to set my watch to the local time when I arrived at the airport.

I wasn't supposed to see Kashan until the following day. But I had to consider all potential scenarios. There was a chance he would arrive early to make sure I didn't have anyone with me. Kashan might suspect that my sudden change of heart toward him could be a ploy to trick him into bringing Lilah into Israel. As paranoid and suspicious as Kashan was, he might also assume I had police, FBI, or even Mossad backup so I could have him arrested. There was even a possibility that he already had eyes on me since my arrival at the airport. I wouldn't put anything past him.

Tal and I had to be inconspicuous. We decided ahead of time that our meeting should appear to be merely a spontaneous encounter among strangers. I would ask her where I could find a gift shop to buy souvenirs, and she would discreetly convey the status of Lilah's passport by using the secret code.

Of course, I already knew Lilah's passport had come in, and I assumed Gina had also informed Tal. But I still planned to meet up with her. I looked forward to seeing a friendly face. But we had to be careful. If Kashan saw me talking to someone, he would become suspicious. And if that happened, he wouldn't take his eyes off me for even a moment. And a moment could be all I needed to break away and disappear into the streets of Jerusalem with Lilah.

As I approached the Damascus Gate, I saw Tal coming from the opposite direction. I wasn't sure she saw me yet. Walking directly toward her, I stared, as if it might compel her to notice me. Once we were within yards of each other, we finally made eye contact, then immediately looked away.

I casually approached her and inquired about a gift shop. Out of nervousness, I choked a little when I spoke, which put both of us on edge. The intensity of the situation caused us to hold our eyes wide open in a weird and abnormal way, as we continuously scanned the area for any sign of Kashan.

With straight faces, we intentionally showed no emotion, as if doing so would blow our cover. Which, looking back at it, I suppose only made us appear more suspicious. Thankfully, no one at the Damascus Gate on that summer night in the year 2000 seemed to notice the two white women displaying rather awkward behavior.

Then, in her proper and prestigious accent, Tal, through lips that barely moved, uttered the secret phrase: "Breanna slept in her own bed last night."

I gave her a slight nod, acknowledging that Gina had already informed me about the passport. But I guess my response wasn't clear enough because Tal's eyes focused directly on mine and opened even wider. Through clenched teeth, she repeated our clandestine code.

"I said, Breanna slept in her own bed last night!"

"Yes, I know, Tal," I said with minimal expression. Then I broke eye contact with her and looked elsewhere. "Gina already let me know the passport arrived while I was waiting to board my flight at JFK," I explained, while casually rubbing my forehead.

I glanced back at Tal long enough to make sure she comprehended what I was saying. She raised her brows and nodded, letting me know she understood. Then we both relaxed a bit.

To avoid further exposure, I suggested Tal come to my hotel room, where we could speak more freely. Once confirming that she was familiar with the location, we parted ways. Soon after I returned to my room, Tal arrived bearing chocolate rugelach, a delicious Israeli pastry. After catching up on the details of each other's lives, we agreed it was best to say goodbye just in case Kashan decided to show up that night unexpectedly.

"Can I pray for you before I leave, Mary?" she reached out toward me.

"Of course you can," I answered. "Please do," I clasped onto her hands.

"Heavenly Father," she began, "I ask for a hedge of protection around Mary and Lilah." "Give Mary peace so that she will be able to sleep tonight. And Lord, please bring them back to the U.S. safely. In Jesus's mighty name we pray. Amen."

"Amen!" "Thank you, Tal," I hugged her.

Tal left the room discreetly. I closed my eyes and let out a breath. The short visit with Tal had been a comforting reminder that I was not alone.

"Lord, thank you that your presence is here with me tonight." "I could never do this without you," I admitted.

Peace lingered in the room as I prepared for bed. My limbs ached as if they were still carrying the weight and the length of my day. But I knew the pain would subside by morning if I could stop thinking long enough to let sleep overtake me. I slipped underneath the comfort of the bed's soft linens and began counting my slow, deliberate breaths as if they were sheep. It didn't take long for me to drift off.

A few hours later, my sleep was disturbed by a repetitive sound. Due to exhaustion, I was a bit disoriented. The clock showed it was only 1:15 a.m. local time, but my phone was ringing nonstop.

"Hello!" I answered rather frantically, imagining there was some sort of emergency.

"I just called to make sure you were okay and that nobody was bothering you," an all-too-familiar voice sounded.

"Yes, I'm fine, Kashan." "No one is bothering me," I reassured him. "I was sleeping."

"Do you promise me? No man has tried to talk to you?" His tone conveyed accusation.

"I promise. Nobody has tried to talk to me. I'm pretty sure they would be afraid of losing their job if they did."

"Okay, habibti. Tisbahina ala khair [good night]. I'll let you go back to sleep. Love you. Goodnight."

"Love you too. Goodnight," I hung up and placed my phone back on the nightstand.

"Whew," I exhaled, relieved that everything was alright.

I lay there for an hour, thoughts swirling in my head. At best, I got only intermittent sleep, waking periodically to check the time and count the hours until I would see Lilah. By 6:30 a.m. I finally gave up and got out of bed.

After showering, I applied my makeup carefully, wanting to look my best. In this part of the world, there were beautiful women everywhere. And with Kashan's propensity for, well… being with women, I knew what I was up against. I couldn't risk him losing interest in me. So, I planned to use every God-given asset I possessed to hold his attention.

Much thought had already been put into my style for the day. A dark, smoky-eyed look was my go-to for giving my rather plain brown eyes a more dramatic appearance. I chose a sheer violet lip color to balance out the deep aubergine shade on my eyes.

The purple fitted top with flowy sleeves I decided on complimented my complexion. It was made of a lightweight cotton material and, for added interest, had an embroidered pattern in a similar hue on the décolletage area. The tassel ties at the collar could be pulled together for a more modest look. Any wrinkles that hadn't fallen out of the shirt overnight could be easily taken care of with a blast of hot air from a blow-dryer.

I pulled the blouse over my head carefully to ensure I didn't mess up my makeup. Then I stepped into my favorite bootleg jeans and pulled them on. A quick glance in the mirror verified that the top fell at a flattering place at my hips. Every little detail mattered, considering what was at risk.

The thought of finally seeing Lilah filled my heart with joy. I almost couldn't contain myself. But no matter how I thought things would go, I knew I could not count on anything—not when it came to Kashan. With him, I never knew what to expect. I always had to hope for the best yet be prepared for the worst. But still, I hoped and prayed the day would be filled with only good things.

Today has to be good. Guaranteed! This is the day I'll see Lilah. Maybe this is even the day I'll take her away from this place. Or maybe it will be tomorrow. Yes... tomorrow sounds a bit more realistic.

"Lord, please let it be soon," I whispered as I walked out of my room and locked the door behind me.

"Labneh and shai [tea] with na na [mint], please," I said to the waiter when he asked for my order.

I tried to relax as I sat there in the warmth of the morning sun. It was difficult, though, because my phone remained silent. Kashan hadn't even called to tell me they were on the way.

That could mean anything or... it could mean nothing.

The idea that I was now within hours of holding Lilah in my arms again felt surreal. Part of me seemed almost afraid to believe it. At one point, I had feared I would never see her again.

But now... the thing that I thought might never happen is actually going to happen!

The waiter returned with my breakfast, startling me from my thought flow. I wasted no time getting back to it.

When I finally see Lilah, I've got to make sure I don't fall apart. I can hug and kiss her, but I've got to show Kashan at least as much attention—if not more—or he may be suspicious of my motives. He has to believe that I'm here to be with him and not simply to retrieve my daughter. My actions have to go along with the narrative I've so earnestly portrayed over the last few months.

After I finished my breakfast, I decided to walk around a bit to kill some time. Realistically, it could very well be several hours still before Kashan showed up. The day was getting hotter, and I was having second thoughts about my choice of clothing.

Down the street, closer to the Old City, there was a small vendor stand. It had tons of brightly colored fruits piled up on display. Drawn in by the fresh aromas and bright colors, I soon found myself at the counter ordering fresh-squeezed juice. Still somewhat dehydrated from my flight, I figured it would do my body good. When I requested both orange and pomegranate mixed together, the shop owner was more than happy to accommodate me. I hoped everything in my day would be that accommodating.

It was already noon, and still no call from Kashan. Waiting like that with no word from him stressed me out. I hated how inconsiderate he was.

Surely, he must know how anxious I am waiting for him here by myself in a foreign country.

After finishing my juice, I decided to head back to the hotel. I didn't want to be too far away in case they arrived suddenly. When I reached the lobby, I sat down on a beautifully sculpted wooden bench. It was far enough away from the front desk that my conversation would not be overheard. I punched in the numbers from the long-distance phone card and then added Kashan's phone number.

"Ring, ring, ring, ring, ring."

No answer.

Inside my room again, I lay down on the bed and looked up at the ceiling.

Deep breaths.

Me getting impatient is not going to make the time go any faster.

I didn't plan on falling asleep, but, sleep-deprived, my body made that call. The next thing I knew, my phone was ringing. Late afternoon shadows had already overtaken the room. I couldn't find my phone right away, so I began to panic. Then I listened more strategically. My ears tracked the sound down to the floor beside the bed. There I discovered my phone, which had fallen when I dozed off. I snatched it up and answered quickly.

"Where are you?" "What time is it?" I asked frantically, realizing the sun was already low in the sky.

"I'm on the way," Kashan's voice sounded in my ear. "I had to go to my sister's house first, but now I'm on the way in a cab. I'm sorry I'm late."

How many times have I heard him say that before? Too many to count, for sure.

Why I expected him to be anything other than late, I cannot say. But I had waited months to see Lilah, so knowing they were just minutes away from me now immediately washed away my frustration. I just wanted to see her, and hold her, and kiss her face.

"How did Lilah do on the bus ride?" I asked. "Was it okay for her?"

"I'll tell you about it when I get there," he said, cutting me short. "What's your room number?"

"108. Go to the left after you enter the front lobby." "I can't wait to see you guys!" I said excitedly.

"I have to go, habibti. I need to make sure this guy isn't taking me the long way so he can charge me more money."

"Hayawan [Animal]!" I heard him say to the driver before he hung up.

I couldn't believe I had slept for almost six hours. In panic mode, I ran to the bathroom to quickly brush my teeth and spritz on some perfume. Then I carefully lined my lips with wine-colored lip liner, reapplied my lipstick, and blended the two together with my finger for a softer look. Some Super Skinny Serum strategically pulled through my hair, added shine, and sufficiently got rid of my bedhead.

It was imperative that Kashan's first look at me after months of being apart would be impressive. Everything was on the line. The minute Kashan was no longer attracted to me meant my chances of getting Lilah from him would take a nosedive. I wasn't about to let that happen. God would do his part, and I would surely do mine.

Just like the FBI suggested: "If your husband still wants to be with you, you could use that to your advantage." That's all I'm doing here. I'm using Kashan's desire to possess me as a tool to help me rescue my little girl. The agents probably never imagined I would actually show up here to implement that plan. They made it very clear that they wouldn't advise me to travel to the Middle East. They warned that it might be an unsafe environment for me. But of course they would say that. It was their job to say those kinds of things.

Fortunately, I don't need their approval. I would go to any country on earth if it meant bringing Lilah back home. But this is not just any country. This is the Holy Land. I've been here before. I'm already familiar with Middle Eastern customs. Besides that, I'm in Israel, where a woman and a mother have rights. I'm in a country that agrees with the Hague Conven-

tion. That means if I make it to the American Embassy with Lilah, I'll be able to take her back home with me!

Pep talk complete, I looked in the mirror, gave a nod, and acknowledged that I was ready.

"Lord God," I sighed, "please make my efforts successful."

> And may the Lord our God show us his approval and make our efforts successful. Yes, make our efforts successful!
> Psalm 90:17 NLT

Just then, I heard footsteps coming down the hotel hallway.

But no... it sounds like only one person's footsteps, so... it can't be them.

Then a firm, "Knock, knock, knock," on the door.

Oh my Goodness. It must be them!

I ran to the door and swung it wide open. Kashan took a step back, startled by my energetic show of enthusiasm.

"Hey!" I exclaimed as I bounded into the corridor.

My joyful greeting echoed into the empty passageway. Kashan stood there smiling. He extended his arms toward me, waiting for an embrace. But I froze when I didn't see Lilah. Afraid to look down the hallway for the little girl who was not there, I simply kept my eyes fixed on Kashan. I knew not to look. I knew right away what was happening. He did not bring her. She was not there. The anguish that came over me was unbearable as my whole world plummeted and fell out of reach yet again. How anyone could continue to be so cruel was something I could, in no way, comprehend.

"I couldn't bring her, Mary," I heard him say. "I couldn't take the chance."

Chapter 13

PROMISES, PROMISES

My mouth remained open, mid-gasp. The searing pain of utter heartbreak surged through my being. A groan came from my throat as I stepped backwards into the room. My knees went soft, and the floor pulled out from under me. Kashan stepped forward and caught me before I collapsed onto the floor.

"You promised, you promised," I said between sobs.

"I couldn't take a chance on bringing her into Israel." "But you can still see her," he said, as he reached behind with one arm and closed the door.

"What?" "How?" I asked, sniffing back my tears.

"I can take you to Amman to see her tomorrow," he said, with an authoritative lift of his eyebrows. "Now be quiet so the people won't hear us." He gave me a firm look, as if that settled the matter.

People hearing us was the last thing I cared about. I was still struggling to accept the fact that I would not be seeing Lilah that day. And since he had not even brought her into Israel, I would not be taking her back to the States with me either—at least not that day.

"You are just a few hours away from her. We can go together and see her tomorrow, habibti. I told her I was coming to get you. She can't wait to see you."

He wore a plastic smile as if what he was doing to his daughter and me was not sick and twisted.

"I know you're disappointed, but you can wait one more day to see her."

When I didn't come around immediately, his eyes narrowed. He raised his chin and looked down at me as if questioning my authenticity.

"You are glad to see me though… aren't you?"

Okay, Mary, remember your role. You were initially disappointed that you didn't get to see your five-year-old daughter who you haven't seen in months. That's understandable. But you are finally reunited with this man who you are deeply and passionately in love with, and you'll get to see your daughter tomorrow. So stop with the tears!

You had no plan to take Lilah back from Kashan. There was no plan that was ruined here—no plan at all. Remember, this is Kashan's world, and you are just a minor detail in it… a variable… a nonessential. You are simply a possession that can be enjoyed by him or thrown away, discarded with barely a thought.

Just because there is a setback doesn't mean the game is over. It doesn't mean the battle is lost. Well… which will it be, Mary? Are you stayin' and playin', or are you going down in defeat?

My determination to not lose my only opportunity to get Lilah back brought clarity and purpose to my mind. Recalling the character I had to portray helped me regain my composure.

It put a stop to my flow of tears. Still in need of a moment to pull myself together, I purposely took my time pushing my hair back from my face. Then, feigning resignation, I looked up at Kashan and spoke softly.

"It's just that… I haven't seen her in months now. And… I missed her. I missed both of you… so much."

The submissiveness of my demeanor compelled him to pull me closer into an embrace. I had not been in compliance with Kashan's directives at this level for some years now. It was the number-one thing he always wanted. Whenever he saw strength, aptitude, or resilience in me, he wanted to bring it into submission. Fortunately, he never stopped wanting that. If he had, I wouldn't have been there, that close to Lilah. I reminded myself of that as I endured his touch.

Still, I found it abhorrent to be in the clutches of a man capable of committing an act so cruel that it caused me to entertain death as an alternative to feeling such pain. His heinous deed resulted in me losing my little girl. It even caused me to question my faith.

When he wrapped his arms around me, I was pulled into a greater depth of torment. His firm hold on me was suffocating. I was enveloped by yet another layer of suffering, one that I never imagined possible; my misery was complete.

But remember, you're not alone. The Lord is here with you. He hasn't left. He knows right where you are. He's here, even now, in this sinister assault—this overwhelming trauma.

Suddenly, a scripture came to my mind. It was the one about flood waters and fires.

> When you go through deep waters, I will be with you.
> When you go through rivers of difficulty, you will not
> drown. When you walk through the fire of oppression, you
> will not be burned up; the flames will not consume you.
> Isaiah 43:2 NLT

Yes! He promised to be with me through every difficulty. I'm sure he's here with me now.

> But you belong to God, my dear children. You have already
> won a victory over these people, because the spirit who lives
> in you is greater than the spirit who lives in the world.
> 1 John 4:4 NLT

That's right! I am the one who has the advantage here, because greater is HE that is within me.

> You will keep in perfect peace all who trust in you,
> all whose thoughts are fixed on you!
> Isaiah 26:3 NLT

My mind must stay focused on the Lord if I'm going to have any peace in this situation. He is the one who is able to see me through this.

> We also pray that you will be strengthened with all his
> glorious power so you will have all the
> endurance and patience you need.
> Colossians 1:11 NLT

That's exactly what I need right now—HIS power, HIS endurance, and HIS patience. I'm not reliant on my own abilities!

Encouraged by these thoughts, I was strengthened by the living and eternal words I had already come to know as truths. I was reassured in a way that simply does not happen in the natural realm. And I knew, beyond a shadow of a doubt, I was being comforted by my Heavenly Father. Peace came over me as I was surrounded by the presence of the Holy Spirit. I was surely not alone.

I looked up into Kashan's dark eyes and smiled softly. It was a show of acceptance, even contentment—one that convinced even me. Kashan was not the enemy. He was a mere puppet. He was a vessel being used by an evil entity. He would be used to cause harm and pain, and then be discarded. He was deceived, having no idea what he was doing or who he was up against. He was to be pitied, not hated.

Yes, I'm the one with the advantage here.

He did not speak. He just looked into my eyes, searching for any sign of distress or resistance. But he saw none, because there was none there. How was it possible? It was only possible because of a power far greater than my own.

> Now all glory to God, who is able, through his mighty power at work within us, to accomplish infinitely more than we might ask or think.
> Ephesians 3:20 NLT

He kissed me, and I closed my eyes. Tears streamed down my cheeks. Holding my face, he kissed my tears away and promised, as he had done so many times before, that everything would be okay. I nodded in agreement, because I knew that it would be.

And then, I was sure that I could hold on. I was confident that I could endure for as long as it took to get Lilah back. I could keep the faith while I waited for God to bring Lilah home.

Chapter 14

INTO JORDAN

At around 10:00, Kashan finally woke up. Beside the bed sat a cup of coffee with cream and two sugars—just the way he liked it. It was already cold since I had gotten it from the hotel restaurant an hour earlier.

Once he sat up and took a few sips, I encouraged him to shower quickly so I could check out on time. Kashan left the room first and waited for me outside by the cypress trees. He didn't want the hotel employees to know he slept in the room overnight, which I thought was ridiculous, especially since we were married. But he knew the area more than I did, so I followed his lead.

Since Kashan was Palestinian, not holding an Israeli passport, he would travel into Jordan on a separate bus from me, an American tourist. That didn't come as a surprise to me because we had made this journey back in '93 before getting married in Amman.

As an American, the separate bus mandate, supposedly set up for security purposes, didn't make much sense to me at first. But under the present circumstances, it was beginning to make much more sense. And it didn't bother me at all that Kashan wouldn't be sitting right there beside me on my bus. It gave me a break from his nonstop monitoring of my every move. When

Kashan reminded me that his bus would be arriving later than mine, I was fine with that too. It gave me a chance to breathe.

I placed my bag on the seat beside me as a deterrent to anyone wishing to sit there. Finally able to relax, I closed my eyes, keeping one hand on top of my purse. The constant hum of the bus motor was like a lullaby drawing me into its sleepy refrains.

Mom always told me that two wrongs don't make a right. There's some truth to that. But regardless, convincing my husband I still want to be with him isn't wrong. I do want to be with him—as long as he has my daughter.

That was the last thought I had before I drifted off to sleep.

"You have to promise me that you won't go into Jordan, no matter what!" I could hear my dad's voice in my dream. "They'll kill you! You'll never make it out!"

"Okay, Dad, I promise." "Don't worry," I told him. "But Dad, I have to go see her! I'm this close to her now. She's just across the border. I have to go! You would do the same thing if you were me. You would go, Dad."

My sleep ended abruptly when the bus bounced over a large bump in the road. Letting out a sigh, I conceded that my cognitive thoughts were probably more productive than restless sleep. I still needed to sort some things out in my mind. Having an agenda for the rest of my time in the Middle East seemed wise.

Later this evening, I'll give Gina a call from Kashan's parents' house. We are seven hours ahead, so it will be earlier in the day there in the States. I'll tell her I decided to go to Jordan after all, without giving her a reason. If I sound very positive, she will assume that Lilah and I are okay. She'll know not to ask the wrong questions. She'll figure out that I decided to go into Jordan because it was my only option. Gina will then call my family to let them know. They'll be worried, but I'll touch base with them periodically to reassure them that everything is fine.

Gina and I hadn't discussed the possibility that Kashan might show up in Israel without Lilah. She may have considered it, but I had not. To consider it would have undermined my momentum.

Just because Kashan showed up in Jerusalem without Lilah doesn't mean I'm out of options. All that time rocking and strategizing on Gina's front porch wasn't for nothing. I know the culture I'm dealing with here. They can't contain me that easily. I still have some tricks up my sleeve.

I nodded, acknowledging the need for an ever-evolving plan. Just because I wasn't aware of what was ahead didn't mean God wasn't. I simply needed to be flexible enough to trust him and go with the flow—no matter where it took me.

There's a chance I can convince Kashan to leave Jordan and go into Cyprus. It's the closest country, apart from Israel, that's party to the Hague Convention. If I can persuade Kashan to go to Cyprus for a change of scenery, his federal kidnapping charges will be recognized, and I'll be able to get Lilah from him.

I imagined how I might present the idea to him. Still remembering what it was like to be at his parents' house, I knew it would entail endless days of never leaving the property. The men left every day to do whatever they wanted. But not the women. After a few days sitting around his parents' house doing nothing, I would complain to Kashan that I was bored. I would ask if we could do something fun, like visit another country. Then I would casually mention how I have always wanted to visit Cyprus. I would ask if he had ever been there before. Of course, Kashan would respond, saying he didn't have the money to make a trip like that. Then, I would offer to pay for it.

Even if it takes every penny I have to get us to Cyprus, at least Lilah and I will be safe. Then I'll run to the shelter of the U.S. Embassy and phone home.

I had it all figured out. I knew my next move.

It will take a lot more than this to make me give up. I am far from hopeless. This is nothing more than a minor setback—a temporary delay.

Speaking of which, I ended up waiting hours for Kashan's bus to show up in Jordan. He had instructed me to speak to no one while I waited. He still felt the need to go over the rules with me as if I were a child. After so many years with the man, I could recite the rules backwards, upside down, and inside out. I knew them in order of priority, and I knew the consequences if they were not carried out to his satisfaction.

I didn't expect an embrace from Kashan when he arrived. For a man to openly embrace a female in public was deemed inappropriate, according to Islam. Unfortunately, that didn't prevent some men from groping you on the sly if they were inclined to do so. The memory of that happening to me was an exceptionally appalling takeaway from my last visit to Jordan. Thankfully, so far, I was able to avoid unwanted contact from degenerates. But still, I knew to brace myself for other unpleasant scenarios that inevitably manifest in an environment so rooted in sexism.

By the time Kashan finally got there to pick me up, he was sweaty and miserable. He didn't even offer a greeting when he saw me, apart from cursing in Arabic, that is. It wasn't directed toward me, but still, it tied up my stomach in knots.

Kashan summoned a taxi and asked the driver how much he would charge for the drive to Amman. Then he cursed some more. Once we had ridden for about ten minutes, Kashan told the driver to stop and let us out. At that point, he hailed another taxi that drove us the rest of the way at a rate Kashan thought was more reasonable. I didn't understand the Arabic conversations throughout the process, but I didn't have to. Kashan's demeanor said it all.

As we walked up the familiar stone stairway to Kashan's family home on the third floor, it was all I could do not to run. But knowing that would be seen as improper, I restrained myself and took some deep breaths. While no one could see us, Kashan grabbed my hand, pulled me toward him, and kissed me, further delaying my long-awaited reunion with my daughter.

Finally, Kashan pulled out his keys and opened the door. Right away, Lilah sprang up from the table where she had been drawing and ran toward me. Nura, Kashan's mother, peered out at us from the kitchen.

"Mommy, Mommy!" Lilah shouted with a slight Middle Eastern accent.

As soon as I heard Lilah's voice, I lost it. Tears flowed down my face like a flood as I held her and stroked her head.

"Thank you—thank you, Lord!" was all I could manage to say.

"Mommy, it's okay. Don't cry. Taeta is cooking us something delicious, and I made a beautiful picture for you. Look!"

She ran to the table to retrieve her artwork and quickly returned to me.

"This is beautiful, Lilah," I placed my hand to my cheek in astonishment. "I love those pretty pink flowers!"

I held her at arm's length to get a good look at her, and pulled her back close again. Besides her hair needing a cut and the unfashionable local threads she was wearing, she appeared to be well. Her cheeks were full and vibrant. Most importantly, she had a big smile on her face.

Kashan's ongoing narrative to Lilah over the last four months had been that they were waiting for Mommy to join them. I was certain that caused her to feel abandoned by me as she wondered why I was taking so long. But if she was damaged by being separated from her mother, she didn't immediately show it.

The rich, red color of the Persian rug on the natural stone floors gave the room needed warmth and a touch of elegance. The main room had much the same furniture as before, although it had been rearranged. The rectangular dining table was pulled to the forefront, while the sculpted sofa and upholstered chairs were pushed back into what had become a sitting room. The goldenrod-colored fabric of the chairs caught the late-day sun, making that area glow. It seemed altogether more inviting than I remembered.

Nura greeted me with a gentle smile, followed by the traditional kiss on both cheeks. She appeared healthy and robust. Her complexion was still youthful and dewy; her black silken hair was tidy and full of shine. Her dark eyes were clear and just as piercing as ever. I looked into them and wondered if she, as a mother, felt any sympathy for Lilah and me. It was hard to tell by her expression, although it was pleasant enough. Nura spoke no English, but I understood enough Arabic to know she was offering hot tea.

Then, without asking if I was ready to disengage from the little girl I hadn't embraced in months, Kashan said, "Let your mommy sit down, Lilah."

She reluctantly let go of my waist and smiled up at me sweetly.

"My mom wants to know if you want tea, honey," Kashan informed.

The familiar scent of maramia [sage] still lingered in the house from the last time Nura served tea. Kashan's mother made tea better than anyone I knew, except perhaps her daughters. It was always the perfect amber-brown color—never bitter and perfectly sweetened.

"Yes, please." I turned to Nura. "Shukran," I added with a smile.

She returned the smile and disappeared into the kitchen. When I sat on the couch, I pulled Lilah to sit down beside me.

"Her name is Taeta," Lilah said, kindly explaining to me how to say grandma in Arabic. "Say it, Mommy. Tay-ta."

"Tay-ta," I said to appease her.

"Very good, Mommy!" she offered with an encouraging grin.

Kashan laughed and said, "Give your mommy a break, Lilah. You can teach her Arabic later."

"It's okay. She's fine." "She can teach me whatever she wants," I insisted.

"You would be surprised at how much Arabic Lilah knows." "My mother is a good teacher," Kashan nodded proudly in Nura's direction.

The joy of seeing Lilah erased many layers of the pain I'd been carrying since she was taken. To see her and know she was okay was such a relief to me. The injury was still there, but now that I was with her, I knew I would come through.

Clasping tightly to Lilah's hand, I settled myself farther back into the couch and absorbed the bliss of being with my little girl. I closed my eyes for a moment and whispered a prayer of thanks. Just as I did, the undeniable scent of Middle Eastern spices wafted from the kitchen.

"Something smells good," I looked at Lilah with widened eyes.

"Are you hungry, Mommy?" "Taeta made something special for you," she said melodically.

"I am hungry, Lilah." "What did Taeta make?" I clasped my hands to my face as if unable to contain my excitement.

She stared at me for a moment and smiled softly as if she were reacquainting herself with my facial features. Then she suddenly darted into the kitchen, uttered something in Arabic to her grandmother, and quickly came back out. Watching her was like heaven to me.

"Maqluba! She made you maqluba, Mommy! Say it, Mommy. Mak-a-lu-bah."

I laughed at how Lilah over-enunciated the word for my benefit.

"Oh." "I think I know that dish," I said, looking at Kashan for confirmation.

"That's right," he nodded. "Chicken upside down."

"Yes," I exclaimed. "Chicken upside down—I love it!"

"She loves it, Taeta! My mommy loves maqluba!" Lilah danced around, singing, "Mommy loves maqluba." Then, with a serious expression, she came right up to my face and informed me, "There is very delicious food here in Jordan, Mommy."

"Yes, I know Lilah. Mommy is very excited."

And I *was* excited. I was excited to be there with her for the next several weeks. And should the opportunity arise during that time, I would be even more excited to get her out of there.

My soul was refreshed, and more importantly, my strength returned. The enemy had tortured me with thoughts of never seeing my daughter again. But the devil was a liar because there I was with her.

I squeezed Lilah again and gave her kisses on her face. She giggled.

"I love you, Mommy."

My eyes welled up with tears again. I looked into her brown eyes and smiled, "I love you too, sweetheart."

I had been concerned about seeing Kashan's parents again. And I couldn't help but wonder if Khuram Shehadeh's absence at the time of my arrival was intentional. Khuram, AKA Seedo [Grampa], was Kashan's father. The last time he and I were together in that house, we were not exactly on good terms. Back then, he was telling me to get on a plane and return to America. But Kashan assured me that everything was fine now. And from the reception I had received so far, it appeared to be so. The house felt somewhat empty, though, since all Kashan's siblings were grown and had left the home by now.

Kashan informed me that Faisha, my favorite, had married a wealthy Kuwaiti man named Nofal. They lived in Abdoun, one of the most affluent neighborhoods in Amman. Samad, the youngest brother, was studying abroad in Qatar. The other six siblings were married with children and lived in either Amman, Kuwait, or Al Azariya in the West Bank.

Faisha was the third from the youngest sibling. She and I bonded when I was there in '93, and I truly looked forward to seeing her. I hoped she felt the same. And I was especially curious to find out what she thought of Kashan's actions.

What reason did he give his family for showing up in Amman with Lilah? Did they even consider it to be kidnapping? Probably not, since he was a man. A man can get away with ANYTHING in this environment.

But kidnap is a word that must never come from my lips in the presence of Kashan or any member of his family. And especially not in front of my overly talkative five-year-old. For me to assign a negative and accusatory label to what Kashan did would reveal my true feelings on the matter. No—I'll never utter that word as long as I'm in their company.

I'm here simply because I'm still so much in love with Kashan. And I want, more than anything, for our marriage to work out. They'll remember the irrational and lovesick Mary who would go to the ends of the earth to be with her man. Well... she's back

Chapter 15

STAGE ONE - ACT TWO

I did not have to wait long to further test my acting skills. With Nura, it wasn't so difficult since we were not engaging in conversation. But Faisha, who was fluent in English, came for a visit the very next day. I was genuinely happy to see her, which made the performance somewhat easier. However, I could not let my guard down like before. I had to assume that anything I said to Faisha would be conveyed to the rest of the Shehadeh family.

Faisha was not the one who betrayed me by exposing Kashan and me. That was Badira, one of his other sisters. Badira suspected that her brother and I planned to be married despite her parents' wishes. Then she tricked me into confessing what she claimed to already know. She was cunning and deceptive. But Faisha possessed character. She was more trustworthy and faithful. However, Faisha would be faithful to her family and customs first and foremost. That was why I could not confide in her. I believed Faisha was fond of me, but her loyalty ultimately lay within the dictates of Muslim beliefs and traditions. That meant she viewed me as an infidel. A friend, perhaps, but definitely an infidel.

I had already fooled his family once when, instead of returning to the States as they instructed, I went into Israel to find Kashan. Then we were married against his parents' will. So, his family would be keeping a close eye on me, for sure. They would be on the lookout for any indication that I was averse to the plans Kashan had for us to remain together, happily ever after, here in Amman.

"I would like to invite you to come to my house for dinner on Thursday," Faisha stated with a rather straight face. "What would you like for me to prepare for you?"

Her neutral expression was not because she was being unfriendly; it was just her way of showing self-control and restraint. I trusted this more than the beguiling smile and alluringly persuasive manner her sister Badira possessed.

"Oh, that would be nice." "Shukran," I smiled. "Faisha, anything you choose to make will be delicious, I know."

On Thursday, Faisha arrived with her husband, Nofal, and their two-year-old son. They affectionately called their son Kashi, a nickname for his given name, Kashan. Lilah fussed over him affectionately. It comforted me to see that she had formed loving family relationships in Amman, rather than suffering from loneliness the entire time.

"Are you ready, Mary?" Faisha asked with a subtle smile.

"Yes, of course. I've been looking forward to it."

We went down to the garage under the building and got into Nofal's Black BMW. Nofal played contemporary American music as he drove us to their home. Realizing this was probably done for my benefit made me feel valued. Kashan planned to come later that evening for dinner. Truth be told, I was glad for any time I had away from him.

When I walked into Faisha's home, I was blown away by how fancy it was. The gold embellishment was a bit too flashy for my tastes, but to each their own. Kashan had previously told me that Kuwaiti citizens were very wealthy people. And, from the appearance of Faisha and Nofal's abode, that appeared to be true. Faisha's home would, in all likelihood, be the envy of most Palestinian wives.

The formal furniture in the adjoining front rooms looked as though it had never been sat upon. Everything was trimmed in gleaming gold, from the chandelier that hung grandly over a highly polished dining table to the white chairs in the sitting area. The rug underneath their glass coffee table had intricately woven patterns of gold, white, and tan, with a gold medallion design at its center.

I wondered if Nofal had a career or if he was just independently wealthy. Thinking about it made me realize that most of the men in the Shehadeh family didn't appear to be gainfully employed. The youngest brother, Samad, was attending university abroad, so it made sense that he did not work. And I had been told that Faraz, who had returned from the States to marry his high school sweetheart, was working at a car dealership. But their father, Khuram, the oldest brother, Omeir, and my husband, Kashan, did not have professions—not ones that I could identify, anyway.

The Shehadehs seemed to be merely managing the money from Khuram's former highway construction business in Kuwait. There were ongoing discussions about possible business ventures as well as conversations on how to save money. So, evidently, a fair amount of Khuram's wealth remained. But based on the appearance of their individual dwellings, they clearly did not have the prosperity Nofal had. Obviously, Faisha had done very well for herself.

Seeing her married and apparently content made me happy for her. I knew enough about the Muslim customs to know things were done differently when it came to engagements. The last time she and I had been together, she was broken-hearted over some boy her parents did not approve of. That made me curious to know the circumstances around her marriage agreement.

As soon as Lilah took Kashi into his bedroom to play, I touched Faisha's arm lightly and asked, "How did you and Nofal meet?"

Present-day Faisha was more guarded and less forthcoming than her younger self. Unlike the girl of the past who entertained romantic notions and enthusiastically shared them with me, she kept her demeanor. After giving it some thought, she blushed and then fondly recounted how she met her husband. She told me they initially noticed each other on campus at the University of Jordan. Later, they were introduced through mutual friends. Nofal eventually confessed to Faisha his love and desire to marry her.

Faisha felt the same way, but knowing her father may not agree, she came up with an alternative plan. She instructed Nofal to come to her house with his parents and formally request her hand in marriage. Then she acted as if she was not interested in marrying Nofal.

I cupped my hand to my mouth in disbelief and listened, wide-eyed as she continued with her story. The young lady before me was both clever and resourceful. I appreciated that she trusted me enough to confide in me. But still… I had to be careful in case this revealing disclosure was simply a trap to get me talking.

Faisha continued with her story, saying that Khuram insisted on taking control of the situation, just as she knew he would. He became furious that she would so quickly dismiss a pursuer, especially when she had no one else knocking at her parents' door asking for her hand in marriage. He reasoned with Faisha that Nofal was a respectable man who was able to support her and that she would do well to accept him. After several weeks of pretending she was against the union, she finally relented and agreed to marry Nofal.

"Oh, wow?" I said, amazed.

"Yes," Faisha answered proudly. "I knew my father would be against us unless he believed it was his idea."

"That's amazing!" "You do know your father, don't you?" I laughed.

"Yes, I do know him very much," she admitted with a grin. "And I am very happy. Nofal is a good man. He is so good to me." "He does not say no to me for—" she paused while searching for the correct word.

"—for anything," I suggested.

"Yes." "He says yes to me for everything!" she said, beaming with enthusiasm.

I reached out and placed my hand on hers, "I'm so happy for you, Faisha." "You deserve the best."

"Thank you so much, Mary. I wish the same for you and my brother."

I took a deep breath in and then released it, nodding my head. She had to know something was wrong between Kashan and me since he brought Lilah to Jordan without me. There was a time in the past when I would have openly confided in her—

but this was not that time. This time I was here to take my daughter back, so I wouldn't take any chances.

"My mother said that you and Kashan were not living together when he left America and came to Jordan with Lilah." She leaned in closer and looked in my eyes, "Mary, did Kashan leave you to… live apart from you?" "Is there a problem with your marriage?"

"Faisha, you know I've always loved your brother," I pressed my lips together as I carefully considered my wording. "But we went through a time when we were not getting along so well. Sometimes it can be challenging to live with… someone. And I was so tired all the time from working in the salon. Also, my mother died. It was a difficult time, and I was not at my best."

"Oh, yes. I heard about that." "I'm so sorry about your mother, Mary," she offered.

"Thank you." I smiled, knowing she was sincere. "Well," I said, shrugging my shoulders, "Kashan and I spent some time apart." "And since then, I have realized more and more how my life is just not the same without him."

Well, that's not a lie. Convincing his family that I don't have an ulterior motive for being here may be easier than I thought. I can speak true statements that go along with the posture I intend to portray—that of a doting wife.

"Do you think you could be happy living here in Jordan, Mary?"

Hmmm. She didn't waste any time getting to the point. Kashan must have instructed her to feel me out on that subject.

"I am happy here in Amman, Mary," she continued before I had a chance to answer. "It is a very nice city. It is much better now than when you were here before, almost ten years ago. It has grown so much and has many new stores and restaurants."

I'm sure there are many things to do in Amman if your husband allows you to go outside of the house whenever you choose. I know how things work around here. And Faisha definitely sounds like she's speaking from a script Kashan gave her.

"I think I could like it here in Amman, especially when I have a sister and a friend like you to spend time with," I smiled sweetly.

"Thank you so much, Mary. I'm also happy to… spend time together," she answered.

We chatted for a while, discussing everything various family members were up to. They all seemed to be content and doing well, which was good to hear. While we were talking, I glanced down at my feet. Noticing how bad they looked, I mentioned that I needed to get a pedicure. I asked her about the nail tech she had taken me to the last time I was in Amman. She placed her glass of water down on the table. Her expression changed to one of excitement.

"Would you like to have a pedicure, Mary?"

"Sure," I answered, not knowing what she had in mind. "I would love a pedicure. Where can I get one?"

"Malaya, come here," Faisha called out firmly.

A petite, barefoot woman ran into the room obediently.

"Prepare to do a pedicure for Lilah's mother," Faisha ordered the young lady.

"Oh… no," I objected, shaking my head. "I can't ask her to do a pedicure for me."

"She is working here for us. She does what I tell her to do. She does a very good pedicure." "All the Filipino girls do," she informed me.

"Well, I insist on paying her then," I stated, with furrowed brow.

"No! We do give her money." "We pay her family every month," she answered with a stern look on her face.

"What?" "I mean… does she even get any of that money?" I demanded.

"Why does she need money?" Faisha asked, holding her hands up toward the ceiling. "She has food to eat, and she is living in a much better house than the one her parents have back in her country."

Faisha's unrelenting expression told me she was not going to change her mind. I regretted that I ever mentioned the word pedicure.

What type of family would sell their daughter into what seems like slavery? And how can Faisha think this is okay? Seems I don't know her as well as I thought.

Malaya returned with a basin of sudsy warm water, some towels, and manicure tools. She smiled, motioned for me to place my feet in the water, then sat on the floor cross-legged. Reluctantly, I placed my feet in the warm water.

For the next hour, Malaya meticulously exfoliated, clipped, and filed in silence. Occasionally, she looked up at me and smiled shyly. I smiled back, although I never really relaxed. But I knew if I protested too much, it would look like I was being non-compliant. And I didn't want that. When Malaya finished with everything except applying the polish, she turned her head toward Faisha and then back to me again.

"Color?" she asked.

Faisha instructed her to retrieve several nail polish colors for me to choose from. Most of the colors she brought were too subtle for me. But thankfully, there was a shimmery fuchsia one in the mix. I picked it up and gave it a good shake before handing it to Malaya. She smiled and got back to work.

When she finished, she looked up at me, her brows drawn together in concern. Wondering if she might be fearful of a scolding if I was not happy with her work, I gave her a reassuring smile.

She whispered softly, "Is good?"

I nodded and quickly tucked a $20 bill into Malaya's apron pocket before Faisha had a chance to turn around.

"Very nice," I stated loud enough for Faisha to hear. "Thank you so much."

Despite the sick feeling in the pit of my stomach, I tried to pour as much enthusiasm into my voice as possible—for Malaya's benefit. I felt practically compliant in this subjugation, as if I, myself, held this girl captive.

Faisha turned to look, then asked, "Do you like it, Mary?"

"I love it!" "Thanks so much," I repeated, hoping to keep Faisha's attention on me and my feet, and off the ear-to-ear grin Malaya was wearing because of the $20 I'd just given her.

Unfortunately, her obvious delight in receiving some duly earned compensation did not go unnoticed by the boss-lady. Faisha's head snapped back over in my direction.

"Did you give her money?" she asked through squinted eyes. Then her eyes fell on poor Malaya in an accusatory fashion.

"Not much," I waved my hand, insisting that it was only a small amount.

"No, Mary." "Do not give her any money!" Faisha said sternly. "This is my gift to you. She will expect it every time if you give her money."

Faisha held out her hand toward Malaya and pressed her lips together, indicating the conversation was over. Malaya's eyes took on an empty look as she reached into her pocket and, in compliance, handed the money over to Faisha.

Seeing it broke my heart, so I couldn't help but give it one last try. "Please let me at least tip her something, Faisha. She worked so hard."

She didn't answer. She simply lifted her eyebrows quickly, coupled with a single, non-wavering *tsk*, and placed the money back into my purse. This sent barefoot Malaya into the hallway where she disappeared with the water basin. Her dutiful effort to be swift, silent, and contained did not go unnoticed by me.

Is she barefoot so that she doesn't make a sound as she obediently moves about the house? Or is it because she doesn't own shoes? Wait, is everyone expected to remove their shoes upon entering this house? If so, I must already be exhibiting infidel tendencies since I neglected to remove my sandals when I got here.

Looking back toward the front door, I observed a row of neatly placed shoes. Then I looked at Faisha's feet and saw she was wearing socks and fancy slippers.

This is not good.

"She does not always work so hard," Faisha spoke, interrupting my thoughts. "Sometimes she is lazy. And once she broke something valuable while she was cleaning. She threw it in the garbage so that I would not know what she did."

Assuming it was Malaya she was speaking of, I nodded but remained silent. It was obvious to me that Faisha was not in agreement with my Western way of thinking. But I needed to be careful not to make waves. I was not there to save the world—I was there to save my child. My heart went out to the young woman, though. I determined that whenever I was around Malaya in the future, I would not add to her burden, as I had unwittingly done by the mere mention of a pedicure.

Lost in my thoughts again, I wondered how many Malayas there were in Amman. Or how many Lilahs and Marys there were, for that matter. I couldn't dwell on that, though. To appear anything other than happy and content could be detrimental to my mission. I checked my expression, making sure it conveyed interest in Faisha's dialogue instead of my concern for Malaya.

The dinner Faisha prepared was a chicken dish called mloukhiya. It was one that I was unfamiliar with, but it smelled wonderful. So far, Kashan had not shown up. I could tell by Faisha's demeanor that she was not troubled by her brother's tardiness.

"We will not wait for Kashan," she said, offering no apologies.

Faisha prioritized feeding her husband and guests at a reasonable hour over waiting for Kashan to arrive. Clearly, she knew her brother as well as I did.

"If you would like to prepare to eat, you can wash your hands, Mary." "There is a washroom there," she pointed in the direction of the hall behind me.

Like her mother, Faisha was an excellent cook. Even the men on her mother's side of the family were known to have great cooking skills. It didn't take much encouragement for me to accept an additional portion. A few minutes later, Lilah requested a second helping also.

"Well, it seems the Americans have brought their appetites to the dinner table tonight," I said, laughing.

Faisha and Nofal laughed.

"Please, have as much as you want," Faisha insisted. "I will also prepare a plate for you to take home with you."

"I won't say no to that," I admitted. "Thank you, Faisha. Your cooking is amazing."

Then, turning to Nofal, I pointed toward Faisha and said, "You found a valuable treasure when you found this one."

He smiled and said, "This is something I know is true."

"God bless you both, and thank you so much for having us as your guests," I told him.

"You are very welcome, Mary," Nofal answered with a nod.

"We love Lilah so much." "You and Lilah are always welcome here, Mary," Faisha said, reaching over and patting the table in front of me.

After dinner, Faisha and I went to sit in their gilded living room, while Lilah played with little Kashi on the floor. I really didn't mind having a break away from Kashan, but I was beginning to feel a little anxious at the same time. He had promised to be there hours ago. When Faisha suggested coffee, I readily accepted, happy to have one more activity to keep us occupied until Kashan's arrival.

And then, as if the smell of Turkish coffee had lured him in from off the streets, the doorbell rang. Hearing the bell, Lilah looked up at Faisha and me, her mouth open with excited expectation.

Not nearly as excited, Faisha and I looked at each other and, in unison, said, "Kashan."

Faisha opened the door for her brother and asked him in Arabic if he wanted to eat. He answered in a combination of English and Arabic, saying that he would eat from the portion she had already wrapped up and placed on the table for us to take home. Nofal stood up and walked into the living room to greet his brother-in-law. Gracious words in Arabic ensued from my husband's mouth. I couldn't understand exactly what Kashan was saying, but, by this time, I was familiar enough with the inflection of his tone to know he was apologizing for being late. At Nofal's suggestion, Kashan agreed to stay for coffee.

Faisha and I looked at each other, but remained silent. We shook our heads and rolled our eyes over her brother's predictable dysfunction. Nofal and Kashan continued to converse in Arabic, which left me totally clueless. Faisha periodically translated the mostly superficial topics being discussed.

Once Kashan deemed it was time for us to leave, I expressed my appreciation to Faisha and Nofal for their hospitality. When thanking Faisha for the pedicure, my cordial expression masked the regret I felt for not being able to properly thank the person who actually did it.

All in all, I considered the visit to be a success, though. I hoped I had managed to lay some groundwork toward gaining the trust of Kashan's family. It was simply a matter of proving myself to be of good character, watching my words, and biding my time. With God's help, I knew I could do it.

> I have strength for all things in Christ who empowers me [I am ready for anything and equal to
> anything through him who infuses inner strength into me; I am self-sufficient in Christ's sufficiency].
> Philippians 4:13 AMPC

Chapter 16

MAYBE NEXT TIME

During the following weeks, Kashan and I received visits from various family members. Most of them were siblings, but some were aunts, uncles, and cousins. Other than that, we did nothing but sit around the house. Well… I did nothing but sit around the house, while Nura stayed busy cooking and cleaning. I was concerned that made me appear as though I thought I was the Queen of Sheba or something, just lounging around doing nothing. But every time I asked Nura what I could do to help, she dismissed the idea.

So, most days, all I did was get up out of bed, shower, and do my hair and makeup, which, no doubt, added incriminating evidence to the notion that I indeed thought I was royalty. However, the more I thought about it, the more I was certain that the Queen of Sheba would have been able to make a plan on a whim and execute it without having to ask a man for permission. She would have gone wherever and done whatever she wanted, proving, without a shadow of doubt, that I was clearly not the Queen of Sheba.

Kashan, on the other hand, left the house every day and went God knows where. He did whatever he wanted and answered to no one but his father, who, obviously, did not have him under house arrest like the females seemed to be.

After several days of nothingness, broken up by intervals of preparing and consuming hot tea with a choice of either na na or maramia, I was ready to implement plan C. And who wouldn't be?

Recap: Plan A was to convince Kashan to return to the States and bring Lilah with him. He gets arrested on charges of federal kidnapping, thrown in jail, and the key thrown away. Or he simply gets deported and instructed never to return to the States. Plan B was having Kashan meet me in Jerusalem, where I would have the right, as Lilah's mother, to return to the U.S. with my daughter. Kashan would have possibly spent some time in an Israeli prison before being expelled to either Jordan or maybe even the West Bank, where he has people.

When I presented the idea of a trip to Cyprus (plan C) to Kashan, he was not immediately opposed. At first, he seemed to consider the idea. He may have been simply feeling me out to see how far I would push it, in order to determine if I had an ulterior motive. But I couldn't leave it alone, or I would never convince him. So I continued to bring it up.

"I just want us to go someplace we've never been before, honey. And I have the money for it." "Doesn't Cyprus sound beautiful?" I asked, while folding clothes. I purposefully avoided eye contact with him as I spoke because I didn't want to come across as being too earnest.

Ultimately, Kashan gave his answer, stating flatly, "I... don't think it's a good idea for me to go to Cyprus."

I froze. But waiting too long to respond could make Kashan think I was devastated. So I continued folding clothes and casually asked, "What do you mean?"

I turned to look at Kashan, but he didn't notice. He was too busy brushing his fingers through his hair and looking at himself in the mirror. Without bothering to make eye contact with me, he finally replied.

"I just don't think it's a good idea," he repeated. "I'm not willing to take that chance."

Then, before I had an opportunity to respond, he coolly walked out of the bedroom. I wanted to cry. My final option for getting Lilah out of there had just slipped through my fingers and dissipated into the dry, hope-consuming, Hashemite air. I managed to pull myself together, though. Kashan was obviously doubting my intentions, so I needed to prove him wrong.

After a few minutes, I joined Kashan and his mom in the kitchen, where they were paying homage to a fresh pot of hot tea. When I walked into the room, Nura was speaking in Arabic to Kashan. He eventually noticed I was there.

"My mother thinks I should take you to some beautiful, historic places here in Jordan," he said, as if his willingness to do so might earn him a nomination for husband of the year. "We have a lot of them, you know," he added.

Somehow, I created an expression—a customized mask, amiable enough to support my role as doting wife.

"Oh, okay." "That sounds great," I smiled.

My final plan had been destroyed by a cruel and evil entity who took pleasure in my agony. That was clear to me. But I took comfort in knowing who would ultimately win in the end. This ride was going to take a little longer than I had hoped. This fight was one that would obviously go several rounds. But the win was not dependent on my strength, my natural abilities, or even my acting skills, as impressive as they were. I was disappointed, of course, but I knew this was far from over. And I was placing my hope in the one who was seated on the throne. He was the one who was in control. He knew just how all this would end.

> I make known the end from the beginning, from ancient times, what is still to come. I say, 'My purpose will stand, and I will do all that I please.'
> Isaiah 46:10 NIV

Kashan continued speaking with a neutral expression as if he were giving a weather report forecasting one hundred consecutive days of no change whatsoever in the barometric pressure. I feigned interest.

"We can rent a car and drive to… various places in Jordan. We'll stay in hotel rooms instead of driving back here every night." "You do have the money for that, right?" he asked with gathered eyebrows.

Kashan knew full well I had the funds. He had asked me how much money I brought with me before we left for Jordan. And he was probably aware that it was meant for two plane tickets to America. But what I saw as a worthy expenditure, he saw as treason. So the money meant for bringing Lilah home would unfortunately fund a holiday for the man responsible for causing us so much harm.

"You know I have the money," I smiled through the pain.

"Okay. Get you and Lilah's things ready, then." "We will leave tomorrow so I can be back before next Wednesday," he ordered.

That wasn't the first time in my life with Kashan that I didn't get my way. And it wouldn't be the last time either. He called the shots throughout our whirlwind trip to Aqaba, Petra, and the small desert village of Wadi Rum. Normally, I would have been delighted with such an excursion. But my time spent with Kashan in Jordan in the year 2000 fell far short of delightful.

Once we returned from our trip, it was already mid-August. The school year would be starting soon. The thought of Lilah attending kindergarten in Amman instead of back home where she belonged was breaking my heart. She was just beginning to learn Arabic, and I couldn't see how she would be able to comprehend what was going on in a Jordanian classroom setting. One evening when Kashan and I were out on the balcony, I brought up the subject of Lilah's education.

"Are there any English-speaking schools in Amman?" I shifted my body toward him so I could see his face as we sat together on the bench.

"Yes, there are," he replied, expertly tapping the end of his cigarette over the ashtray.

"Oh." "Well… can we go and visit some schools while I'm here?" I asked, hoping to have some input.

"Okay, sure," he answered without looking at me. "We can visit some schools. They will be private schools, though. My daughter won't be attending a public school here in Amman."

I assumed that meant Lilah would be in a nicer learning environment than the public school system in Amman had to offer. That sounded good to me. If she had to be in Amman for kindergarten, I felt a private school would be a better choice for her.

"Alright then." "When can we go?" I asked, standing up in excitement.

"We'll go tomorrow," Kashan grumbled, not sharing my enthusiasm.

He smashed his cigarette down into the ashtray, then walked back into the house. I wondered why he didn't want to discuss it further, but it wasn't for me to ask.

The next morning, I was up early, eager to visit some schools. Kashan informed me that there were only two private schools in the area, so I knew it wouldn't be a full-day excursion.

The first school we visited was an English-speaking school. The interior of the school was brightly painted and cheerful-looking. The vice-principal who gave us the tour was very friendly. She explained that the school offered the highest level of learning in an inclusive classroom environment. She made it clear that the school provided an atmosphere where students were encouraged to work together and focus on the things they had in common, while also appreciating diverse ethnicities and varied cultures. I was excited and a bit surprised to know that a school like that existed in Amman. But I could tell by Kashan's demeanor that he did not share my enthusiasm.

The woman informed us that many of the students' parents came to Amman from around the world to work at the various embassies, universities, and hospitals. Some of the families, she explained, stayed long term, while others were only there for a short time.

Kashan asked what religion was taught to the students. She stated that the school did not adhere to any specific religious practices, but was respectful of different belief systems. Kashan's demeanor stiffened at hearing this. From that point, I knew it was going to be a no. Why I even fooled myself into believing I would have a say in the matter, I do not know.

The next school we visited was a private Muslim school. The building had an antiquated feel about it. The dismal entryway was arched and came across as more foreboding than welcoming. The interior was drab and lacked color. The hallways and classrooms were plain, dark, and bland, especially when compared to the school we had just left. To me, the choice was clear.

The female administrator was covered with a hijab and a long plain dress. Kashan spoke with her in Arabic. He did not even bother to include me in the conversation, which gave me a bad feeling in my gut.

Kashan stopped talking to the woman long enough to look at me briefly and say, "This will be Lilah's classroom."

It was decided then. Lilah would attend the gloomy-looking private Muslim school, with an atmosphere that felt and smelled like a dungeon.

"I see," I said, faking a smile.

On the way back to the house, I didn't speak. Kashan didn't bother to ask me what was wrong. I prayed overnight that God would soften Kashan's heart to be more reasonable. But the next day, when I tried to bring up the subject of Lilah's schooling, Kashan shut me down right away.

"Khalas [Enough]! My daughter will be going to a private Muslim school." "No discussion!" he glared, daring me to mention it again.

I walked back to the bedroom, closed the door quietly, and cried, knowing there was nothing I could do or say to change his mind. The cultural and religious belief system my husband adhered to gave him the advantage, while it placed limitations and restraints on me as a female. It was not fair. Disappointment had me hemmed in on all sides.

Why had he given me hope that it was open for discussion? Why had he even taken me to see the other school?

"Oh, Lord, please help me get Lilah out of here soon," I cried.

Kashan made no attempt to console me. It was just as well, though. It gave me time to nap, which provided a needed break from conscious disappointment. A couple hours later, I was awakened by a knock on the door.

"Taeal [Come]. Qum [Get up], Miriam."

It was Kashan's mother calling me to eat. She hadn't called me by the Arab version of my name since I was a guest in her home back in 1993.

When I entered the kitchen, Khuram was seated at the head of the table. Lilah was already eating.. Nura placed a plate on the table across from Lilah and motioned for me to sit. Khuram grumbled a greeting of sorts.

"Hi, Mommy," Lilah said sweetly with her head slightly tilted to the side. "Did you have a nice sleep?"

"Yes, honey, I did," I said with a smile that was meant to portray that everything was just fine.

Chapter 17

JUDGMENT AT WORK

By early September, I was already back in the States without Lilah. But seeing her had provided me the assurance of at least knowing she was okay—or as okay as a five-year-old could be while living far away from her mommy in a land that was vastly different from the one she was accustomed to.

Holding her and hearing her sweet voice in person had applied a much-needed healing balm to the deep wound within my soul. It had thoroughly removed the despondence from my heart and bound it with a covering of fresh hope. It had done a lot toward building my stamina to see this through. I fully believed it was simply a matter of time until God brought Lilah back home.

> But those who trust in the Lord will find new strength. They will soar high on wings like eagles. They will run and not grow weary. They will walk and not faint.
> Isaiah 40:31 NLT

I wished I could have stayed with Lilah, but I knew doing so would cut me off from the resources needed to get her out of Jordan. Being there without a lucrative way of producing income would prove to be debilitating. And it would prevent me from freely communicating with my spiritual and moral support system here in the States—namely, Gina.

Gina was the friend I needed when I was at my weakest. But since seeing Lilah, I felt strong enough to live on my own again. Shortly after I arrived back in the States, I let Gina know I was ready to move out of her place and find an apartment to rent.

"Are you sure about this, Mary?" Gina stood before me, her hands on her hips as she scrutinized my decision to move out.

"I'm one hundred percent sure," I reassured her. "Seeing Lilah and spending time with her has done me a world of good. It's only a matter of time now until God brings Lilah back home. I really appreciate you taking me in like you did. I can't tell you how much that means to me." "You guys are just… the best." I hugged her and wouldn't let go until she relented and hugged me back.

"Well, I'm glad you're doing better, but… you know you can stay as long as you need to, right? You know we're always here for you."

"I know you are," I smiled.

The duplex I moved into was within three miles of Gina's house and just four miles from the salon. Once I got my stuff out of storage and filled up the space, it was more than adequate. And the rent was reasonable enough that I would be able to afford periodic travel back to the Middle East to see Lilah.

I still had not found a new church since the small one Janis and I attended closed its doors. None of the churches I'd visited in the area felt right to me. But eventually, at the recommendation of a friend, I visited a small non-denominational church closer to the beach. The pastor's messages resonated truth and challenged me to trust God no matter what. I thought it was a good fit.

Talking to God was something I was struggling with, though. At home, every time I sat down with the intention of praying, I simply fell apart and cried. So, I purposely avoided conversations with God for a while, as crazy as that sounds. It was an attempt, I suppose, to keep my head above water without thrashing amid the waves of emotion. If only I could have raised a hand to signal for help. Instead, I became paralyzed in an ill-fated attempt at self-preservation. But God, in his mercy, helped me with that. One day, I clearly heard the Lord speak to my spirit.

Finish everything you say to me with the words: "as I put my trust you."

I wrote the phrase on a piece of paper and placed it in my Bible. Then I began adding it to my petitions each time I prayed. This enabled me to express my feelings and utter actual words to God instead of simply sobbing. Over time, as I continued to make the proclamation God had given me, my faith increased. Eventually, I was able to pray multiple sentences at a time. It was like learning to walk again.

God was so kind and loving. He was faithful not to leave me on the side of the road alone, afflicted, and impaired. He understood why I was struggling to talk to him, and he didn't take it personally. He knew just what I needed to get back on track.

> When I am afraid, I put my trust in you.
> Psalm 56:3 NIV

It was never easy. Encountering each additional day without my daughter was a brutal battle. But knowing God had the final say gave me the purpose I needed to remain alive. I had to keep going so that I would see the day when Lilah was home again.

> Yet I am confident I will see the LORD's goodness while I am here in the land of the living.
> Psalm 27:13 NLT

For the most part, I didn't waste much time or energy blaming myself for Lilah's kidnapping. But that doesn't mean blame was not directed my way. Although my true friends, especially those who were self-aware and admittedly the recipients of God's grace, defended me and did not judge me. Over time, I came to realize those same friends protected me from knowing all that people were saying behind my back.

However, in the salon, I was often openly confronted with judgment. It was both haughty and cruel. The way it came after me when I was already so wounded and brokenhearted left no doubt as to where it originated. It came straight from the pit of hell—callous and unrestrained. Proper and dressed-to-kill, it wore an age-old variant of self-righteousness which draped down from its factitiously inflated chest. It had an unpleasant stench about it, like that of a dated perfume.

The enemy's intention was clear—to impair me with debilitating blows, then totally destroy me by causing the kind of severe pain and anguish that shame mercilessly and relentlessly inflicts on a human soul. Perhaps, for the perpetrators, it was done simply for the sinister pleasure of watching someone in a weakened position suffer. But they couldn't have known the evil they were coming into agreement with when they threw stones in that way. If they had, they themselves would have cried foul. If I did not have the Lord standing with me in my defense, I may have faltered. If I had not already been with my daughter and seen that she was okay, I may have lost it completely.

> But in that coming day no weapon turned against you will succeed. You will silence every voice raised up to accuse you. These benefits are enjoyed by the servants of the LORD; their vindication will come from me.
> I, the LORD, have spoken!
> Isaiah 54:17 NLT

※ ※ ※

Jen, my 1:00 appointment, sat in the reception area waiting to be called back. When she saw me coming toward her, she started to lift her hand and wave, but then, as if second-guessing herself, awkwardly clasped her hands together and smiled instead. I escorted her to my chair, waited for her to sit, then fastened the cutting cape around her neck.

Looking at my reflection in the mirror, she said, "Mary, I'm so sorry to hear about what happened." "I mean, about how your daughter was, uhm… kidnapped and all." "What in the wur-orld?" she added with a Southern drawl. "Is there anything that can be done about it?"

I did not know Jen very well, but she was pretty easy to read. The lack of concern on her face and the way she pressed her lips together while she waited for information told me that she didn't really care. She appeared to be more interested in knowing the dirty details than she was concerned about my daughter's well-being.

"Well, unfortunately, the government isn't able to do much for us," I answered.

Her eyes widened with enthusiasm. I continued to pull the paddle brush through her thick, coarse hair as if I didn't notice.

"Oh, my goodness! So… do you think you'll ever see her again?"

Wow. What a horribly insensitive question. Do you think I'll ever see YOU again, might be a more appropriate thing to ask.

Placing the hair brush down on my station, I carefully laid out my cutting shears on a rubber mat specifically made to protect the blades from getting dinged. I realized there were some things I could control, and some things I could not.

"Well, I have been able to go see her. I'm just not able to leave Jordan with her. It doesn't work like that over there."

After securing a towel around her neck, I motioned for Jen to walk with me to the shampoo area. The sound of the chrome chair base wobbling against the tile floor and then settling back into place let me know she was following behind me.

"What?" she practically skipped to catch up with me, not wanting to miss the slightest detail. "You mean you've gone over there to see her? He let you see her?"

"Yes, he let me see her. Kashan would like to reconcile the marriage. That's the only reason I was able to see her."

I turned on the faucet and placed my hand under the running water while adjusting the temperature. It took a while to fully saturate her hair. As I worked some rosemary and mint scented shampoo into a lather, she looked up at me, indicating that I should continue with my story.

"If Lilah's father thought I didn't want to get back together with him, he wouldn't allow me to see her at all. The FBI says that's an advantage most women in my situation don't have.

The government can't help me get Lilah back, Jen. That means I must do whatever I need to do to get her back myself."

Once we were at my station again, I picked up a bottle of cutting lotion and squirted four pumps into my hand. Most clients' hair only required two pumps, but I knew Jen's hair would soak up this serum like a dry sponge and be cryin' out for more.

"You mean, you are going over there acting like you still love him? You're still… being with him?"

The moment that question came out of Jen's mouth, the entire salon went quiet. All the other stylists, along with their clients, tuned in to hear our conversation.

Not entirely oblivious that she had everyone's attention, Jen cried out, "Eww," and wrinkled her nose in disgust. "I don't know how you do that! Especially after what he did to you."

After a brief moment of silence, murmuring ensued from behind me. But each and every statement reached my ear as clearly as if it were spoken directly beside me.

"Well, that's what got her in this position. She done it to herself."

"Ha!" someone scoffed. "She married an A-rab. What did she think was gonna happen?"

"Yep." "You got that right," one of my co-workers sneered, with a snap of her fingers.

That brought about laughter from the other stylists. Gradually, the blow dryers were turned back on and the noise drowned out their residual condescending comments. I knew what the unified sentiment was though: "She married a d*#n foreigner, and she got exactly what she deserved."

Shifting my attention to the task at hand, I meticulously shaped Jen's hair, making sure it was well blended and properly detailed. After I finished with the blow-dry, I brushed the hair off her neck and removed the cape.

"How does that look?" I asked with a smile, deliberately showing no outward sign of the emotional beating I'd just taken.

"Looks wonderful, as usual. Thank you, Mary. Oh, and I need to set up my next appointment. We're taking my little girl to Disney next month, and I want to get my hair touched up before I go."

Not all my clients were as insensitive as Jen. Most who were aware of my situation were quite sympathetic. One woman even offered to give a large amount of money toward bringing Lilah back home.

"Mary, my husband and I talked about it," she had said. "If something were to ever happen to Sloan, we don't know how we could bear it. She's our only child. That's why we want to offer you up to $5,000 to help bring Lilah home from the Middle East."

"Oh, Katherine! I really appreciate that. That's so generous of you. But money isn't going to bring Lilah back home. It's got to be God who brings her back, or it can't be done." "And he hasn't even given me the plan yet," I shrugged my shoulders. "But when he does, I'll definitely keep your offer in mind."

Weeks passed. I constantly anticipated my next trip to see Lilah. Going back at Christmastime made sense so that she would not be alone there in a home where the holiday, not to mention the Savior, was not even recognized. While I waited for God to show me his plan to bring Lilah back, I worked hard and put money aside so I could stay with her for an entire month. This kept my hands busy and my mind occupied. It served as a worthwhile diversion.

Chapter 18

CHRISTMAS IN THE MIDDLE EAST

December finally arrived, which meant I was only weeks away from spending Christmas with Lilah in Amman. Not only would I be there on Christmas day, but also for her birthday in January. Over the last couple of months, I had worked hard to save up money for another overseas flight. Rent and regular bills always needed to be paid, whether I was home or not. In addition to that, I had the added expense of Christmas and birthday gifts for Lilah. But God was faithful, so all the money I needed came in through my work at the salon.

In Jordan, unlike a typical childhood experience in the States, Lilah was required to spend most of her time indoors. She loved to play dress-up, though, so I decided some frilly costumes would be a perfect Christmas gift for her. In addition, I planned to bring the movies *Toy Story*, *The Sound of Music*, and *Home Alone* on VHS to help her remember English and her American culture.

I couldn't wait to be back in Amman with Lilah. But recurring thoughts of being harmed by Kashan if I returned to the Middle East played over and over in my mind. I felt my pretense of wanting to reconcile the marriage was always at risk of being uncovered. The likelihood of suffering dire consequences for my trickery seemed imminent. But God was with me in those moments when fear crept in. He spoke to me through the words of the prophet Isaiah.

> The Lord has said to me in the strongest terms, "Do not think like everyone else does. Do not be afraid that some plan conceived behind closed doors will be the end of you. Do not fear anything except the Lord Almighty. He alone is the holy one. If you fear him, you need fear nothing else. He will keep you safe."
> Isaiah 8:11-14 NLT

His words held me together. They strengthened me and stopped my trembling. They encouraged me to not shrink back in fear. They propelled me forward. They reminded me that he was with me in the midst of it.

When I arrived in Jordan a couple days before Christmas, Kashan picked me up at the airport in his father's car. As we approached their neighborhood, I noticed lights displayed on the patios of many apartments. They were rather plain, lacking the color and vibrancy of Christmas lights in the U.S., but it was still nice to see. It took me by surprise as I had not expected this in a predominantly Muslim country.

"Oh, look at those Christmas lights!" I said to Kashan.

"It's also Eid, a Muslim holiday. It's occurring during the Christmas season this year." "It doesn't usually happen at the same time," he explained.

"Oh, the lights of the crescent moon with a star must be for Eid," I said, realizing that the majority of the lights were actually celebrating the Islamic holiday and not Christmas.

"That's right." Kashan reached his hand out and placed it on top of mine. "Lilah is going to be so happy to see her mommy," he said, changing the subject. "We have missed you so much."

"I've missed you guys, too. It's so good to be here."

It was good to be there. To be there for my daughter, that is. My first trip to Amman after Lilah was taken had been difficult on all accounts. But over time, my role of being a loving wife who longed to be with her beloved husband was becoming easier for me to play.

My second trip was more relaxed since I didn't have an active plan—a current operative. I had no expectations either. I was simply there to spend time with my daughter while waiting for God to show me a way to get her out. I hoped Kashan's family would allow Lilah and me to celebrate a Christian holiday in their home. The extent of our festivities would be the presentation of Lilah's gifts, which didn't seem like too much to ask. The closer we got to Kashan's family home, the more I realized there was no time like the present to inquire. So, I went for it.

"I brought Lilah some Christmas presents to give her on the 25th." "That's okay, isn't it?" I pulled my eyebrows together with a pleading expression.

"Of course, that's okay. Do you think my parents are monsters or something? They love Lilah. They'll be happy for her to get some gifts from her mommy." He wrinkled his forehead, as if my question was absurd. "Silly," he added, as he returned his focus to driving.

But I knew it was unwise for me to assume anything. To do so could jeopardize my objective to get Lilah home. The more I showed an attitude of submission and respect, the more they would trust me and let their guard down, which was my primary objective.

A foundation of trust had to be established between Kashan's family and me so they would continue to welcome me as a guest in their home. It was imperative that I portray an interest in assimilating—somewhat—to the Muslim culture, in hopes of obtaining credence with them. That meant making more of an effort to learn the Arabic language and possibly even taking on some of the daily chores around the house, if Nura let me.

I produced a smile and squeezed Kashan's hand. Obtaining permission to acknowledge Christmas at their house was a legitimate reason to smile. It could have gone in a different direction. He could have been vehemently against it. I was relieved and very thankful.

Once we arrived, Kashan parked the car but held onto my arm, preventing me from exiting the vehicle. He pulled me toward him. I braced myself for what I would be continually subjected to for the remainder of my visit.

Afterward, I reapplied my lipstick and adjusted my clothing. A quick look in the mirror to make sure I was presentable enough, and I was finally able to get out of the car. Nothing about this was easy. But I believed if I waited, there would be a day when it would finally be over.

The steps it took to walk up to the apartment seemed endless. I couldn't reach the top soon enough. Lilah ran to greet me as soon as she heard her father open the door.

"Mommy, you're here! Taeta, come see. Mommy is here!"

By this time, Lilah's accent had changed a lot. She was really rolling her r's now. And it was evident that speaking English was becoming increasingly more difficult for her.

On Christmas morning, Lilah hugged me profusely for her gifts. She put on the play clothes as she unwrapped each one.

By the time she finished, wrapping paper was all over the floor, and Lilah was layered in a princess gown, a tutu, a crown, and a cape. She was more than happy to pose as I snapped photos of her that I knew would be treasured once I was home again without her.

Before the new year arrived, Faisha extended another invitation for us to come visit. She called and spoke with Kashan first, to obtain his approval, and then asked to speak with me.

"Will you come to my house today? I would like to prepare a meal for you and Lilah." "And my brother also, if he returns on time," she added with a laugh.

"Yes, of course," I readily accepted. "I would love that."

I was genuinely fond of Faisha, despite our difference of opinion on some pretty important subjects. But she was brought up in a different world than me. And who's to say that I would not have come to the same conclusions she had, if I were her?

"Okay, Kashan will bring you after my father returns home with the car," she informed.

When we arrived at Faisha's home, we were greeted by the smell of delicious food. Lilah removed her shoes at the door and went to embrace little Kashi.

"Something smells zaki [delicious]," I said, hoping I was using the word correctly.

"Thank you, Mary. I hope you will like it."

"I'm sure I will, Faisha," I said, kissing her on both cheeks.

Kashan offered some excuses to his sister for why he couldn't stick around. Faisha smiled, seemingly as undisturbed by her brother's departure as I was.

"Come and sit here in the salon [living room]," she motioned toward one of the fancy sofas. "I've prepared some shai if you'd like some, Mary."

After instructing Malaya to take the children to play in another room, Faisha sat down across from me. Lilah took her cousin by the hand and followed Malaya down the hallway.

"Are you enjoying yourself in Amman, Mary? Inti mobsutta [Are you happy]?"

It was a question I was often asked by the women in the family.

"Na 'am [Yes]," was my reply in Arabic. That's what my reply would always be. That's what it had to be.

"When will you come here to live, Mary? When will you leave America and make your home here with us in Jordan?"

"I'll come as soon as I have everything situated in the States," I explained. "I need to save up money because, when I come to Jordan, I'm not sure how I will make money. I don't know if Kashan will want me to work when I'm living here."

"There are ways you can work without going outside the house," Faisha said, enthusiastically. "Maybe my brother will allow you to cut hair for women at your home," she suggested. "Many husbands in Amman are allowing their wives to have a job in their home. Some women are selling beautiful dresses." "Nofal told me he will allow me to do this also," she lifted her head proudly. "When Kashi attends school, I will begin this work."

How good of the men to allow their wives to have a job. And how convenient that they won't even need to leave their homes. Sounds phenomenal.

"Oh, that's so nice," I said with a smile that almost convinced myself.

"Yes, women now have many opportunities to have a career in Amman. Amman is a very nice place to live." "I think you will be very happy here," she reached out and touched my arm. "There are so many American women living in Jordan now, Mary."

Yeah, the American women who came here with their husbands and never managed to make it back out. I have higher aspirations for me and my child, thank you very much.

My eyes widened as I played along. Faisha continued to enlighten me.

"My friend's brother married an American woman, and she is very happy here. She says she likes Amman much better than she likes America. She has converted to Islam now."

Uh oh. Here we go.

I pressed my lips together as I contemplated my response.

"Oh, really?" I asked with a smile.

"Yes." "She was a Christian, and now she is Muslim," Faisha claimed.

Well, I'm pretty sure she wasn't a Christ follower if she converted to Islam. I mean, Christ is either the Messiah or he isn't. If someone knows that Christ is truly the Son of God, they can't simply unknow that truth.

"Wow," was all I managed to say.

"Yes, this is true," Faisha insisted. "I spoke with her, and she told me she is very happy to be Muslim now."

"Is that so?" I responded, clearly seeing the flaw in her story.

I knew what she was saying had no merit whatsoever. Someone with a genuine relationship with the Savior would be unwilling to deny Christ for any reason, including a Muslim conversion. This brought me to the conclusion that although the woman she was referring to may have come from a country founded on Judeo-Christian values, such as the U.S., she was probably not a Christ follower prior to her conversion. Any person who knew Christ was truly who he said he was—the way, the truth, and the life—could never deny him.

> Jesus told him, "I am the way, the truth, and the life. No one can come to the Father except through me.
> John 14:6 NLT

But Faisha wouldn't have understood that. Only a devout believer in Christ would understand that. And a devout believer would refuse to entertain the claim that God couldn't have a son and that Jesus was merely a prophet. To profess Mohammad as superior to Jesus Christ would be considered blasphemy for a sincere, God-loving Christian.

Knowing the truth of the Gospel and having faith in Christ provides the only clear and plausible way to prevail against a demand to submit to Islam. So it was completely understandable that women from the largely secular Western world might relinquish their freedoms, not seeing any way around it.

I realized Faisha could have been instructed by Kashan to bring up the subject of conversion. Or perhaps she believed me converting to Islam would smooth things out between her brother and me. Either way, the direction this conversation had taken was very disconcerting. But at least I knew what they were thinking. I hoped I still had plenty of time before Kashan's family began to put any real pressure on me to convert.

"Should we check on the kids?" I asked, looking away from Faisha's intense gaze and back toward the hallway.

"No, they are fine. Malaya is with them."

Intent on introducing an alternative topic of discussion, I said, "Oh... how nice it is that Malaya helps you so much."

"Yes, that's true," she conceded. "But these Filipino women can be trouble. So many of them get pregnant after they arrive in Jordan."

Unable to imagine where she might be going with this, I leaned closer to get a better understanding.

"They... get pregnant?" I peered at her through squinted eyes. "How? I thought they don't ever leave your homes."

"Yes, this is true. But they are evil, and they are tricking Arab husbands to be with them. Many of them were becoming pregnant. Because of this problem, we make them take birth control medication as soon as they arrive in Amman."

"Oh, my goodness!" I put my hand to my mouth in horror.

"And Mary... I have seen the way Malaya looks at Kashan when he comes over." "You cannot trust these Filipino women," Faisha said firmly.

I felt sick to my stomach when I realized what she was saying. If what Faisha told me was accurate, Filipino women were not only being sold as slaves to work here in Jordan, but they were also being raped by the husbands and possibly any other males who had access to them.

The decision to immediately place them on birth control was, no doubt, done to cover the sexual crimes being committed by the men. The wives were either falling for this deceptive reasoning contrived by their husbands, or they were knowingly complicit.

I found the fact that Malaya was acting differently around Kashan to be very telling. His sister may have given him the benefit of the doubt concerning this matter, but I knew him better than that. Malaya was the clear victim, not the men she was subjected to.

Oh Lord, I have to get my daughter out of here!

Lilah was now six years old. And what's more, she had turned another year older while away from her homeland. She fluently spoke a language that had once been unknown to her, with rare opportunities to speak English. I had no knowledge of, or input into, what she was taught at the Muslim school she attended. And I had to leave her there once again, living each day without me. My prayers constantly covered her. My tears were continually before the Lord. If it were not for the grace of God, I would not have been able to endure it.

> You keep track of all my sorrows. You have collected all my tears in your bottle. You have recorded each one in your book. My enemies will retreat when I call to you for help. This I know: God is on my side!
> Psalm 56:8-9 NLT

Chapter 19

CUSTOM-MADE CAGES

Every four months, I returned to the Middle East to see my daughter. I considered my time apart from Lilah to be a means to an end—working hard, saving up money to fund my next trip overseas, and praying for a miracle. At times, my plight felt insurmountable. The only reason I endured was because of God's Spirit continually imparting strength within me.

The more time I spent in the Middle East, the more I knew the rules. I diligently performed all mandatory functions correctly and without resistance.

- Do not make eye contact or speak to men outside of the immediate family.
- Do not touch Kashan after he made himself clean for prayer by ritual washing.
- Do not assume you have a say in decisions concerning your child.
- Do not open the door or attempt to leave the house
- Do not show legs or cleavage.
- Do not walk past or near a man who is praying.
- Do not leave the bedroom when a man outside of the immediate family is present.

- Do not move your hips when you walk.
- Do not break the rules.
- Do not question the rules.

If I thought Lilah and I would have to abide by these edicts for the rest of our lives, I would have gone off the deep end. Perhaps I would, at some point, be driven to plunge a knife deep into the heart of the man who placed my little girl and me in that environment. Although that would have brought on tragic consequences for both my child and me.

I could not imagine the Sharia court system in Amman ruling in my favor and granting me a verdict of "not guilty by reason of insanity," or giving me a lesser sentence due to it being a "crime of passion." And the chances of my American family being able to obtain custody of Lilah after I was imprisoned or executed were slim to none, thanks to Islamic family law.

No, for the most part, I did not entertain such reckless thoughts. Wisdom kept me from doing that. Wisdom encouraged me to use self-control and stay the course. Wisdom constantly whispered in my ear, making me wiser than my enemy.

> Wait patiently for the LORD. Be brave and courageous.
> Yes, wait patiently for the Lord.
> Psalm 27:14 NLT

Believing our situation was not permanent helped me adhere to the rules. I fully expected the Lord to deliver us one way or the other. I always believed that we would leave that way of life and never return to it, although I couldn't help but sympathize with the women we would leave behind in this tyrannical social structure. I tried my best to come to terms with it.

I just can't understand how they endure this way of life. How do they spend their entire lives following degrading regulations contrived by some kind of vile and depraved evil entity? But it's the only life they know—they were born into this system. They were indoctrinated from the time they came into this world. Still, there must be something inside these women that cries out for justice. Did they become marginalized and dominated that easily? Were they subdued and oppressed without even a fight? Surely not! It can't be as neat and tidy as they make it out to be.

Living under the subjugation I experienced in Amman was difficult for me. Due to my experience living as a woman without constraints in a free society, I was unwilling to accept that degree of confinement. However, many of the women in that part of the world didn't seem to realize they were captives. But I was certain there must be something, albeit beaten down and buried deep within them, that cried out for fair treatment.

My heart broke for them. I wanted to inform them of their chains. I wanted to tell them that they were actually created in the image of God and therefore equal to their husbands.

> So God created mankind in his own image, in the image of God he created them; male and female he created them.
> Genesis 1:27 NIV

> And God saw everything that He made, and behold it was very good (suitable, pleasant) and He approved it completely.
> Genesis 1:31 AMPC

> Thank you for making me so wonderfully complex! Your workmanship is marvelous - how well I know it.
> Psalm 139:14 NLT

I desperately wanted to reveal to them that they were living in bondage, under false doctrine, and that there was a better way. I wanted to announce to them that they were not merely possessions but amazing women, worthy of honor, respect, and love. I wanted to let them know they deserved to have the liberty to speak and to do and to go as they pleased. I wanted to say that they had a right to unlimited privileges—well beyond those granted to a young child.

> There is no longer Jew or Gentile, slave or free, male or female. For you are all one in Christ Jesus.
> Galatians 3:28 NLT

But I couldn't say a word concerning those things. Not at that time and not under those circumstances. Mentioning it would have made waves and harmed my chances of escaping with my child. And even if I were to say something to the women concerning their restraints, they probably wouldn't have been receptive, at least not initially. They may have felt insulted or become angry that I had the audacity to speak against their religion. They might have even reported me to the men.

I pondered how it was that some were born into freedom and others were delivered into bondage due to their parents' geographic location and culture. It brought tears to my eyes. My heart ached for this broken world. Acknowledging the power of God and his faithfulness in answering prayers, I prayed that these women would one day realize freedom for their souls.

> His purpose was for the nations to seek after God and perhaps feel their way toward him and find him - though he is not far from any one of us.
> Acts 17:27 NLT

ಬಿಂ ಬಿಂ

I poured more hot tea into my cup. Sprigs of mint swirled around inside. The steamy liquid encouraged the aromatic herb to release just a little more flavor, as a goodwill offering.

"How is it that you started wearing a scarf to cover your hair, Faisha?" I inquired. "When I first met you back in '93, you still lived at your parents' house, and you were not covered."

I stirred a quarter teaspoon of sugar into my cup, then watched it dissolve before I gradually looked up to hear her reply. She looked at me for a moment, as if determining where I was coming from, and then produced an amiable smile.

"I decided it was wise for me to be covered while I was outside of the house attending university," she answered. Then she got up from the table and walked to the kitchen to place some cookies on a platter.

"No one told me to begin wearing a scarf," she elaborated. "I went to my father and told him I wanted to wear a scarf."

She placed the platter on the table and took her seat again. I nodded as if I believed her story, but I cannot say that I did. It was understandable that a woman in Amman might choose to be covered to protect herself from being ogled by degenerates. I had learned that the first time I visited Jordan. And, even up until then, I continued to witness unsavory conduct when I was out in public. Kashan had almost come to blows with numerous men because they were leering at me.

But I had a hard time seeing the Faisha I knew resorting to the extreme measure of covering her hair as a deterrent to would-be offenders. I knew how capable Faisha was at putting a presumptuous man in his place. I had seen her do just that back in '93 when she and I had been granted permission to walk down the street unescorted. We were on our way to her brother's house when a young man we passed dared to address us. Faisha wasted no time reprimanding him and putting him in his place.

I wondered if something might have happened to Faisha that caused her to cover herself. But I suspected that despite what she told me, her father had actually forced her to cover. Or perhaps even her husband. I didn't expect to get any more information from her on the subject. So, I left it alone.

"I see," I answered.

Faisha shifted slightly in her seat, then continued speaking.

"Some women who are covered are not good Muslims." "Just because a woman wears a scarf doesn't mean she is good," she paused to make sure I understood her point. "Radiya, my brother Omeir's wife, was not covered before they got married," she began to elaborate. The judgment in her expression was evident by the way she pursed her lips together and tilted her head to the side.

"Oh, really?" My eyebrows lifted, realizing my question had opened up a can of worms.

"Radiya used to wear short skirts and lots of makeup," Faisha divulged.

I tried to imagine Radiya in a short skirt. It wasn't easy, though, since I had only ever seen her in a long, loose garment. And I realized that my definition of a short skirt likely differed from Faisha's by... several inches.

"When we were growing up, Omeir was in love with Radiya. She is our cousin, from my mother's brother, you know."

"Yes, Kashan told me that," I listened intently as she continued.

"Omeir was always doing nice things for Radiya and bringing her gifts. He told my parents that he wanted to have Radiya, even if the test showed that they could not have children."

"The test?" I put two fingers to my temple and contemplated what she may be saying.

"Yes, the genetic test to determine if the children will be—" she paused.

"—disabled in some way?" I helped her come up with the words in English. "I mean… having a mental or physical disability or maybe a genetic disorder?"

"Yes, like this," Faisha nodded, "…having something wrong." "Omeir said that he would rather not have any children if there would be a problem. But he still wanted to take Radiya for his wife."

"Wow." "He must have really loved her," I acknowledged.

"Yes," she nodded. "So my parents and her parents agreed they could be married."

And just as I was settling in for a happy ending, she added some critical information.

"After they were married, Omeir told Radiya that he wanted her to be covered. She told him no! She did not agree to do it. So, he had to beat her."

Faisha held her head high; a satisfied expression came over her face. She placed the shame on her sister-in-law for not wanting to cover, rather than on her brother for being physically abusive. What Faisha was so proud to admit, I found to be so inherently wrong.

"What?" I leaned forward, in shock.

"That's right. He had to beat her and make her cover herself. Otherwise, she would not have done it. So… she is not good like you think, because my brother had to force her to cover. A good Muslim woman will make the decision to cover for herself—not because she is forced to do it. I decided to be covered by my own choice." "No one had to make me do it," she smiled and lifted her brows toward the self-appropriated halo on her head.

"I see," I nodded.

I felt sick when I considered how Radiya was forced into submission. And I suspected that Faisha was coerced into making the decision to cover rather than face the humiliation and embarrassment of being forced, as Radiya had been.

"Do any women ever change their mind about being covered?" "Does that ever happen?" I was almost afraid to hear her answer.

"No," Faisha stated flatly. "A woman can decide to cover, but after she makes this decision, she can never decide to be uncovered. This cannot happen."

"Oh, okay. I understand."

I understand, alright. I love Faisha, but—note to self—I definitely cannot trust her to help me in any way. Whatever the men were selling, she was buying, however little the return was. All the women in the family seem to believe lies that leave them in deficit of respect, perceived value, mobility, career, voice, choice, and freedom.

Are these women even aware of their plight? Or have they all drunk the Kool-Aid? (A little of both, probably.) Was Faisha saying these things to me as a scare tactic? Was she simply following orders and saying what she was told to say? Surely Kashan wouldn't have wanted Faisha to tell me how his brother had beaten his wife into submission, though. Or would he? I can't tell for sure, so... I'm not taking any chances.

"Would you like another cookie?" Faisha asked, without expression.

As far as I was concerned, she may as well have said, "Do you understand?" But I could play this game too. I simply had to play it better than them, which was challenging since they were the ones in possession of the rulebook. And the rulebook was sinister!

That's okay. I'm a quick study, and I have more at risk here. So while they're busy playing checkers, I'll be playing chess.

"Oh, yes, please." "Shukran," I answered with a sugary sweet smile.

"Afwan [You're welcome]," she replied.

I continued to behave as before: friendly, respectful, and adherent to the rules. I planned to bide my time until God showed me what to do next. Each encounter I had with the evil, woman-hating entity who deceptively hid behind the guise of religion left me with an increased sense of urgency.

Oh, Lord, please get us out of here before I'm pressed to convert to Islam or forced, God-forbid, to wear one of those unbecoming robes!

Before long, the subject of cousins came up again. It was the evening of Kashan's birthday. Omeir and Radiya came to visit with their five children. Taeta asked the men to go out and get some knafeh—a delicious dessert made of soft cheese and topped with sweetened, shredded phyllo dough and chopped pistachios.

Everyone was so excited! It was the equivalent of having a cake and ice cream party in the States—perhaps even better. The noise level in the house was louder than I had ever heard it.

The kids were having a blast and running all around. I was surprised Nura was allowing it. If Khuram had been there, it probably would not have been tolerated.

I noticed that Lilah seemed especially delighted when Omeir's kids arrived at the house. It was obvious to me that she was sweet on Masood, who was close to her age. They attended the same Muslim school, although they were not in the same class since he was a year ahead of her. Masood tolerated Lilah chasing him around, but I could tell he was annoyed. The adults seemed to think her infatuation was amusing, even cute. I, however, did not.

"Lilah, leave Masood alone." "I don't think he wants to play," I said, hoping to deter her.

"Lilah always wants to be near to Masood," Radiya smiled.

"They are cousins," Kashan interjected. "It's good for her to have cousins in her life." "This is the way it's supposed to be," he said, smiling.

"Um hum," I said. "I know."

And I did know. I was all too familiar with the custom they had of cousins marrying cousins. The conversation I'd recently had with Faisha came to mind. Kashan and his family believed it was okay for cousins to marry. They seemed to prefer it, by the way they spoke. One of Kashan's older sisters, Johara, was married to their cousin Aadil. They lived in Al Azariya, near Jerusalem. But I didn't want little Masood's DNA anywhere near my daughter's DNA. I thought it was absurd to even consider it.

I had to get Lilah out of there before she came of age: of age to be told what length her skirts needed to be, of age to be forced to wear a scarf to cover her beautiful hair, and of age to be told who she would marry.

Lilah, oblivious of what life in Amman would mean for her future, continued to chase her cousin around the dining table. She was too young to understand. But I understood. I knew what needed to happen. I needed to get her away from this place!

My God, please keep Lilah safe while I'm away from her.

❧☙❧☙

Tears streamed down my face as we stood at Queen Alia Airport a couple weeks later. Lilah hugged me tightly and kissed me on the lips.

"Mommy, when you come here to live in Jordan with me and Daddy, you won't have to cry anymore."

"That's right, Lilah. I won't have to cry anymore when I'm with you all the time." I brushed the tears from my face and smiled at her innocence.

"Yes, Mommy." "When is that going to be?" Kashan whispered sarcastically in my ear.

"Soon, I promise. I just have to save up more money and figure out what to do with all my stuff. You don't want me coming over here empty-handed, do you?"

I kissed Lilah again and squeezed her one last time before I went through security.

Three trips in, and I still hadn't received God's divine plan to get Lilah out. Kashan was adamant that I return to be with him for my birthday in about four months. Not so much because he wanted to see me, but more to ensure I would not spend my birthday with another man. We each had our priorities. We each had our agendas

Chapter 20

SEPTEMBER 11, 2001

It was one of the rare occasions that we were outdoors doing something fun. Kashan took Lilah and me to visit an area along the Jordan River, not far from the Dead Sea, where there had been recent archaeological finds. Remnants of a Byzantine Christian church built between 491 and 518 AD had been uncovered near the location where, we were told, Jesus himself was baptized by John the Baptist.

It was great to be out of the house on an excursion. For a small fee, a guide took us, along with a European family, to the various stations of discovery. He explained the significance of each one as we toured the site.

It was late afternoon, around 4 o'clock or so. Kashan's cell phone rang. Seeing it was his oldest brother, Omeir, he stepped aside and took the call. After a short conversation, he turned to me with a rather grave expression on his face.

"A plane crashed into a building at the World Trade Center," he informed me.

"What?" I asked, shaking my head. "What do you mean?"

"Omeir said that a plane crashed into one of the buildings at the World Trade Center in NYC." "That's all I know," he admitted, shrugging his shoulders.

We continued with the tour, but I was no longer hearing the tour guide's commentary. My concern for the people involved in the accident in New York had me distracted. Kashan's eyes shifted back and forth as he looked here and there, rather than focusing on the tour. He rubbed his lips with his hand as if in contemplation. Neither one of us knew what to make of it. Before too long, his phone rang again.

"It's Omeir again," Kashan whispered to me.

We locked eyes for a moment before he stepped aside to answer. I grabbed Lilah's hand and followed him.

He spoke in Arabic, so I wasn't sure what he was saying. He turned and looked at me. By the odd expression on his face, I knew something was terribly wrong.

I squinted my eyes and shook my head in question. "What is it?" I asked, impatient to hear.

He said goodbye to his brother and then answered me.

"A second plane crashed into another building at the World Trade Center."

Trying to grasp what it all meant, I looked around at the landmark location of the early church where we stood. I remained silent for a moment, then quickly realized I could not continue with the tour.

"Maybe we should go back to the house and watch the news to see what's going on," I suggested.

"Come on," Kashan said, indicating that we should follow him toward the dusty parking lot where he'd parked the car.

On the drive home, Kashan and I discussed who we thought might be responsible. Still uninformed of the details, I was under the impression it was two private planes that had plunged into the buildings.

"It's probably some crazy guys like those responsible for the bombing in Oklahoma City in '95. I'm sure anybody can learn to fly one of those small private planes." "I'll bet they stole the planes from some tiny airport," I surmised.

"No." Kashan's eyes widened. "They were not small planes, Mary." "They were large commercial aircraft," he informed me.

"What?" I asked, looking at him in disbelief.

We sat in silence for a while, attempting to figure things out. The more I tried to comprehend the situation, the more questions I had.

Were these flights filled with passengers? How had these people gotten their hands on major airline passenger jets? And who were they? It's unlikely that they were simply some angry domestic idiots. This seems too sophisticated a maneuver to be carried out by a handful of self-isolated citizens with visions of murderous and suicidal grandeur.

Then I began to ask myself more serious questions. Questions that would help pinpoint the mindset of the perpetrators.

Who hates the U.S. so much that they would be willing to go to this length to kill as many Americans as possible, along with themselves? Who would be capable of such evil? Who would have a network of hate so calculated and vile that they would carry out this degree of destruction to my country?

There was only one person who came to mind. And I considered my husband to be familiar enough with this person to provide further insight.

"The only person I think is capable of doing something like this is Osama bin Laden," I said to Kashan.

He turned and looked at me with a glint of surprise in his expression. Then a more serious look fell over his face. He nodded in agreement.

"I think you're right," he said.

We didn't speak much on the drive home. Kashan knew my mind was busy, so he didn't try to engage in conversation. I didn't know what Kashan's opinion was on the incident. I knew he and many Palestinians regarded Bin Laden as a type of hero. Why that was, I could not fathom. And at that moment, I really didn't care why. I just needed to know what level of damage had been done to my country and how many innocent lives had been lost.

Periodically, I expelled an audible sigh as I worked through things in my mind. The drive home took us an hour, but it felt like an eternity. I couldn't get back to the house fast enough. I had to know what was going on. It felt horrible to be away from my country when it was hit by what appeared to be a terrorist attack. But there I was, in a land where the authors and creators of such attacks often originate.

When we got back to the house, Kashan translated the condolences offered to me on behalf of his mother. Then Nura said something else to him in Arabic. I detected the urgency in her voice and asked Kashan what she said. He told me she asked him if this was *it*—if this was the war they had been waiting for.

I had a flashback of Kashan's cousin, Aadil, in Al Azariya, telling me that, in the end, the blood of the infidels would run knee-deep. "Why not sooner than later?" he had suggested. It appeared that Nura held to the same belief.

"What'd you tell her?" I asked bluntly, not in the mood to mince words.

"I told her I didn't know, but maybe."

Kashan changed the television channel to CNN, the only news station that was broadcast in English. I sat on the floor in front of the television and watched previously recorded video footage of United Airlines Flight 175 crashing into the South

Tower of the World Trade Center, which at that point had already collapsed. Horrified, I covered my mouth with both of my hands. Tears of anguish and outrage flowed down my face.

The North Tower was still standing. Black smoke billowed from it. It had been struck earlier by the hijacked American Airlines Flight 11. All passengers on both flights were assumed to have been killed on impact, as well as thousands of others who worked in the buildings that day. Despite what I saw playing out before me, I couldn't help but hope that somehow, some of the passengers on Flight 11 might still be alive.

Then, to my horror, the North Tower collapsed as I watched. Heavy metal and concrete crashed to the ground, spewing debris as brave first responders and would-be survivors were, in seconds, buried beneath a massive amount of concrete and steel rubble. People ran through the city streets, unrecognizable due to the white powdery substance that covered them. The dust detailed an expression of desperation on each of their faces, causing them to share the same ghastly resemblance.

And then the nightmare continued when the reporter informed viewers that the Pentagon had taken a hit as well. American Airlines Flight 77 slammed into the Headquarters of the U.S. Department of Defense, presumably killing everyone on board and numerous others on the ground. Fully in shock at that point, I listened in disbelief as yet another plane crash was announced. United Flight 93 was down in an open field in Shanksville, Pennsylvania.

Thousands of lives were taken that day. Millions of hearts were broken. Torrents of tears streamed over my burning face and down onto my shirt. Horrendous images played repeatedly on the television screen while the news reporter described more details as quickly as they came in. A fire burned within me. Seeing my country, which was, up to that point, so naïve to this level of wickedness, caught off guard and attacked by such magnitude of evil—it affected me in a way words cannot describe.

I didn't think I had any more pain to suffer. But that hit me hard and below the belt. It marked me. Kashan's mother placed some tissue in my hand, but I didn't turn to acknowledge her. I simply was unable to break myself away from viewing the current news broadcast concerning my country.

A desperate cry came from my throat, "Oh, my Father God!" I began to shake my head. "Lord Jesus, please."

Lilah, sitting close enough to hear, tried to comfort me. "Mommy, don't cry. It will be okay, I promise."

I turned around and pulled her toward me into an embrace, "I know, honey." "It's going to be okay. Everything is going to be okay."

I kissed her cheek and held her small head in my hands, then looked into her eyes to reassure her. "Mommy's okay." "She just needs to watch this right now," I whispered in a somber tone.

Kashan took Lilah by the hand and suggested, "Why don't you go see if Taeta needs some help in the kitchen?" "Maybe she has a snack for you."

"Okay, Daddy," she bounced to her feet and ran into the kitchen.

Without looking at Kashan, I turned back to the live broadcast. For many hours, I stayed glued to the television. Thankfully, no one stopped me.

The smell of food wafted into the living room, but I barely noticed. I didn't want to notice. I didn't want to accept that life would simply go on as usual under those dire circumstances. It couldn't. It shouldn't. And no, it wouldn't! Not for me anyway.

Not for my country. We would be forever changed. A line had been crossed; a boundary had been breached.

I cried out to God in anguish over the brutal and unjust act that was committed against my country. And when I did, a higher level of conviction came over me. Something rose up in me that day. Something shifted. That September in Amman, sitting there on the floor in the living room, a fierce determination took root within me. I became more convinced than ever that I could and would do whatever it took to end the injustice in Lilah's and my life. I was never more determined that I would indeed live to see the day that I got my child out of there.

I will see it—or I will die trying!

"Ta' ali, kum," Nura called out, motioning for us to come to the kitchen table.

Reluctantly, I went to the bathroom and splashed cold water on my face. When I came to the table, Nura patted the place beside her, inviting me to sit there. Her show of compassion threatened to make me start crying again, but I resisted the urge, and it went away. She placed several warak dawali [stuffed grape leaves] on my plate.

"Tanawal el ta' am," she said, insisting that I eat. She then added some pieces of leftover baked chicken and salad onto my plate. I appreciated the sentiment.

"Shukran," I said without looking up.

Just the day before, Kashan's sisters, Faisha and Ciara, came to the house to help prepare those stuffed grape leaves. It was a happy time, with the women gathered around the table together. Lilah and I were allowed to contribute, despite our lack of ability in forming the cylinder-shaped rolls. The others made it look easy as they skillfully formed the meat-filled grape leaves. I was amazed at how quickly and meticulously they worked.

What attention to detail they showed. I couldn't think of any traditional American dishes that required quite that much effort.

The conversation among them that day appeared to be lighthearted, by the way they were laughing. It was nice to see them together, enjoying themselves. Periodically, I asked what was so funny, since I still had little comprehension of the language. Faisha was always willing to interpret.

"It is a saying we have: 'It takes the women a very long to prepare the grape leaves, but it takes the men very little time to consume them.'"

I appreciated her interpreting so I would feel included. Though at times, I was suspicious that their jokes were actually about the two novices at the table. Not that I really minded. And neither did Lilah, evidently. She was fluent in Arabic, so she understood everything they were saying. She continued to proudly add her contributions to the bowl of wrapped grape leaves, regardless of their chatter. So I did too.

An additional comment was made by Nura, which caused her daughters to erupt in laughter. Lilah simply smiled and kept working.

After adding another oddly formed contribution to the ever-growing collection, I looked at Faisha and asked, "What did she say?"

Faisha was laughing so hard she could barely get it out. That caused Nura and Ciara to laugh even harder.

Faisha wiped a tear of laughter from her cheek with the back of her oily hand and answered, "My mother said, 'You can tell which ones are made by Lilah and Mary.'"

We all laughed at that. Then Nura said something else. They began laughing again. I looked at Faisha for insight.

"My mother suggested that Kashan could eat the ones prepared by you and Lilah. Then Ciara said that Kashan would be very hungry since Mary and Lilah are so slow at rolling them."

"Ha!" I laughed. "That is funny."

"And then my mother said that would be fine because Kashan wouldn't be home soon enough to eat any. She said my father would eat them all before Kashan arrived home."

"Oh, that's probably true," I said, nodding my head in agreement.

I admired the women of Kashan's family for the strength and endurance they exhibited under the confines of Islam. I loved them. But I could not forget that I was not one of them. I couldn't trust them with my secrets. I couldn't expect them to do anything to help Lilah and me get away. Not because they didn't have compassion, but because their belief system basically deemed me an infidel. I was Christian and not Muslim. That meant they considered me to be in defiance of the teachings of their prophet, Mohammad.

The memory of the women's laughter faded in my mind as I ate the food in front of me. The saying, "What a difference a day makes, came to mind."

That was just yesterday. It was a day filled with bonding and laughter. But this is today. And there is no laughter for me and my country. There is only heartbreak and tears.

Before long, Kashan's father came home and offered me his condolences. I respectfully thanked him while questioning his sincerity. In the days that followed, more of Kashan's siblings came to visit, and they too offered their sympathies. Sometimes they would even throw in some conspiracy theories for good measure.

"Did you know that there were no Jews in the Twin Towers on that day?" "It is because the Jews are responsible for this attack, but they are trying to blame it on the Muslims," claimed Faisha.

"Oh, really?" I responded flatly. By that point, I wasn't capable of feigning interest in their opinions on the subject.

"Yes, the Jews are evil people." "They will do anything to hurt Muslims," she tried to convince me.

Nothing I heard from Kashan's family surprised me anymore. Unable to produce an expression that indicated I gave any credence to her claims, I listened to her rhetoric with a solemn face.

"I wish I would have the chance to kill even one Jew. We consider that killing one Jew is worth losing the lives of many Muslims." "The more babies we have, the more of us there will be to kill the Jews," Faisha professed.

Who would follow the kind of God that placed such little value on human life, specifically the life of his own followers? As long as this kind of mindset continues, the killing will continue—all in the name of Allah.

When the following Friday came, I was sitting in the living room watching TV with Kashan and his father. Khuram had turned on CNN for me so I could stay informed on what was going on in the States. Once I got caught up on the latest news, I handed the remote back to him and thanked him for his consideration.

A little later, Kashan began pacing back and forth while he and his father engaged in conversation. Khuram's voice took on a stern tone. His face appeared irritated, his bushy brows furrowed. He occasionally glanced over at me. I had no idea what they were discussing, but I could see that Kashan was hyped up about something. Then he abruptly stopped speaking with his father and turned to me.

"Would you like to go to prayers with me today?" he asked.

His smile was twisted into a wrathful, yet satisfied grin. He looked directly at me, but his gaze was distant, as if imagining some gratifying event. His question took me by surprise. He had never invited me to Friday prayers. I was actually considering it, just to get out of the house.

Before I had a chance to process what Kashan's motive might be, his father looked at me, shook his head, and said, "Do not go."

Then Kashan turned and walked out of the condo, slamming the door behind him. His footsteps echoed in the corridor as he briskly went down the stairs. His father grumbled some curse words, then returned to watching television.

The next day, the television showed footage of celebrating in the streets outside a mosque after Friday prayers. Because of the black and white patterned hattahs many of the men in the crowd wore, I assumed they were Palestinians. They were burning the American flag along with an effigy of President Bush. It sickened me. The evil smile on Kashan's face when he had extended the invitation for me to join him for Friday prayers remained fixed in my mind.

Being there in the Middle East and apart from my people during the attack made me feel as if I had betrayed my country somehow. It didn't really make sense, but nothing did. At least I had been allowed to call my dad, though. I heard the urgency in his voice when I talked to him.

"Please be careful, Mary. For God's sake! There are reports of people over there celebrating the terrorist attack against the States."

"Dad, I'm fine. I just worry about you guys."

I snatched a tissue from the box on the table beside the couch and wiped the moisture from my face. The tears I had shed since the attack on my homeland seemed to have an endless reservoir.

No matter how many times I was offered condolences from Kashan's family, I would not be fooled—I could not be fooled. For me to let my guard down and believe they had good intentions could very well be the death of me. I realized that now more than ever. It made me wonder how much *my* death would be worth to them. I didn't ask, though. Instead, I politely accepted their claims of sympathy, while regarding each one as… mostly insincere.

❧ The Assignment ❧

One afternoon, Lilah came home from school and asked Taeta for some colored markers from the large chest of drawers. She appeared eager to begin work on her homework assignment.

By the way Taeta pointed her finger toward the table, I assumed she was instructing Lilah to refrain from damaging the tabletop. Once she was set up at the table with all needed supplies, Lilah got busy. With a finger resting on her cheek, she pursed her lips and moved them from side to side as she contemplated her next move.

"Lilah, what's your homework assignment today?" I asked, wondering if I could help. "What are you drawing?"

"I'm drawing the flag for Israel. Or… I can draw the American flag. I can choose the one I want to draw. That's what my teacher told us."

I was pleasantly surprised to hear that her school was teaching the children to be mindful of other countries and cultures. I thought, perhaps, that the devastation in the U.S had been a wake-up call for school administrators at the private Islamic school Lilah attended. With some amount of optimism, I surmised that the radical terrorist strike on my country had created an initiative, perhaps by order of King Abdullah II himself, to teach a more nondiscriminatory attitude toward nations with customs and beliefs different from those in Jordan.

"Oh, that's so nice, Lilah." "What will you be doing with the flags when you take them back to the classroom?" I inquired. "Will the teacher put them up on the wall?"

Kashan, hearing the conversation, came from the kitchen. He stood with his back leaning against the kitchen door frame. "Lilah, tell Mommy what you will do with the flags in the classroom, habibti."

Kashan looked toward the blank paper on the table. His eyes were glazed over. His lips curled with sinister satisfaction.

"We will tape the flags to the ground and stomp on them, Mommy," Lilah answered matter-of-factly.

"What?" I asked, shocked by her answer.

When I looked up at Kashan for clarification, he kept the same smug look on his face, but his eyes were focused on me. He glared, daring me to say anything.

Clasping my hand over my mouth, I turned and ran down the hall to the bedroom. The door slammed harder than I intended, but I couldn't have cared less. The sound of Nura rapidly spilling out words of disapproval carried down the hallway, hitting their mark. I lay on the bed, knees to chest. The thin pillow I'd wrapped around my head to cover my ears wasn't substantial enough to block out the sound of a completely broken world.

What kind of people teach children to hate others in this way? What kind of twisted evil is this? And here I am, in the midst of them, as my country is being attacked... by them! I'm away from my people, here in the Middle East, in the company of those whose so-called religion calls for such depraved, murderous acts. First, this evil ideology stole my daughter. That nearly took me out. And now this!

I have to get Lilah out of here before her principles and sense of self-worth are totally destroyed and replaced with lies—lies about her own people, lies from the enemy of her soul. But I need to get control over my anger now, or I could mess everything up. I can't let them believe that I wouldn't ultimately submit to the living conditions here, as horrendous as they are. No, I have to be smarter than that. I have to use wisdom.

Under the present circumstances, it's understandable that I reacted in this way. I mean... my country has just been attacked. My display of emotion shouldn't come as a complete surprise to them. It actually makes sense. It makes me look authentic. Yes—that's it. I had a good cry, and then when I was finished, I pulled myself together. That's the conclusion they'll come to. I haven't ruined anything yet. I just need to get myself together and show some self-control before I mess up the plan.

> A person without self-control is like
> a city with broken-down walls.
> Proverbs 25:28 NLT

I took a deep breath in and then slowly released it, hoping to expel all my negative and counterproductive emotions. It helped.

The more I appear to assimilate, the better for both Lilah and me.

I began to go over the next step in my plan. A detailed description of my role played on repeat in my head. But it kept slipping farther away, just out of reach, as my overworked mind drifted between varied planes of consciousness. Leaving Lilah to return to the States always broke my heart. But since the attack on my country, I was pulled in two directions. Part of me couldn't get out of there soon enough.

These people hate my people. They hate everything we stand for. I have to get us away from here.

My eyelids fluttered shut as if pulling me back behind a heavy, weighted curtain. I forced them back open.

Surely, this wouldn't have happened had I not been out enjoying myself that day... had I not looked away. Surely, there is something I could have done to protect my country... to warn them.

My thoughts made no sense. Still, they continued.

But I'm here in the Middle East... here in the midst of those who celebrate the attack on my country. I need to put some distance between me and this place before I do something reckless or say something brazen... something brash.

The details of my current assignment became more hazy and obscure in my mind. I tried to gain clarity. Before I could get very far, sleep spread itself out over me like a soft peace offering, providing me temporary solace from my struggles. Sleep promised to walk me through a full dress rehearsal of my next step, if I would only be still and allow it to.

My flight out of Amman was set for Friday, October 5th. The aircraft would make a stop in Shannon, Ireland. There, I would deplane. At least, that was the plan. But nothing in the world was certain—not anymore.

So much had been taken from me. So much had been lost. At that point, I was on fire. I was burning. I felt wildly desperate for God to act justly on behalf of me and my country.

> Yet the Lord longs to be gracious to you; therefore he will rise up to show you compassion. For the Lord is a God of justice. Blessed are all who wait for him!
> Isaiah 30:18 NIV

Chapter 21

A REPRIEVE

Realizing my flight home would stop to refuel in Shannon, Ireland, I had asked my younger brother, Tieger, to meet me there. He and my older brother, Conor, had already visited Ireland a couple years prior with my father. But I had never been there myself.

My plan was to deplane in Shannon and then take a flight into Dublin, where Tieger would meet me. It was unlikely that Kashan would call me so soon after I left Amman. That would give me a desperately needed respite from the constraints of the regime I'd just spent the last thirty days with.

Kashan was unaware of my plans to stay in Ireland for the weekend. If I told him, he would be convinced I was meeting up with a man for a passionate encounter. Hours of excruciating interrogation would likely follow. So I took all necessary measures to make sure he didn't find out.

Prior to leaving the States, I booked a room at a Dublin hotel. I put the name to memory and kept no written documentation of my reservation. Realizing I needed the confirmation number to check in, though, I wrote it on the back of an inconspicuous business card. But assuming Kashan and his family might go through my purse, I made it look like a phone number by prefacing it with a South Givenia area code.

Tieger and I had planned to meet at the William Hotel in Dublin on October 6th. We agreed to have no contact whatsoever during the entire time I was in Jordan for... obvious reasons. But since four U.S. flights had recently been hijacked, I was concerned that my brother wouldn't be willing to board a plane. And I wouldn't have blamed him.

Before leaving for the airport with Kashan, I said goodbye to Lilah and promised her I would be back as soon as possible. She was becoming somewhat used to me leaving her by now. Smiling sweetly, she reminded me of the ever-growing list of things she wanted from the States.

The car radio played contemporary Arab music as we drove to the airport. By then, I had become accustomed to the local rhythms. I still couldn't understand most of the words, but I got the gist of it. Based on everything I had observed of the Muslim culture, the song seemed disingenuous and insincere to me, though. The man's words vowed true love, which I believed could never actually be realized within a belief system that placed so little value or respect on women.

> Nevertheless, in the Lord woman is not independent
> of man, nor is man independent of woman.
> For as women came from man, so also man is born
> of women. But everything comes from God.
> 1 Corinthians 11:11-12 NIV

In my opinion, the lyrics that professed devotion were deceptively cloaked in a facade of genuine affection. The source of the deceit was not merely man's desire to dominate. It was much darker than that. I felt the words were designed to distract a suppressed female population from seeing their true worth, like a lullaby aimed to placate. I saw it as a strategic maneuver implemented, not by man, but by the true enemy of our souls.

Perhaps the direness of my situation had brought me to a place where I felt compelled to look behind every curtain to expose hidden agendas. Regardless, I would not be taken in by the ardent declarations that came through the speakers that day. Any civilization that represses its women and kills those who believe differently from them, I felt, wasn't capable of true love.

My flight to Ireland departed on time and appeared to be as smooth sailing and uneventful as my previous flights. At least initially. I was seated next to a young Arab man who was quite fidgety. He made eye contact with me (a female) several times, which was not the norm in that part of the world. Since he had already broken social protocol with his behavior, I decided to ask him where he was from to get a better idea of his mindset and intentions. He stated that he was from Yemen.

I remember Yemen. October, 2000. Al-Qaeda bombed the USS Cole by suicide attack. That was not long ago. Of course, I know Yemen.

He explained to me that his parents were sending him to the States to live with an aunt and uncle because he had been using drugs. I found it odd that anyone would confide in a complete stranger like that, especially within the conservative Muslim environment we were in. I reasoned that the drugs he was on might be altering his behavior. Deciding he was relatively harmless, I attempted to close my eyes and get some sleep. The only thing I wanted to think about at that moment was exiting the plane and placing my feet upon friendly soil.

But before I had a chance to drift off, my troubled neighbor placed a blanket over his head, clenched his fist, and began pounding on his armrest. Considering his current drug addiction, I suspected that he was going through withdrawal. I also concluded that he was, quite possibly, very close to losing it. That was enough to put me into complete panic mode. Especially so soon after the terrorist attacks.

I made the decision that sitting there beside him was no longer a safe option. So I politely excused myself, then carefully squeezed past the angry man under the blanket. I walked down the aisle of the plane and motioned for one of the flight attendants, letting her know of my concerns. To my relief, she immediately relocated me to a seat at the opposite end of the plane.

Once we landed in Shannon, I quickly found my gate. My next flight was scheduled to depart within the hour. During the forty-five-minute flight to Dublin, I went over the prearranged details. I hoped all would go smoothly and that Tieger would be waiting for me at the hotel.

The woman I spoke with when I made the reservation had assured me that the William Hotel was well known. She said that all taxi drivers in the area would be familiar with the location. As soon as I retrieved my luggage, I hailed the first taxi I saw.

I was certain that I remembered the name of our hotel correctly. I purposely hadn't written it down because I didn't want to raise any suspicions. However, the name I had impressed in my memory must have been incorrect because the cab driver claimed he'd never heard of the William Hotel. I tried to call my brother Tieger, but I wasn't getting an answer.

For over thirty minutes, the cab drove me around looking for the hotel. Eventually, because I was feeling both sorry for the guy and stupid at the same time, I told him to let me out on a random curb. Then I hailed another taxi. I told the next cab driver my sob story about how I couldn't find my hotel or my brother. I sat in the back seat of the cab feeling defeated and increasingly hopeless.

With an expressionless look on my face, I admitted, "If I wasn't so exhausted, I'd be cryin' right now."

"Ah, but you can't be cryin' now, Mary. You're in Ireland." "If you're going to be cryin', you'll have to do it with some laughter," he declared, in an Irish sing-songy way.

His positive attitude was contagious, so I rallied a bit.

"Now here's the Fitzwilliam Hotel, Mary. Could that be the one for you, by chance?"

"Oh, yes." "Possibly!" I sat up and grabbed my purse. "Will you wait for me while I run in and check, please?"

"Of course I will, Mary," he smiled. "I'll be right here."

His dark eyes twinkled, fine lines gathered at their edges. If I wasn't so preoccupied with the mission at hand, it may have occurred to me that he was, quite possibly, an angel sent from heaven.

I jumped out of the vehicle, crossed the walkway, and entered the reception area of the Fitzwilliam Hotel. The ginger-haired woman at the front desk was able to find my reservation right away. By hearing her voice in person, I could tell she was the same woman who had taken my reservation.

I realized that between her Irish accent and a bad phone connection, I had misunderstood her. When she was saying "Fitzwilliam Hotel," it sounded like "it's William Hotel" to my American ear. I thought putting an "it's" before the name was simply the Irish way of prefacing things.

"It's William, you're saying?" I had asked.

"Yes, Fitzwilliam." "That's it," she had confirmed.

"Okay." "Thank you very much," I replied, thinking I had understood clearly.

The cab driver could tell by the pep in my step that I had finally found the right hotel. By the time I got to the car, he was already in the process of retrieving my bags from the trunk (or the boot, as it were).

After paying him in Irish pounds, I walked back into the hotel lobby. The interior was nice enough, but I was too concerned about finding my brother to take much notice of the décor. Tieger was out there somewhere searching for a hotel that didn't exist, and it was all my fault. I tried calling his cell phone again, but there was still no answer.

Needless to say, I didn't sleep well that night. In the morning, a red light flashing on the phone beside the bed caught my attention. With hopeful expectation, I picked up the phone and rang the reception desk to inquire.

A man's voice answered, "Mrs. Shehadeh, you have a message from Donna Kennedy." "She says to call her as soon as possible. She left this number for you."

"One minute, please," I said as I pulled the drawer of the bedside table open. Thankfully, there was a pen and pad inside. I couldn't imagine how the wife of my older brother, Conor, found me, but I was glad she did.

He read out Donna's number and then added, "You will dial 00 plus 1 to ring the States."

"I'll be using a calling card," I informed him.

"That's perfectly fine. Have a nice day, ma'am."

After punching in the required sequence of numbers, I finally heard ringing from the other end.

"Hello."

"Donna! Oh, my goodness, how did you ever find me?" I placed my hand on top of my head.

"I just did some searching online to find a hotel with a name close to Williams."

She acted like it was no big deal. But it was huge to me.

"You're a genius, Donna!" "Thank God the hotel was willing to confirm I was here," I shook my head and sat down on the bed.

"Well, after I explained the situation, they were more than willing to help," she laughed.

"Poor Tieger. I feel horrible about this. Where did he spend the night? I've been trying to call him since I arrived, but I couldn't get through."

"I was able to help him find a hostel to stay in," she reassured me. "Here's the address."

I shook my head again in grateful disbelief. "You're amazing, Donna. What would we do without you?"

"He should be checking out soon, so if you get over there now, you might catch him," she said quickly.

"Thanks!" "Love you," I said, with high-pitched enthusiasm.

"Love you too," she answered.

I hung up the phone and hurriedly threw on some clothes. I was out on the curb hailing a cab well before my 11:00 a.m. checkout time. As I was getting out of the cab, I spotted Tieger exiting the hostel. If I had arrived one minute later, I would have missed him.

"Tieger, Tieger!" I yelled to him as I ran across the grass, still wet with dew.

The look of relief on his face said it all.

"Oh, my goodness, I'm so glad to find you," I hugged him tightly. "I'm so, so sorry I gave you wrong information. It's a miracle that Donna figured out what hotel I was at and got in touch with me."

"Yeah, I didn't know what I was going to do since you had made all the hotel reservations," he replied, somewhat sullenly.

"Well, I'm just glad you were brave enough to fly over here to meet me. I didn't know if you would even be here. And I wouldn't have blamed you at all for not showing up."

"I almost didn't come," he admitted. "But I didn't have any way of getting in touch with you. I didn't want you to come here expecting me and then be all alone."

Once we got our bearings, we decided to grab a bite to eat. With his tweed cap and green canvas bag slung over one shoulder, Tieger could have passed for a local. But the sound of my suitcase wheels rolling over the cement as I scurried to keep up with him gave us away.

Lugging baggage around town didn't bother me as much as it typically would have. I was just happy to be with family in a friendly land. After we walked for a couple of blocks, Tieger saw a pub that looked familiar to him from his previous trip there.

"I think that place has traditional Irish music," he said, quickening his pace.

Tieger pulled the heavy wooden pub door open for me. The atmosphere inside was lively and cheerful. Most of those present were most likely tourists. But I didn't mind. It was still a stark contrast from the environment back in Amman. As an American in Amman, I had felt merely tolerated and at times downright unwanted and despised. But on that afternoon in Dublin with my brother, I felt safe and welcomed.

> A cheerful heart is good medicine.
> Proverbs 17:22 NIV

Our next reservation was at a family-owned bed and breakfast close to Iveagh Gardens. After checking in, we decided to shower and head back out. We wanted to experience as much of the Gaelic culture as possible—while surrounded by hundreds of other foreign travelers, much like us. If we had more time, we would have ventured out of the city. But that night, we didn't mind staying within the boundaries of Dublin proper. Just having the opportunity to take our minds off the tragedy of the terrorist attack for a while was enough of a blessing.

On the evening of October 7th, 2001, my brother and I were back at our nightly accommodation, enjoying dinner. The TV attached to the wall was broadcasting live news. Normally, I would have been annoyed by the presence of a TV in a dining area, but this time I didn't mind. Part of me had enjoyed the couple days' break I'd taken from watching the news. But part of me felt irresponsible for doing so. As I sat there contemplating, a special report interrupted the regular news program. President George W. Bush came on the air and announced that the U.S. military had begun strikes on Afghanistan in response to the September 11th attacks.

And instantly, we were pulled back into the heartbreaking reality of our broken world. The last couple days in Ireland had served as a reprieve, of sorts, for my brother and me. But for me, that reprieve remained just below the surface, so it was easy for me to transition back into full cognition. I was already deeply vested in the battle between good and evil and had been for the past year and a half since Lilah was taken. I believed Islamic terrorists had severely hurt my country, and I wanted them to answer for it.

"Oh, Lord, please protect the U.S. forces and let them be successful," I prayed.

My brother flew out from Dublin the next day. I planned to fly out from Shannon one day later, which provided me an extra night on the Emerald Isle. When it was time for me to check out of my hotel in Shannon, I realized I had over five hours to kill before my flight departed. So I summoned a cab and asked the driver if there was a castle nearby that he could take me to. He informed me that Bunratty Castle was not too far away and offered to drop me there. He promised to keep my bags in his car and return to retrieve me after a couple hours. When we arrived at the castle grounds, I began to step outside the vehicle, and then paused. "You aren't going to forget about me, are you?" I asked with brows drawn.

"How could I be forgettin' about ya now, Mary?" he promptly replied.

I smiled in response. The Irish were so friendly. I made a vow to myself to return one day under different circumstances.

Choosing to forgo the proper tour, I walked around snapping pictures of the castle's ancient walls set against the backdrop of the surrounding Irish countryside. Inevitably, I found my way to the castle's gift shop, where I purchased a hammered band of Irish silver, just the right size for my thumb. It felt so comfortable there, I decided I'd never take it off.

Satisfied with the experience a day in Shannon had provided me, I left the shop and walked toward the road where the cab driver had dropped me off. There he was leaning against the car waiting for me, just like he promised. He smiled and winked as I approached, then opened the car door for me.

I hopped in and got myself settled in the back seat. The fresh country air was scented with a lovely balance of rich soil and green grass. It blew in through the window and brushed through my hair while I twisted my new silver ring around and around on my thumb.

I've got to come back here someday. Someday, after God sorts everything out. Yes, someday after Lilah is back home.

Chapter 22

ENGAGEMENT

I was glad to be back in the States again with my people. The terrorist attacks had caused much damage and had taken many souls from us. And those taken would never be returned to their mothers and fathers, their brothers and sisters, their children, grandchildren, and friends.

I abhorred the wickedness that placed little value on human life but great value on the destruction of it. I reviled the demonic abomination that saw my people and me as infidels and longed to see a day that our blood would run knee deep. Many Americans still failed to understand the evil entity that caused this type of damage. But I understood it. I lived in its environment during every trip I made to see my daughter. I had abided by its misogynistic mandates and endured its twisted lies.

I missed Lilah, but I knew I had to get control of my emotions before I returned to the Middle East for my next visit. The short-lived satisfaction of losing my temper and going off on Kashan would surely sabotage my intended outcome to bring Lilah back home.

The holidays came and went. I sent Lilah a huge box of gifts and made excuses to Kashan for why I was unable to visit. I prayed and continued waiting for God to show me what his plan was. Meanwhile, the image of those celebrating in the streets after the attack on 9/11 was etched deeper and deeper into my memory. It played on constant repeat.

Lilah had already turned seven. She was growing up so quickly while away from me. She was, no doubt, wondering why it was taking me so long to join her in Jordan. Each time I spoke to her on the phone, I could hear her Middle Eastern accent becoming progressively more pronounced.

Am I losing my little girl to the Middle East? What's the plan, Lord? Will Lilah remain in Jordan forever? How could that be your will? Why is this taking so long?

I questioned the Lord, yet heard no reply. Beyond weary and emotionally drained, I no longer had the stamina to imagine how I would get Lilah out of the hands of the enemy. Knowing there was nothing I could do, I began to shut down. But thankfully, hope did not. Hope wouldn't let go of me. Regardless of how impossible things looked, I could not be separated from it. It had become an intrinsic part of me. It was as if hope was now woven into my DNA. The waiting was slowly killing me. Yet hope remained, refusing to die. It held me up, in spite of myself.

> And hope will never let us down.
> Romans 5:5 NIV

For Valentine's Day, 2002, I had proactively made plans to cook dinner together with my girlfriend Stephanie. She was a client-turned-friend who had recently gone through a divorce. She and I spent many evenings together with the intention of encouraging each other.

More often than not, those nights turned into me attempting to drown my sorrows and numb my pain with overindulgence of wine. It never worked. It merely resulted in me greeting the next day with a hangover. It was never appropriately addressed either.

On the rare occasion that I acknowledged my intemperance with remorse, friends would give me a pass, saying, "Oh, I don't blame you at all—it's totally understandable under the circumstances." Broken, fallen, and seemingly down for the count, I regret that anyone saw me in such bad shape.

After work that day, I counted up my earnings. It was just enough to cover my overseas flight and the bills that had to be paid ahead of time. I knew I should have already purchased my next plane ticket, but I dreaded going back to Amman. I desperately wanted to see Lilah, but at the same time, I had little desire to return to the camp of the enemy.

Too much time had already passed since I'd seen Lilah. I knew I needed to be there in the Middle East to reassure her. Additionally, I had to maintain the counterfeit relationship with her father. It was the only reason I was allowed to see her. If I didn't have an ongoing relationship with Kashan, she could be lost to me forever. And I had really dropped the ball by neglecting to cater to his ego lately. My calls to him had become less frequent. And by this time, his calls to me were few and far between. As a result, I should not have been so surprised at what happened next.

I arrived at Stephanie's house around 5:30. She gave me a hug, then pulled out the cutting board and placed a knife on it. The onions and garlic were already on the countertop, awaiting my arrival. She and I always worked well together in the kitchen.

"How was your day at the salon today?" she asked while opening a bottle of Rodney Strong Cabernet.

I grabbed two wine glasses from the china cabinet and began to pour. Just as I was telling her about my day, my cell phone rang. It was Kashan. I hadn't spoken to him for weeks, and my stomach tightened at the thought of hearing his voice. I knew he would be both angry and accusatory.

"Ugh, it's Kashan," I said to Stephanie.

"Go ahead and answer. I'll get started on the salad while you take care of that."

"Okay, thanks," I said, then reluctantly took the call.

"Happy Valentine's Day, Mary," Kashan said coldly.

Oh, this doesn't sound like it's going to be a pleasant conversation. Lord, help me.

"Happy Valentine's Day," I replied, feeling increasingly nauseous.

The previous weeks of not speaking with him had given me a much-needed break. But hearing his voice snatched me right back into my horrible reality. I began to tremble. Stephanie noticed and offered a reassuring look.

I expected to be reprimanded for not calling over the past weeks—that would have been bad enough. But I was in no way prepared for what Kashan was about to say.

"The first time I told you I loved you was on Valentine's Day." "Remember?" he asked.

Before I had a chance to answer, he raised his voice and spoke over me, "Listen to what I'm telling you now!"

I looked over at Stephanie, who was no longer cutting vegetables. She had her hands placed flat on the counter as if bracing herself for whatever kind of support she may need to give me.

Kashan continued in a hateful tone, "You will never see your daughter again!"

"What?" I placed my hand over my heart as if securing it from shattering completely.

"Too bad you decided to abandon your husband and your child," Kashan snarled. "Now I have become engaged, and I'll be marrying a Muslim woman."

"But... *I'm* your wife." "What are you saying?" I asked, desperate for him to retract his words.

"When I marry this woman, we are going to move out of my father's house, and you will never see your daughter again." "And this is all your fault!" he insisted angrily.

My mind tried to process what he was telling me. But I was still in disbelief. "No, Kashan! Please don't do this!" "Don't do this to us!" I pleaded.

"It's too late, Mary. For almost two years now, you have promised to move here. But you did not come. I haven't even heard from you in weeks. Obviously, you didn't want to be with your husband and your daughter. I have to go on with my life, Mary. I'm marrying a Muslim woman who my family approves of. It's already been settled. It's too late now." "You made your decision, so I made mine," he said heartlessly.

"Please, Kashan! Please forgive me, honey." "I love you and... I—I can't lose you!" I pleaded with him between gut-wrenching sobs.

"You did this to yourself, Mary." "My family welcomed you in their home and treated you well, even when they didn't have to," he reminded me.

"I know, I know. And I appreciate that so much! I'm... so sorry, Kashan, please! Please forgive me and give me another chance. I've been trying to get everything settled here so I can come there. And since 9/11 happened…. I mean, it was so traumatic for my country. I—I just wanted to spend some time in the States and… with my family before I left." "But…" I continued to cry, "I'll—I'll drop everything now and come… right now." "Please… please, Kashan!" I fell to the floor, clutching the phone to my ear.

"It's too late! The deal has already been made. The arrangements between my family and hers have already been agreed upon." "There is nothing I can do about it now," he said coldly.

"Sweetheart, please. I'm coming there now. Please! Please don't do this!"

"I said it's too late, Mary."

I could tell by the way the sharp edge left his voice that he was satisfied with the amount of pain he inflicted on me. It was exactly the reaction he hoped for. Once again, his wicked actions provided evil gratification to the dark source that governed him.

It reminded me of the call he made from the airport in Paris when he told me he had taken Lilah. At that time, he claimed it was all my fault. And there we were, two years later, with him still in possession of my daughter, him seemingly holding the winning hand. But he himself was being played, a mere puppet of the devil who ruled him. I had to remember that.

"Well, I can't stop you from coming." "But it won't change anything," he informed me. "I can't back out of this. And I'm not sure if my parents will welcome you into their home anymore since I'm engaged to another woman."

"Well, I'm coming anyway, so you can go ahead and prepare them for that. I just have to get my plane ticket and tie things up here. I can't bear the thought of you being with another woman. Please, don't do this."

How long will I have to play this game? How long will I have to pretend to be in love with a man who is this cruel to me? But I already know the answer. As long as it takes. That's how long.

I had dropped the ball by not having daily contact with him after 9/11. But knowing that Kashan supported the terrorist attack against America caused me great anguish. While nursing my wound, I had failed to keep up the facade. I had become weary. How unwise I had been not to consider that his parents might persuade him to marry a Muslim. I had foolishly allowed my emotions to become a diversion, to knock me off course, to distract me from the only plan I had to get Lilah back.

I had blown it. My chances of bringing Lilah home had crumbled and fallen to the ground. I had nothing—no reasonable plan of action. And, more critically, I had no master plan from the Almighty. There was no time to dwell on that, though. I had to get to the Middle East and break up that engagement!

"Mary, I don't advise you to come, because there's nothing that can be done about it now. It's too late." "You did this, Mary, not me," said Kashan, in a hateful voice.

"Well, regardless, I'm coming." "So, you may want to let your parents and your fiancé know, because… I'm showing up," I advised him.

Kashan knew me well enough to know I meant it. How he would manage the fiasco that would be incurred by me being there was his problem.

"Bye, Mary."

He hung up the phone as if he did not acknowledge my coming there. As if he thought it would be that simple to get rid of me. As if!

For a moment, I sat there on the floor in silence. There were no tears. There was no time for that. I placed the phone in my purse, and I looked up at Stephanie, who had been patiently waiting for me to fill her in on what was going on.

"What's happened, Mary? What is it?"

"He's engaged to be married to a Muslim girl who is, no doubt, much younger than me. He says once they are married, I will never see my daughter again. I have to go. I have to go back to Amman now."

"Oh, Mary, I'm so sorry. Do you think you can change his mind?"

"I don't think so, Stephanie," I shook my head. "The deal has already been made between the two families. I think money has been promised and papers have been signed."

"What are you going to do?" she asked.

"I don't know. All I know is I have to go."

"If there's anything I can do, my friend," Stephanie hugged me. "You know I'm here for you."

"Pray for me, Stephanie. Just pray."

"You know I will," she promised.

As I drove back to my house, I began to make a mental list of things that needed to be done before I left.

- Give notice to my job and my landlord.
- Put my things in storage and pay for as many months ahead of time as possible.
- Leave my vehicle at Gina's house—thank goodness it's paid off.
- Make another list of things I should take with me in order to convince Kashan that I plan on staying in Jordan permanently, which... isn't necessarily so.

   a) A couple of my good cutting shears.

   b) My most conservative clothing.

When I entered my apartment, I wasted no time before engaging with my Heavenly Father. The adrenaline in my system caused my hands to tremble and my voice to waver.

"Father God," I said while pacing back and forth on the living room floor, "you have not shown me your plan for bringing Lilah home." "I have been waiting nearly two years now. I don't know what your plan is. But you know me, Lord. You knew me before I was born."

> You made all the delicate, inner parts of my body and knit me together in my mother's womb. Thank you for making me so wonderfully complex! Your workmanship is marvelous - how well I know it. You watched me as I was being formed in utter seclusion, as I was woven together in the dark of the womb. You saw me before I was born. Every day of my life was recorded in your book. Every moment was laid out before a single day had passed.
> Psalm 139:13-16 NLT

"You even know what I'll do before I do it. And you know that I am not willing to leave Lilah in the Middle East by herself. So, here I go back to Jordan. This is no surprise to you. And I know you can take care of us there, or you can bring us back here to the States. It's up to you, Lord. I don't know what you'll do, but I trust you. Now you do what you'll do, Lord. And I'll do what you already knew I would do—I'm going to be with my child! We have nothing and no one but you, Lord, and I have put my trust in you. And I know that you are able to save us."

> Surely the arm of the Lord is not too short to save,
> nor his ear too dull to hear.
> Isaiah 59:1 NIV

Once I had discussed with the Lord what my intentions were, I was able to get the rest of my affairs settled in a short amount of time. Before I knew it, I was saying goodbye.

My flight would depart from Prominence Metropolitan Airport on the morning of February 24th. Janis and Gina drove me to Providence the night before so I could have dinner with my family at Carrabba's. I could tell that my father and my siblings were afraid for my life. They didn't hold out much hope that I would ever return, much less return with Lilah. But they did their best to put on a brave face.

"You all need to believe that God will bring Mary and Lilah back," Janis stood up and boldly addressed my family as we waited for our food. "Continue to pray for them because God can do this, and I believe that he will do this."

Some nodded in agreement while others sniffed back tears. My heart went out to them. With lips pressed together tightly, my dad attempted to subdue a display of emotions. I knew he was thinking that it may be the last time he would see his youngest daughter.

The sky was clear, and the stars twinkled brightly as we stood outside the restaurant on that cold Givenia night, saying goodbye. I was deliberately cognizant of where I was and who I was with, knowing I would cherish those final moments of being Stateside with my family.

Chapter 23

ASHES ON THE ALTER
A Poetic Affirmation

Another flight. Looking out of the window, I saw no turbulence there. Not a cloud in sight. The skies, even the heavens it seemed, offered no resistance to the aircraft as it swiftly cut through the blue toward its destination.

This time I'm going back to stop a marriage... I'm going back to this land for... how long this time? Quite possibly forever.

I nodded in agreement as these thoughts crossed my mind.

All plans to bring Lilah back home by human endeavor had failed. Two years of exhaustive efforts and futile attempts to bring my child back, this precious little girl who called me Mommy.

Two years with nothing to show.

All strategies were shattered now. They were killed and laid to rest. No longer did they fill my thoughts or hold my attention. No longer did they consume my energy.

My plans are nothing but ashes on the altar of my God.

And now, having no fight left in me, I rendered no defiance.

My thoughts cleared; my mind emptied. A deep breath in and then out slowly.

A quiver came over my body as a final token of resistance—a last attempt toward strife. It was as if my humanness, my very flesh, was reminding me of its existence, determined to be heard… to be attended to… to be appeased.

Peace, peace. Be still and know that I am God.

Then… stillness.

Mortal effort having been exhausted, depleted. Tears streamed down my otherwise expressionless face as if I were mourning the passing of an old friend.

I was certain, so certain that I was exactly where I was supposed to be—here, at the end of myself.

The tears on my cheeks began to dry up as if they had been cut off from their source: disconnected from all the lies and all the fears that had produced them, fueled them, fed them. Lies that I would lose Lilah, fears that I would lose my life.

Kashan's words proclaiming that I would never see my daughter again sounded faintly in my ear. But the words rang hollow now, waning in volume as they echoed and disappeared back into the darkness from which they came.

I had finally arrived at this place, although not willingly. I had fought it. I had cried out. I had protested. But all my efforts failed to produce. They came up empty. They breathed their last breath. They finally died.

It took me two long years to irrevocably relinquish this to him. Two agonizing years to get to the end of me.

No stress. No anguish now.

Oh, the peace that comes from the ceasing of strife! The liberty of giving everything to him. Knowing with all my heart that I can trust my God.

Every part of my mind, every thought directed toward him for clarity and healing. Every fiber of my being submitted in utter dependence on my Heavenly Father.

On this altar, the ashes became a beautifully draped cover of peace that warmed and comforted my soul. And from that peace, an eternal hope sprang forth. First, slight and deep within my being, then growing ever stronger: a hope not dependent on human strength to see it through.

No more striving.

Now, an emboldened confidence began to build within me. A confidence in someone greater, so much greater than I. A confidence whose source of existence is found in knowing God's love, faithfulness, and unmatched power—all these being immeasurable and without limitation.

A Loving Father, a Mighty Savior who is for me: someone willing to go before me and fight my battles, because he loves me. Because he loves my child.

Whatever becomes of us is completely in the hands of the Almighty. My confidence is in him!

And he is ever here with me… because it is in his presence that I am. Always with him, and he, always with me. Apart from him, I am lost. But in him, I have found favor, and in him resides all hope.

My head raised, my spirit strengthened for whatever would come.

As I put my trust in you.

Yes. As I put my trust in you.

Declared throughout realms unseen, these words—now delivered with finality into the heavenlies.

Chapter 24

A DARK PROPOSAL

Spring was upon us. Normally, I would relish the thought, but not here, and not now. It meant very little to me since I rarely left the house.

At least his parents welcomed me, though. Well, maybe not welcomed, but… at least they allowed me to stay in their home. They could have easily revisited the position they held back in '93 when they suggested I return to the States.

I wonder whose idea it was to let me stay this time. Whoever it was, Khuram had the final say.

Kashan was becoming anxious and increasingly more agitated with me. I could feel how much I was unwanted. By his demeanor, I could sense that the thought, *What am I going to do with her?* was predominant in his mind. There was an urgency in my spirit to be on guard for my life.

The new wife in Kashan's proposed future made me expendable to him. She would be charged with taking care of our daughter. She would easily outperform me in the area of procreation. And she would willingly do her part to perpetuate the teachings of Islam—to achieve its purpose on earth. But I, on the other hand, had been deemed to be much more trouble than I was worth. Knowing how easy it would be for Kashan to do away with me was terrifying. A feeling of imminent danger resonated in my gut.

We were alone in the house. Nura and Khuram were visiting Kashan's sister in Kuwait. There would be no witnesses. Lilah could easily be sent over to her cousins' house for a visit. Kashan could make up a story of how I accidentally met my demise. It wouldn't be questioned by anyone or even looked into by the Jordanian Public Security Directorate (PSD, the police). Never before had I felt such eminent danger.

Despite those feelings, I did my best to function as normally as possible. I woke each morning and secretly had my quiet time with the Lord while Kashan was still sleeping. Sticking to my routine helped me to get through each day. And I regarded each new day as one more that I was allowed to spend with my daughter. One afternoon, while I was making a fresh pot of coffee, Kashan began calling me from the living room.

"Miriam!" Kashan said firmly. "Come here. I want to talk to you."

I immediately came into the room, being careful not to spill his coffee on the way. He lit up a cigarette and relaxed back onto the sofa with an air of arrogant self-satisfaction. His expression of smug gratification showed how he loved knowing I was at his beck and call.

"We need to talk about something, sweetheart." He strategically flicked his finger on the lit end of his cigarette so the ashes would fall neatly into the ashtray. "I'm doing my best to make everyone happy. Isn't that what you want: to be happy together with me and your daughter?"

"Of course, that's what I want," my stomach tightened.

As if picking up on my tension, Kashan pursed his lips together. He forced air out through his nostrils, showing his annoyance, his disrespect for me becoming increasingly evident. Admittedly, I struggled to retain respect for myself. There's something so degrading and dehumanizing about being totally under someone else's control. I was weary and broken, but I did my best to convey that I was in no way giving up on our marriage.

In hopes of somehow protecting myself from where the conversation was going, I pulled my head back slightly. He noticed and took hold of my chin, guiding my face back over toward his. I breathed in short, staggered gasps of air.

"You know I have to marry this woman, don't you?" He didn't wait for me to answer. "It doesn't mean that I love you any less."

His eyes widened as if daring me to contradict his sadistic expression of devotion. My entire body stiffened.

"I am willing to remarry you, though," he grinned.

"Remarry me? What do you mean?" "Why would you have to remarry me?" My brow wrinkled incredulously.

"I divorced you because you didn't come when you said you would," he stated flatly.

I wasn't sure if he was telling the truth. I hadn't been served any papers.

"Oh, it's that easy?" I said curtly.

He squeezed my face to show his impatience. "Yes." "It's that easy," he said between clenched teeth. "But I am willing to remarry you so we can remain living together—all together as a family."

"You're willing to remarry me?" I pulled my face away from him. "So I can be *one* of your wives?" My lips curled in disgust. "How can you even suggest such a horrible thing, Kashan?"

Not really expecting an answer, I kept my eyes on his face, imagining how this potential living situation might actually play out:

The young wife would be given instructions to always keep an eye on the first wife—namely, me—and report any suspicious actions to the husband. The first wife would promptly hit the young wife over the head or, better yet, slip something into her tea.

"Would you like na na or maramia in your tea?" I would ask. "But of course," I would answer. "It would be my pleasure," I could hear myself saying. After binding her limp, young arms with a strong cord, I'd gag her, then proceed to disappear into the Amman streets with Lilah.

Lost in thought, I didn't immediately notice the snarl of disdain that had overtaken my beloved's—the betrothed one's—face.

"Mary!" he yelled, then reached out his hand to grab my arm.

Abruptly awakened from my daydream, I flinched back out of his reach, inadvertently knocking into the coffee table. This caused Kashan's cup to topple and spill its contents onto the Persian rug.

He jumped up in anger to come after me as if I were a child he was reprimanding. Seeing the determination in his face, I swiftly moved away from him to the opposite side of the coffee table. Around and around the table we went. He tried changing direction, but each time, I was faster than him and managed to steer clear of his extended arm.

He almost got me, but at the last second, I flew across the room and jumped up on an upholstered bench at the far wall. That move took him by surprise.

"What are you doing?" Kashan said with a smirk. "Get down from there—we're just talking," he claimed.

Realizing I had nowhere to hide, I reluctantly agreed. He took hold of my arm, pulling me down off the bench and over to the couch. He firmly grasped my hands to convey his affection as well as his control.

"Now… as I was saying, I have to remarry you for us to be able to live together. And the only way my parents will approve of us getting married again is for you to become Muslim."

There it was. The danger I sensed, now boldly exposed, stared me in the face. I could feel a tremendous surge of evil energy. It was brazen, as if laughing and reveling in the moment.

Now we have her. This will be the end of her!

I clearly understood what was being presented to me: a compromise, a sure way to stay with my child. But I knew that was a deal I could never make. If I gave my concession, it would surely mean my eternal separation from God. It would mean death for me. I was fully aware that the vows spoken when converting to Islam renounce Jesus as being the Son of God, the Savior of the world. But I knew, beyond a shadow of doubt, that there was no other name by which man could be saved. I knew that Jesus was truly the Messiah. He had proven himself to me repeatedly. I could never, in a million lifetimes, utter blasphemous words denying those truths, not even in pretense, not even with my fingers crossed.

> Salvation is found in no one else, for there is no other name under heaven given to mankind by which we must be saved."
> Acts 4:12 NIV

My gaze fell on the overturned coffee cup and the brown stain surrounding it. I didn't really see it, though. It didn't matter anyway. It was the least of my worries. Instead, I imagined what might become of me once I refused to comply with Kashan's demand.

Will I be put on a plane headed back to the States? Will I be put out on the streets of Amman to fend for myself? Or will I be dealt with and disposed of, never to be seen again?

I was more terrified at that moment than I had ever been in my entire life. Lilah's life and my very soul were both on the line. Still, I would not take the bait. I would not fall for the lie that renouncing Christ was the only way I could be with my daughter.

And even if it was the only way, I still couldn't do it. I wouldn't do it! But somehow, I just knew God would come through for us. If this was a test, I was determined to pass it. I would not give up on God. I remembered God telling me that if I would not fear people doing me harm, and if I would acknowledge the Lord himself as the ultimate power, he would keep me safe. It was that promise from him that made me brave enough to continually return to the Middle East. It was the scripture that encouraged me to trust him, even when I was terrified. He promised to protect me if I put my confidence in him.

> The Lord has said to me in the strongest terms, "Do not
> think like everyone else does. Do not be afraid that some
> plan conceived behind closed doors will be the end of you.
> Do not fear anything except the Lord Almighty. He alone is
> the holy one. If you fear him, you need fear nothing else.
> He will keep you safe.
> Isaiah 8:11-14 NLT

My hope is in him—my only hope! He is my Heavenly Father. He is my Savior and my Lord. He is the only one who is able to save Lilah and me.

The extreme pressure of the ultimatum Kashan placed on me had me in deep distress. In response, my body began to tremble involuntarily.

"Why are you shaking?" Kashan asked with a scowl. "What's wrong with you? You act like I've given you a death sentence."

"You have," I answered in a low, wavering voice, "because Jesus said anyone who denies him here on earth, he will also deny before his father in heaven."

> But everyone who denies me here on earth, I will
> also deny before my father in heaven.
> Matthew 10:33 NLT

Kashan shook his head and rolled his eyes. "That's ridiculous. I don't have time for this." "We'll talk about it later," he motioned toward the cup on the floor as he stood up. "Get that cleaned up. My mother will kill me if she sees it."

He didn't wait for my response. Instead, he callously turned and disappeared down the hall like a snake slithering back into its hole.

"My time is up, Lord!" I whispered an urgent prayer. "Please get us out of here, now!"

Chapter 25

SHOW ME THE WAY I SHOULD GO

The warmth of filtered sunlight resting on my cheek awakened me the following day. Kashan lay beside me, still asleep. My first thought was of our conversation and the ultimatum he had delivered. While the house was still quiet, I silently rolled out of bed and went into the kitchen to talk to God. No matter the circumstances, he never failed to provide encouragement and a faithful reminder of his love.

> Let the morning bring me word of your unfailing love, for I have put my trust in you. Show me the way I should go for to you I entrust my life.
> Psalm 143:8 NIV

While waiting for my coffee to brew, I looked out of the kitchen window and prayed under my breath. I noticed the progress being made on a construction site below. There was an apartment building going up in front of ours. The exterior stone wall, which would eventually separate that property from ours, was nearly finished. There was only a small portion of the wall left open so that the construction workers could go in and out. A plank of wood had been placed over the ditch in front of the wall so they could cross over.

As I watched them work, I wondered how much they were being paid for their labor. I imagined it wasn't much at all. From what I saw, it was a difficult life for the poor in Amman, Jordan. Sometimes I had seen entire families picking fruit from the trees in our neighborhood just to have food. In other areas of town, young boys in dirty clothes would approach vehicles offering to clean the windshields for pay.

Just then, the kettle began to whistle, reminding me that I was heating water to wash my face. Each time I visited Amman over the past two years, I had maintained my practice of daily grooming. It not only gave me something to do, but it also helped me to remain attractive in Kashan's eyes—which was of the utmost importance.

By then, I was a pro at adhering to the cultural norms. That's why I was still allowed to remain in the household with my daughter. However, if I was going to live there long term, I decided it was best to cover up like the other females. So I had asked Kashan to take me out to purchase some long robes and headscarves. He was more than happy to accommodate me. I wore my new attire anytime I was around men or whenever I left the house.

The first time Kashan's family saw me wearing the robe, they were so excited. They kept telling me, "Mabrouk, mabrouk." Kashan found it very amusing.

"What are they saying?" I had asked. "What is mabrouk?"

"They think you converted to Islam," he answered with a sly grin. "They are saying congratulations."

"Well... please tell them I have not become a Muslim," I had insisted, somewhat concerned over the misunderstanding.

My time of grace was coming to an end. I'd been backed into a dark corner by Kashan insisting that I convert. He had not minced words. He had been blatant about his expectations. His words still ran through my head. They were disturbing to the core. And I considered it abhorrent that he claimed I would be the *favorite* of his two wives.

However, being a primary member of Kashan's proposed harem was the least of my worries. The punishment of being separated from my daughter for refusing to convert to Islam would be unbearable. Nura and Khuram would be returning to their home within days, presumably with the expectation that Kashan had already convinced me to convert to Islam. But my belief in Christ was firm and uncompromisable. I shuddered to think about what would happen to me when his parents found out I refused to convert. My time in the Shehadeh household must come to an end before that happened, and I was not willing to leave without Lilah.

"Oh God, please help me," I whispered as I silently carried the pot of warm water into the bathroom.

After washing my face and brushing my teeth, I returned to the kitchen. My conversation with the Lord that morning was direct and to the point. Time was running out. Lilah and I needed a way out of there, and God was the only one who could make that happen.

"Open the door for our escape, Lord. You are our only hope."

After wiping tears from my face, I gulped down the rest of my coffee. Without disturbing Kashan and Lilah, I grabbed a robe from the closet and went to the bathroom to dress. Then I crept back to the kitchen to prepare breakfast. I never knew when Kashan would wake up, but it was imperative that I give him all my attention when he finally did. Day-to-day life with

Kashan was demoralizing, which left me vulnerable to a barrage of negative thoughts.

Kashan always requires all your attention. It's draining, isn't it? Talk about a low-paying job! Subservient—that's what you are.

"Lord, help me make it through this day. Remind me of who you say I am. Keep me, Lord, and lead me. Oh God, how I need you."

I continued praying under my breath, so I wouldn't get caught. All I needed was for Kashan to sneak up behind me and overhear the conversation. If he didn't comprehend what I was saying, he would likely demand I tell him what I was praying for. And I knew I couldn't do that.

I kept my Bible hidden under the mattress where Kashan was sleeping. When he was away from the house, I would pull it out and read it aloud. Little did he know of the power tucked away beneath his sleeping head. Little did he know that I had prayed over and anointed all the doorways in the house with the holy oil a Christian woman from the States had given me. Little did he know that the Holy Spirit was far greater than the spiritual powers and principalities that held Lilah and me captive in that home.

My intimate moments alone with the Lord were vital for my survival. Thankfully, the peace that surpasses all understanding was always available to me. I simply had to give my worries to God and acknowledge his spirit residing within me. Not that it was easy—especially after Kashan's dark proposal.

> And the peace of God, which surpasses all understanding, will guard your hearts and your minds in Christ Jesus.
> Philippians 4:7 ESV

As I cleaned up the dishes, my attention was again drawn to the laborers below and the wall surrounding the new apartment building. I considered how solid the wall would be when it was finished. A stone wall that nice wasn't something one saw a lot in the States, at least not in the houses I had grown up in. It was made with fresh adobe bricks, still bright in color. I noticed that the wall was just high enough that going over it would be quite a challenge for anyone trying to get inside.

The part of the wall that would separate that property from Jasmine Street on the opposite side had not been built yet. That section still remained wide open. I thought about how close we were to potential freedom. It was just beyond the ditch, through the opening in the wall, and across the field.

It wouldn't take much for a person to walk from our building to Jasmine Street and immediately blend in among the pedestrians and fast-moving traffic. So close, yet sadly, inaccessible to Lilah and me. Especially since Kashan made sure to lock us in the apartment every day when he left.

I hadn't walked on Jasmine Street alone since 1993. How I longed to be there now. But we never walked that way. We weren't allowed to. Whenever we went to the main street, we were always accompanied by Kashan and went by car. I couldn't help but envy the people as I imagined them moving about, going from shop to shop.

Are they as confined as we are? Is this their rare weekly outing they had been so looking forward to? Are they moms with kids shopping for clothing? Maybe they are a husband and wife looking for a dress shirt for an important business meeting. Or are they shopping for a gift to bring to a wedding?

Perhaps they'll purchase some of those fancy European chocolates available here—the ones that are so beautifully packaged in elegant boxes and adorned with metallic bows. Or maybe they are just two men enjoying Turkish coffee with hummus and warm falafel. I wonder if my old friends Lazhar and Madani are on Jasmine Street right now.

I hadn't thought about them in a long time. I felt guilty for not thinking of them more often and even worse for not trying to get in touch with them. They had been such a help to Kashan and me when we were in Amman the year we got married. But since I had left Jordan in October of that year, Kashan had forbidden me to mention their names.

"What do you have to do with them anymore?" he had demanded. "Who are they to you?"

It had been eight long years since I'd seen them. And those eight years had been filled with both devastating tragedy and incredible blessing.

And now this...

I wondered if Lazhar and Madani ever thought about me—the reckless woman I once was. I was the crazy American woman who had come to the Middle East to marry Kashan—the passionate woman who would go to the ends of the earth for the one she loved. I was the one who refused to take no for an answer when Kashan's family was against our marriage—the determined one who would not accept defeat.

Standing there alone with the Lord and my thoughts, I realized I was much the same woman in many ways. Even then, I was being true to my nature, true to how God wired me to be.

How foolish I had been then. I was so lost. I was going in the wrong direction, following the wrong path. But God allowed me to go my way. He watched as I walked away from him. He lamented as I went astray... as I broke his heart. He never left me, though. I walked away from him, but he never left me. His love chased after me. He relentlessly pursued me.

So I returned to him. And when I did, he lovingly restored me. He turned me around. He spoke truth to me that set me free. He opened my eyes and gave me clarity. His love didn't leave me as I was. I no longer chased foolish dreams.

I did not deserve that kind of love, yet he lavished me with it anyway. He totally won my heart. He even wrote vows of his love upon my heart. And he assured me that no matter what, I would never ever have to be separated from his love. He promised he would never leave me or forsake me, and that he would always be with me, even to the end of the age. He was everything I needed him to be, and more. Even then.

> And surely I am with you always, to the very end of the age.
> Matthew 28:20 NIV

As I thought of his love for me, peace filled the room. Tears fell from my face. I was so lost in the moment I forgot to whisper.

"Thank you, Lord," I spoke aloud.

"Who are you talking to?" Kashan's voice abruptly sounded behind me.

I startled, as if I'd been caught doing something wrong. "No one," I said automatically, then quickly brushed away my tears before turning around to face him with a smile.

"I thought someone was here." He looked at me with scrutiny in his eyes.

"Your coffee is ready if you'd like a cup," I offered before he had a chance to question me further.

"Sure." "I'll have it on the balcony," he answered coolly, then walked out of the kitchen.

As Kashan got ready to leave the house, I kept myself busy wiping down the kitchen countertops. I was relieved that he hadn't brought up the subject of me converting to Islam so far.

"I won't be gone long," he assured me, as he breezed past the kitchen doorway.

I didn't believe him, though. Prior to his engagement, Kashan had opened an internet café. Since my return, he had been routinely absent from the house for up to 24 hours at a time, using his business as an excuse.

"And remember, don't answer the door to anyone," he ordered as he walked out into the breezeway.

"How can I open the door without a key, Kashan?" I responded impulsively.

He turned back around and gave me a warning glare. "And don't go out onto the balcony," he reminded me.

Then, *click,* the unpleasant sound of the door being locked confirmed he was gone. Once again, Lilah and I were locked inside.

"God forbid we have a fire," I grumbled under my breath as I walked toward the kitchen.

I opened the freezer to see if there was meat for dinner. If Kashan actually did return that evening, he would find dinner prepared for him. And if he didn't return, Lilah and I would eat in peace. As if summoned by my thoughts of her, Lilah came skipping down the hall toward the kitchen.

"Can I draw, Mommy?" her big brown eyes pleaded, as if her life depended on my saying yes.

"Of course you can." "Let me set some things out for dinner first, and then I'll get the paper and colored pencils for you," I turned from her to open the freezer door.

"It's okay, I'll get them." Too excited to wait, she ran into the dining room.

"Lilah, don't go into that drawer!" I called after her. "You know you are not allowed to go into that cabinet."

The next thing I heard was the large, heavy drawer of the cabinet being pulled open. I quickly pulled some chicken from the freezer and put it down on the counter so I could go help her. When I turned around, Lilah was right behind me and we collided.

"Lilah!" I scolded, shaking my head. "You nearly knocked me over."

"Mommy, Mommy look!" She held her hand open flat so I could see what was in it. "It's the key, Mommy. I found the key to the door!"

Chapter 26

AND A LITTLE CHILD WILL LEAD THEM

Taking it from her hand, I reprimanded her, "Lilah, don't touch that key!" "You're not supposed to be going into those drawers."

"It's the key to the door, Mommy," Lilah smiled, undeterred. "Now we can go outside!"

Lilah was not allowed to go into that cabinet by herself, and we definitely weren't supposed to have access to any keys. I quickly placed the key back into the drawer. Before fully processing what just happened, I pulled out some paper and colored pencils for Lilah and got her set up at the table. Then I closed the drawer and immediately backed away from it. It was hard for me to believe that the key Lilah found was the key to the front door, although she insisted that it was.

She has never been allowed to touch the key, much less use it. Why would she be so adamant that it was the actual key? And how could Kashan, or any member of his family, for that matter, be careless enough to leave the key where I could find it? No... there's no way they would do that.

"It's not the key, honey. Let's not talk about it anymore. Do you hear me? Let's not say anything to your daddy about this." "Okay?" I looked at her sternly.

"Okay," she said somberly. "But don't you want to go outside, Mommy?"

"It's not the key, honey," I assured her. "Let's just forget about it." I pulled some colored pencils out of the box and placed them in front of her. "Here, these colors will make some pretty flowers," I smiled. "Don't you think?"

Lilah finally settled down and got busy with her artwork. But I was still trembling.

What if it is the key, though? I won't ever know unless I try it. But what if I try the key and Kashan comes home at the very moment I'm opening the door? Or... what if it's not the key? If it's not the right key, it could get stuck in the door when I try to use it.

And what if Kashan comes home and sees a key lodged in the keyhole? He would know that I tried to escape with Lilah. If that happens, he'll never leave me alone with her again. Then I might never get a chance to get away with her. One wrong move, one wrong decision, and I could mess this whole thing up.

I tried to calm myself and think carefully, strategically. I considered calling Gina to tell her but I didn't want to get her hopes up in case it wasn't the key. I didn't want to get my hopes up either. But I just couldn't shake the feeling that it might really be the key.

Gina will know what to do. I should probably call her right away. But if I call her, they will eventually see the phone call on the phone bill. Then they'll be suspicious and wonder why I called the States from the landline without permission. They'll think I'm planning something. I'll lose their trust. There will be consequences. Kashan will probably interrogate me.

Terrifying images of Kashan slapping me and holding me down came to mind. I froze in place as I imagined it.

I'll be put out of the house. All my chances of getting Lilah out of here could be lost forever. But, on the other hand, if this is the key, then we would be long gone before that phone bill shows up. They will be furious with me, of course. Kashan and his father would curse in Arabic. But Lilah and I wouldn't be there to hear it.

My thoughts were all over the place. I was too anxious to think clearly.

I'm overthinking this. But no... not really. I have to think this way in order to not mess everything up. I'm not being paranoid, I'm being wise. Okay... breathe, Mary.

Critical considerations loomed in my head. I listened to each one as they made their case. I scrutinized them for legitimacy. Then I made a firm decision.

I'm going to do this! I'm going to call Gina and let her know what's going on. If we don't make it out, I'll confess to Kashan that I made a phone call before the darn bill comes in the mail. He'll be angry, but perhaps my punishment won't go much farther than him cursing at me.

Is this really happening? Yes—it's happening. A key has been found. But is it the key to the door? Is this what I've been praying for? Could this be God providing us a way out? If so, now is the time for me to act. It's time for me to make my move. I can't mess this up! Oh, Lord, help me think clearly. I need to talk to an ally. I need to talk to Gina.

It had been seventy-four days since I arrived in Amman, and I hadn't talked to Gina in all that time. Kashan had only allowed me to email her from a computer at his internet café. And he watched over my shoulder and read every word as I typed it. But I had never requested to call her. "There's no reason to spend money on a phone call," he would have said. And even if he had let me make the call, he would have been right there listening.

But he's not here now. He's not here for me to ask permission. He's not here to listen to my conversation. So now is the time to make that call! And I should do it quickly before he comes home.

I made sure Lilah was busy with her artwork, then took the handset into the kitchen so she couldn't hear me. I punched in the country code, the area code, then Gina's number. My heart started pounding with fear as the phone began to ring.

Am I really doing this? Oh Lord, please let her answer.

"Hello?" she answered.

"Hello, Gina?"

"Mary, is that you? Mary, how are you? He let you call me?"

"No, he doesn't know. Gina, listen. I think Lilah may have found the key!"

"What key?" she asked.

"The key to the apartment door! He keeps us locked in here. And his parents are gone, so there's nobody to keep an eye on us while he's away. Lilah found the key in a drawer. I'm not sure it's the right key, though."

There was a pause in our conversation as if Gina was trying to understand my rationale. Then she proceeded, slowly.

"You haven't... tried the key yet, Mary?"

"No, Gina. I'm afraid to try the key."

"What do you mean, Mary?" "Go try the key!" she said, with urgency in her voice.

"But you don't understand. I'm afraid it's the wrong key, and I'm afraid it will get stuck in the door. Then Kashan will find out I tried to escape."

"Okay, Mary," she said gently. "Listen to me. Are you listening to me?"

"Yes," I answered robotically.

"Mary, I promise you, the key will not get stuck. I'll stay right here on the phone with you. Now go and try the key. Right now, Mary." "Go try it!" she said emphatically.

After another moment of silence, I answered, "Okay, I'm going to set the phone down so I can use both of my hands to open the heavy drawer it's in." I began to shake uncontrollably.

"Okay. I'm right here praying." "I'm not going anywhere," she promised. "Go do it now."

My entire body felt numb—I was lightheaded from adrenaline. Somehow I made myself walk over toward the cabinet. Not wanting to be noticed by Lilah as she sat there coloring, I crept stealthily behind her. The last thing I needed was for her to inform Daddy that Mommy tried the key to see if it worked.

Without making a sound, I carefully pulled the drawer open and grabbed the key. As I glided swiftly away from Lilah and over toward the door, I kept imagining Kashan walking in and catching me—I was terrified. When I reached the door and tried the key, it slid smoothly and effortlessly into the keyhole. Then I quickly pulled it back out. To my immense relief, it had not gotten stuck. But in my haste, I neglected to verify that it would actually unlock the door. With trembling hands, I slipped the key back in and carefully turned it.

Click. The door unlocked. I tried the knob, rotating it slowly to avoid making noise. It turned, and the door opened. Immediately, I shut and locked it again. Once I removed the key, I turned the doorknob again to make sure it was locked.

Then I went back over to the cabinet and replaced the key. Instead of leaving it in plain view, I put it under some papers in the far-right corner of the drawer. I didn't want Kashan to find the key in the drawer. If he noticed the key there, he would likely take it from the drawer and hide it from me.

But maybe he already knows the key is in this drawer. Maybe he's testing me to see if I'll take it. No... that couldn't be. He would never risk me finding it and escaping. He doesn't know it's there!

After hiding it, I closed the drawer without making a sound. Then Lilah noticed that I was behind her. She didn't look up from her coloring, though.

"What are you doing, Mommy?"

"Oh... nothing, honey." Then, promptly redirecting her attention, I said, "Oh, my goodness, I love that picture!" "It's very pretty."

"Thanks, Mommy."

I stealthily backed away from Lilah and crept back into the kitchen, as if making an unsteady move would cause my efforts to topple and ruin my chances for success. Covering the mouthpiece of the phone with my hand, I whispered into it.

"Gina, are you there?"

"Yes, I'm here!" she answered.

"It's the key, Gina. It's the key and it works!"

"Praise God!" "Okay, what's your next step?" she asked, hurriedly.

"Well," I considered, "I can't try to leave today." "Kashan could come home any minute now. I'll have to wait until he leaves for work tomorrow. But I'll go ahead and pack up a bag and hide it somewhere. As soon as he leaves tomorrow, I'll try to make it to Jasmine Street with Lilah and then catch a taxi to the Embassy. I have to hang up now before he walks in and catches me on the phone!"

"Okay. Call me if you need me. Call me as soon as it's safe." "Hey," she paused before continuing, "I'm praying for you, Mary." "It's going to be okay. And remember, God is doing this. You are just following his lead."

"Yes, I know." "He is doing this," I answered, grateful for the timely reminder. "Okay, I love you," I said as if unsure we'd ever speak again.

"Love you too, Mary. I'll be talking to you soon."

"Bye," I quietly hung up the phone.

Taking another deep breath, I looked back out into the dining area where Lilah sat drawing. She hadn't even noticed I was on the phone. And miraculously, she hadn't seen me try the key. She knew nothing. She could tell nothing.

Now, to prepare for tomorrow.

My mind was so blown by Lilah finding the key that I had a hard time deciding what to pack. The risk I was taking to get us out of the building and over to Jasmine Street without being stopped was daunting, to say the least.

An American woman and child on the streets of Amman attempting to catch a taxi to the Embassy would appear suspicious. We could be discovered by the Jordanian Public Security Directorate (PSD). Kashan would surely notify them as soon as he realized we were gone.

And even if we did gain entrance into the U.S. Embassy, there was no guarantee they would help us. When Lilah was first taken, the FBI made it clear to me that the U.S. was unable to help in situations like ours.

Then I remembered what my Palestinian missionary friend Issam told me back in the States: "If you ever make it to a U.S. Embassy with Lilah, you must shout loudly that you are an American and you need help. They won't turn you away if you do this. Otherwise, it may be difficult for you to get inside without an appointment."

Nothing was certain, but I knew if I focused solely on the risk I was taking, I would become paralyzed with fear and never attempt to leave the house. And I couldn't allow that to happen. God had provided us a way out, and I had to take it. He provided an open door for me, and I had to make my move. This was exactly what I had been praying for. If I missed my opportunity to flee now, there was no guarantee I'd ever get another one.

> "Keep on asking, and you will receive what you ask for. Keep on seeking, and you will find. Keep on knocking, and the door will be opened to you. For everyone who asks, receives. Everyone who seeks, finds. And to everyone who knocks, the door will be open.
> Matthew 7:7-8

"Lord, thank you for providing the way out." "Please watch over us and help us get out safely," I whispered.

With trembling hands, I began packing a bag of bare necessities. Then it occurred to me that we would have to walk right past Omeir's house to get to Jasmine Street.

Oh, no! They'll see us for sure. Unless...

I ran to the kitchen window to see if there was still an opening in the wall around the new apartment building. That plot of land was positioned directly between our building and the main street. I looked down and there it was—the unfinished portion of wall allowing the construction crew to go in and out. It was still open!

"Oh, thank you, Lord. Please let it remain open until we leave tomorrow so we can make it all the way to Jasmine Street

Chapter 27

DON'T FORGET TO BREATHE

It didn't take long to pack two outfits, an extra pair of shoes, and pajamas for both of us. That left just enough room for our toiletries. Adding anything more would have caused the small canvas bag to tear apart at the seams. I regretted not being able to take Lilah's toys with us. But I was more than happy to leave behind my long robes and headscarves. They had become the most important part of my wardrobe in Amman, but I wouldn't be needing them back home in the States.

I left my cutting shears out of the bag, also. But I had already planned for that. Then I remembered my Bible. There was simply no room for it in the bag. It had served me well while I was here, but I had to leave it behind.

For a brief moment, I paused to imagine how angry Kashan and his family would be when they finally found my Bible hidden between the mattress and box springs. I could see an enraged Kashan throwing it across the room with callous disregard. It would probably be weeks or even months before it was found, and we would be long gone by then.

In sha Allah [God willing]. Yes, God willing. But my God, not theirs!

Once our bag was packed, I stowed it underneath a pile of clothing in an old armoire. There was little chance Kashan would find it there. Realizing there was still some warm water left in the tank after Kashan showered, I ran a bath for Lilah. As I washed her hair, I wondered when she would have an opportunity to bathe again. By the time I showered, the water was cold, but I barely noticed.

I still needed to make dinner so everything would appear normal to Kashan when he got home. Water had begun to pool on the kitchen counter where I had placed the frozen chicken. I quickly checked the refrigerator for things to make a side dish. There were cucumbers, tomatoes, and some parsley—everything I needed for a salad. After dicing the vegetables, I whisked together some olive oil, lemon, and salt for the salad dressing.

All I needed beyond that was some rice or potatoes to serve as a side dish. I looked in the cabinet where the rice was stored. There I found another type of grain. It wasn't labeled, so I wasn't sure what it was. I guessed it might be freekeh and decided it would be an excellent choice for a final meal under that roof.

I wasted no time bringing a large pot of salted water to boil. When the bubbles began to break on the water's surface, I placed the chicken into the pot and added a reasonable amount of rinsed freekeh. Then I placed some fresh garlic, onion, and cumin in as an afterthought. Normally, I would have sauteed the garlic and onions and added them later, but on that day, I was too distracted to care.

When the freekeh was tender enough, I took it off the heat to sit until the remainder of the liquid was absorbed. Sitting at the kitchen table, I went over a projected timeline in my head.

- Try to get at least five hours of sleep tonight.

- Wake up early tomorrow and get ready so we can leave as soon as Kashan walks out that door.
- Prepare Kashan's coffee and breakfast.
- Make sure Lilah is dressed, with teeth brushed and hair combed, ready to go.

Once Kashan left to go to work the following day, Lilah and I would carefully make our way out of the building. It was imperative that we be discreet since Kashan had probably instructed Wali, the young man who looked after the building, to keep an eye on us. Kashan would have likely told Wali to call him if he ever saw me leave the building.

"Oh, Lord, please make us unnoticeable when we leave here tomorrow!"

Our next step would be to get to the street and hail a taxi. I had five JD [Jordanian dinars] in my wallet. I hoped that was enough to get us there. In order to gain entry upon our arrival at the Embassy, I would begin screaming that I'm an American citizen who needs help. Just then, Lilah walked into the kitchen.

"Mommy, I'm hungry."

"Oh, of course, honey," I smiled. "Let's have dinner."

Being mostly unmindful of the task, I cut up the cucumber, tomato, and parsley for our salad. The main dish was still warm in the covered pot. I scooped some up with a large wooden spoon and put it on a plate for Lilah.

"Do you want your salad in a separate bowl, Lilah?" I asked.

"No, Mommy, it's okay. You can put it here on the side of my chicken." "Seedo says it all goes together in the tummy anyway, so it's okay if it touches," she smiled sweetly, as if it was her pleasure to be accommodating.

"When can I go to Omeir's house to play, Mommy?"

"I'm not sure, Lilah. We'll see, honey."

I began cleaning the kitchen, knowing it was very likely she would never see her cousins again. Unless we didn't make it out, that is. If we didn't make it out, she would not only see them again, but she would likely be married off to one of them.

At bedtime, I tucked Lilah in and kissed her forehead. "Sweet dreams, honey."

"Goodnight, Mommy." "Mommy," her large, dark brown eyes pleaded with me again, "can we do something fun tomorrow?"

"Oh, I'm planning on it, honey. Now you go to sleep and dream of all the fun things God has for you to do tomorrow."

I turned off the overhead light and walked down the dark hallway to the kitchen. For some time, I sat at the table and prayed for God's protection and favor. I searched my mind for any detail I may have neglected to mention. The ticking of the clock on the wall reminded me it was getting late, so I decided to put my nightgown on and lie down. I reasoned that I could do my planning and praying in bed and perhaps even fall asleep. Sleep didn't come easy though. Eventually, the clock chimed from the kitchen, announcing 9:30 p.m.

The next thing I knew, I was abruptly awakened by the sound of the front door slamming shut. I gasped and sat upright. Then, realizing it was Kashan, I got out of bed and went out to greet him.

"What's that smell?" "It smells delicious in here," he said, walking past me without a glance.

"I made something." "I think it's freekeh," I shrugged.

I pulled out the covered bowl from the refrigerator, spooned a large portion onto a plate, and heated it in the microwave for two minutes.

"You think it's freekeh?" he wrinkled his brows.

"Well... I'm pretty sure it is," I admitted.

"Thank you, sweetheart," he said as I placed it on the table in front of him.

He pursed his full lips, indicating that I should come in for a kiss. I obediently complied, doing my best to appear as if I hadn't a care in the world. Kashan took a bite of his late-night dinner, then immediately dropped his fork onto the plate and looked at me in dead seriousness. For a moment, I was taken aback.

"My sister was here!" "Faisha was here, wasn't she?" he insisted.

"No," I protested. "She hasn't been here—I promise!"

"My sister didn't make this?" his brows lifted. "You made this, Mary?"

"Yes, I made it." I relaxed.

Kashan lifted his palms up at his sides and asked, "How did you know how to make it?"

"Well, I didn't really know. I just guessed. Did I make it right?"

"It's delicious!" he said, taking another bite. "I thought my sister came here and cooked it for you. You are full of surprises, aren't you, honey?" "What other surprises do you have for me?" he asked as he got up from the table and pulled me close to him.

I fumbled for words. "Uhm... I don't know."

"I'll bet you do know, and you better tell me," he kissed my neck.

I managed to fake a giggle, but my stomach tightened at his touch. Finally, he released me and returned to his dinner. Afterwards, he stood up from the table, pulled a new pack of Marlboro Lights from his front shirt pocket, and began packing them against the palm of his hand.

"I'm going to sit on the balcony," he said as he walked out of the kitchen. "Will you make me some coffee, please?" He didn't bother waiting for my reply.

I got the coffee started and began clearing off the table. The last time Faisha stopped by for a visit came to mind. It had happened while Kashan was away from the house. She confided in me that the oldest brother, Omeir, had decided that Kashan was "the bad one," while I was "the good one" in our relationship. I was surprised to hear her admit it. It gave me some satisfaction to realize that however skeptical of me they had been previously, God had ultimately presented me favorably in their eyes. I couldn't help but wonder what they would think of me once I successfully departed with my daughter.

Will they conclude that God favored me by permitting our escape? Probably not.

It was nearly three more hours before we went to bed that night. As I listened to Kashan breathe, I prayed it was the last night I would ever share a bed with the man. Comforted by that thought, I eventually drifted off to sleep again.

At around 7:30, I was awakened by the sound of a bird cooing outside the window. Kashan and Lilah were still asleep. The chances were good that he would sleep well into the afternoon. For so many years, I had endured his habit of sleeping in. Most days, I found it annoying. But on that day, I was grateful for it. It allowed me the time I needed to get Lilah and myself ready to go. Then there would be nothing for me to do besides prepare his food and coffee when he finally woke up.

"Thank you, God, for this day," I whispered in hopeful anticipation.

Lilah was up by 10:00. I had her fed and ready to go before 11:00. Then, since Kashan was still asleep, I quietly placed our toiletries into the bag I'd hidden underneath the pile of clothes. Not knowing what to do with myself after that, I put on a pot of water for tea. Once it steeped long enough to reach the perfect color, I added maramia instead of mint, hoping to calm my nervous stomach.

The hours passed. Kashan continued getting his beauty sleep while I continued to go over the timeline of events, making sure I hadn't overlooked potential snags in my plan. Unable to think of anything, I decided to make that list of items for Kashan to pick up for us. If he was considerate enough to get them on his way back home—which was doubtful—it would buy me some more time, should I need it. The list consisted of nine grocery items. And just for fun, I put a star next to the three items we needed most.

It was nearly 4:00 p.m. by the time Kashan finally woke up. I already had the coffee maker set up and ready to turn on, so it would be fresh for him. When he finished with his breakfast, I mechanically began to clear the table and dispose of anything that could not be saved for a later meal—a meal that Lilah and I would hopefully not be there for.

"Come here, sweetheart," he walked toward me, interrupting my kitchen duties. I took a deep breath as I prepared myself for another unwelcome embrace. Just then, his phone rang. Looking at the incoming number displayed, he muttered some profanities in Arabic, then turned away from me to answer the phone.

I could only understand an occasional word. It was something about an espresso machine, and then he mentioned some numbers. I thought he might be negotiating the price of a new machine. Or perhaps he was giving an employee instructions on what price to charge for the various coffees they served.

Not that I was intentionally listening to his conversation. Neither was I paying attention to the dishes I was washing. Instead, I was focused on the wall outside. The opening appeared to be somewhat smaller. But it was still there! And there didn't seem to be any workmen around.

Thank you, Jesus!

"In sha Allah, in sha Allah, goodbye," Kashan said, finishing up his phone call.

Lilah ran into the living room and said, "Daddy, Daddy, can I go to Omeir's house?"

Oh no! That will ruin my plan to get us out today. Please let him say no. Please let him say no.

"No, honey, I'm sorry," Kashan told her. "Omeir and Radiya are busy today. But I'll take you over there tomorrow, okay?"

Gosh. That was close.

I brushed a tendril of hair away from my face and took in a breath of relief. The next few hours would be touch-and-go until we made it out of there. Anything could happen to destroy the plan.

Then Kashan said, "Why don't you draw something for Daddy?" "Come to the table. Daddy will get your paper and pencils for you."

To my horror, Kashan walked over to the chest where the door key was. I stopped breathing again as he pulled the drawer open.

Oh God, don't let him move those papers I hid the key under. Please don't let him see the key. Don't let him realize it's there.

Then it occurred to me that Lilah knew the key was in the drawer Kashan was opening. If she was reminded of how she found the key and tells her daddy all about it, he would take the key and make sure I never had access to it again. I couldn't take that chance. I couldn't let that happen.

"Lilah," I loudly interjected, "I think that's a great idea!"

Kashan startled a bit, then looked back over his shoulder toward me.

"Why don't you draw Daddy a beautiful picture—" I spilled out rapidly, "—like the one you drew for me the other day?" "You could use his favorite colors!"

"Okay!" Lilah smiled, wide-eyed, as she was caught up in my sudden show of enthusiasm. "What's your favorite colors Daddy?"

"Red and blue with just a little bit of green," he answered as he closed the drawer. "That would be very nice of you to do for Daddy."

"Okay, Daddy. Are you going to stay here and watch me draw it for you?"

"I'm going to be right over here in the living room. Daddy has some phone calls to make. But I'm right over here. Okay?"

"Okay, Daddy," she answered sweetly.

I closed my eyes. My heartbeat pounded loudly in my ears.

Whew. Okay. Everything is alright. Nothing has happened to change my plans. We'll make a run for it as soon as

Kashan leaves for work. Hopefully, it won't be too late. Hopefully, Lilah will still be awake.

There were so many hypothetical scenarios contending for the top position in my critical thinking process—so many details that could potentially go wrong. A couple hours passed. Kashan still showed no signs of leaving the house.

Oh, come on. Just leave already.

I reheated some freekeh from the day before and made a fresh cucumber salad to go with it. Kashan didn't complain about having leftovers, he was just happy to be served. While we ate dinner, I mentioned the list of groceries I wanted him to get.

"Will you please get these things for us when you go out? I put a star by the most important ones. But we're out of everything on the list, so… whatever you can get will be appreciated, honey."

He took the list from my hands and uttered an overly drawn-out, "Suuuure."

I knew exactly what he meant: he'd get some of the things on the list when it was convenient for him to do so. However, he would only get the items he deemed necessary.

"Thank you, honey," I said, pretending to take him at his word.

Finally, at 8:30 p.m., he began to get ready for work. He took what seemed like an extremely long shower. Then he put on his favorite white, short-sleeved, button-up shirt. I sat on the bed and watched, cheering him on to the finish line.

After shaking out the creases in his khaki slacks, he pulled them on, buttoned them, then threaded a belt through the loops. He fumbled to get his belt buckled as if he had never done it before. I considered asking him if he needed some help just to hurry him up. He then pulled a brush through his hair until he was satisfied with the way he looked. I couldn't help but wonder what in the world he was going to do when he had to find a new hairdresser.

And for the finale, Kashan applied enough Drakkar Noir cologne to last him through the long night and well into the early morning hours. After a few final moments of admiring himself in the mirror, he turned and looked at me. I looked up at him with a neutral face. It was the best I could manage at the time.

"Aww, ya hayati [my life]," he said. "You always get sad when I leave. I know what you're thinking. But I am not going to be with her. Not tonight. It's too late anyway. But listen to me. You know that I will always love you more than her."

"I just hate the idea of having to share you with another woman," I said, following his lead.

"Sweetheart, the most important thing is that me, you, and Lilah will be together. Come here." He opened his hands, summoning me. "Now, I told you what needs to happen so we can all be together." "And if you love me as much as I know you do, you will make the right decision." Then, just like that, his voice transitioned from loving to cold.

"I have to go now," he said impatiently. "I have a guy waiting for me."

"Don't forget the stuff on the grocery list, please," I managed a half-smile.

"I won't." "I have it right here," he patted his shirt pocket.

"Thank you, honey. Bye"

"Bye, Daddy," Lilah chimed in.

"Ma salama, bye." He closed the door.

Click. He locked it.

I listened until I heard Kashan's footsteps reach the bottom of the stairs. Then I waited a few minutes longer to make sure he wasn't going to come back upstairs to retrieve something he may have forgotten. The thought of running into Kashan as we made our way downstairs terrified me.

Chapter 28

NARROW IS THE GATE

It was already approaching 10:00 p.m. Without further delay, I walked behind the dining table to the chest and opened the drawer. The papers in the far-right corner remained undisturbed—exactly as I had placed them. I lifted them up and fumbled around for the key. Once I held it firmly in my hand, I began calling for Lilah.

"Lilah! Come here, please, sweetie."

She came running out from the bedroom. "Yes, Mommy?"

"Now, Lilah, I want you to listen to me. We are leaving here and going back home to the States. God is getting us out of Jordan."

Her face went blank for a minute as if questioning if she had heard me correctly. Then she brightened.

"Really, Mommy?"

"Yes, honey. Really." I ran back to the bedroom and grabbed our bag. My heart began to pound rapidly within my chest. I exhaled, trying to slow it down.

Lilah's flip-flops were on the floor beside the door. I pointed to them and said, "Get your shoes on quickly, please."

"Okay!" she flopped down on the floor.

But then, after putting only one of her sandals on, she stopped. Her shoulders slumped as she looked down at the floor.

"What's wrong, honey?" I asked. "C'mon, we have to hurry!"

"I cannot go," she said sullenly.

"What do you mean, you cannot go?"

With a solemn expression, she continued to hold her head down. "My father will be angry," she replied with rolled r's.

"Honey, honey—listen to me!"

I got down on the floor in front of her and looked directly into her eyes. With my hand on one of her shoulders, I smiled softly to reassure her.

"Daddy brought you here without Mommy's permission. It was a very bad thing for him to do." "Now God is saving us and getting us out of here," I nodded my head to reassure her.

But still, she sat there despondent, as if it were impossible for her to even consider leaving.

"Honey, please!" I persisted. "It's going to be okay. I promise. You're not going to get in trouble."

I knew what she was feeling. I had been afraid to even try the key for fear of being caught and punished. My poor baby, having been kept there under her father's control for over two years, was afraid to leave with her own mother. I hadn't even considered that Lilah might have that reaction. But we had to go! And I couldn't very well drag her out kicking and screaming.

"Oh, dear Lord, help me, please!" I cried.

We could not delay. Kashan could have returned home unexpectedly for any reason whatsoever. Realizing we were running out of time, I ran to the phone and dialed Gina's number.

She'll know what to do.

Three rings.

Please answer!

"Hello."

"Gina—it's Mary," I said quickly. "Lilah is refusing to leave."

"She's what?"

"She's refusing to leave. She's afraid her father will be angry with her!"

"Okay, calm down, Mary," Gina directed. "Put that child on the phone and let me talk to her."

I immediately pulled the phone away from my ear and turned to Lilah.

"Lilah, Ms. Gina wants to talk to you."

Lilah immediately perked up.

"Ms. Gina?" "Ms. Gina, from America?" she asked, her jaw dropping open in surprise.

I smiled, excitedly. "Yes, Lilah. Breanna's mommy, Ms. Gina. She wants to talk to you. Hurry, she's waiting!"

Wearing only one flip-flop, she ran to the phone. "Hello, Ms. Gina!" her expression transitioned to an ear-to-ear smile.

"Yes... Yes... Really? Oh, thank you, Ms. Gina. Okay. Bye. Here's my Mommy." Lilah handed me the phone and scrambled to get her other sandal on.

"Gina, what did you say to her?" I asked as I watched Lilah moving faster than ever.

Before she could even answer, Lilah said, "I'm ready, Mommy!"

"Okay, honey, just a minute," I held up my hand, signaling for Lilah to wait. Then, turning back to the phone, I asked, "Gina, what in the world did you say to her?"

"I told her I was going to throw her a big party when she got here, and I told her that we would all go to Disney together," Gina stated, matter-of-factly.

Lilah began pulling on my shirt.

"Mommy, I'm ready!"

"Okay, honey, just a minute—PLEASE!" I placed my hand on Lilah's head to calm her. "Wow, Gina, thank you! She's all ready to go now."

"Well, I know children, so I knew what to say. Now, you and Lilah get out of there so we can take that trip to Disney!"

"Thank you, Gina. We're leaving right now." "Please pray that the Embassy will let us in!" I added.

"Jev's on the phone with someone from the State Department right now asking them to inform the Embassy in Amman that you're on your way." "And you remember what to say when you get there, right?" Gina asked.

"Yes, I know what to say. I'll get in touch with you when I can." "Love you, bye!" I placed the phone back on the base and took another deep breath.

It all seemed surreal. But it was real, and I had to act fast.

"Now, Lilah, we must be very quiet as we go down those stairs. We don't want Wali or anyone else to notice we're leaving, or they will tell your daddy."

"Okay, Mommy." Lilah was getting more excited by the minute.

"Father, protect us," I said as I unlocked the door and turned around to grab my bag.

Before I could stop her, Lilah ran down the stairs, clomping her feet loudly as she went. When she reached the bottom step, she shouted back up to me.

"Mommy, come on! It's okay. Nobody is here to stop us. Hurry, Mommy!"

"Oh, dear Lord!" I whispered.

I closed the door and started to run down the stairs. But then I turned back to lock it. I decided it was best for Kashan to come home to a locked door. That would buy us some time before he realized anything was amiss. It would take him a few minutes to discover we weren't home. And those few minutes could make the difference between us making it all the way to the Embassy or not.

"Yallah [Come on], Mommy. Come on!" Lilah continued to call loudly from below.

I ran down the stairway as swiftly as I could, imagining that Wali or one of the neighbors may come out at any second to discover what was going on. The small canvas bag bobbed up and down on my back, kicking me with the shoes packed inside. I wasn't deterred. When I reached the bottom of the stairs, Lilah was anxiously waiting. I grabbed her small hand and led her away from the building.

"Honey, be quiet, people can hear us," I said in a firm, low voice as I pulled her close to me.

Then, as quickly as possible, I led her toward the construction site, being careful not to make her trip and fall. When we approached the trench in front of the wall, I realized it was much deeper than it appeared to be from our third-floor view. And the board placed over the ditch was much more narrow than I thought. If we weren't careful, we could easily fall off into the ditch.

I put my foot on the board to test its sturdiness. It wobbled a bit, but then returned to its original position. I knelt down so I could look directly into Lilah's sweet little face. It showed no trace of the heartbreak she had suffered during the last two years of being separated from her mommy.

Her large brown eyes, wide open with excitement, mirrored the streetlights as if they were reflections of fireworks exploding over Disney's Magic Kingdom. She tried her best to look serious, but a smile overtook her face. I presumed she was imagining all the fun she would have once we arrived in America. Hoping that she would understand the gravity of our situation, I spoke to her in a stern voice.

"Okay, Lilah. I'm going to hold your hand, and I want you to walk after me very slowly and very carefully. Do you understand? We are not running over this board because if we do, it will topple over and we will fall right into that ditch." "Okay, honey?" I squeezed her hand for confirmation.

"Okay, Mommy," she said with an enthusiastic nod.

"Okay." "Here we go—very carefully now!" I said as I led her onto the plank.

Inch by inch, we shuffled slowly across the piece of wood.

"Take your time, but keep moving. Mommy's got you."

"Okay, Mommy," Lilah answered. Her voice began to tremble as she moved carefully behind me.

"It's okay, honey," I reassured her. "We're almost there now."

When both of my feet were on solid ground, I turned and took hold of Lilah's other hand, then pulled her firmly toward me. As her feet disembarked, the worn piece of wood wobbled and then settled back into place.

"We did it, Lilah!" "Good girl," I said as I led her through the narrow opening in the wall.

Once we were in the open field, I quickened my pace with Lilah in tow. "Now, let's go find that taxi!"

"Mommy, do we have money to pay the taxi?"

"Yes, Lilah," I assured her. "Mommy has five dinars. That should be enough."

As we made our way toward Jasmine Street, I glanced back to see if anyone was following us. I detected no movement from the apartment building which now stood behind us in the shadows.

Jasmine Street was still alive with vehicles and pedestrians, even though it was late in the evening. As we approached, I saw a cab coming toward us. I quickly held out my hand and the vehicle pulled over right away. I opened the back door, guided Lilah into the back seat, and slid myself in beside her.

Not wanting to appear as if we were Americans running for our lives, I said, "U.S. Embassy," as casually as I could.

Then, wearing a nonchalant expression, I looked out the car window. If the driver became suspicious, there was a chance he would refuse to take us to the U.S. Embassy. I made a slight lift of the chin to appear unapproachable in hopes of dissuading the man from engaging in conversation.

He set his meter, pulled back onto the road, and drove with the flow of the late-night traffic. Without moving a muscle, I let out a silent sigh of relief. Then I reached beside me to grab hold of Lilah's hand. She was sitting straight up, wide awake with excited anticipation.

We did it! We made it out of the house and into a cab. And no one stopped us. Thank you, Jesus!

Each mile we traveled from the apartment building made me feel increasingly more safe. But I knew not to let my guard down. We still had to make it inside the American Embassy.

"You're American," the driver said, interrupting my thoughts.

Well, so much for my poker face. There's no getting around this. I'm going to have to engage.

"What… brings you here… to Amman?" he asked in a broken but friendly attempt at speaking English.

Oh, no! I didn't plan for this. Let's see now… what brought me to Amman?

Then, to my astonishment, I heard a clear and concise response coming from my mouth.

"I came here with an American company. We are educating the women here in Amman on the importance of prenatal health—the importance of good nutrition during pregnancy."

Wow. I'm not sure where that came from, but that was a great answer!

As I was busy congratulating myself on my quick response, Lilah chimed in and began speaking in fluent Arabic to the man. I immediately panicked.

Oh gosh. There goes our cover. Having a child who is so fluent in Arabic certainly does not go along with my narrative. And to make it worse, I have no idea what she said! Oh, Lord, please don't let him turn us in. If he has any doubts about the story I produced, it is all over.

He could easily take us to the nearest PSD station, where I'll be interrogated! Meanwhile, in perfect Arabic, no less, Lilah would gladly fill them in on our entire plan. I can imagine the questions they'll ask her: "What's your last name, habibti? What is your father's name? Ah, I see. Where are you going with your mommy tonight? Back to America? Very nice. Oh, yes, Disney. That sounds like so much fun," they will say.

At the same time, I'll be getting questioned in a separate room. I know how this will play out. We will be held while they wait to receive the report of a runaway wife and child. Then, Kashan will be contacted to come reclaim his property.

Sharia law was the law of the land. That meant that a wife or daughter bearing an Arabic last name, regardless of citizenship, could freely leave the country without permission from a husband or a father. Kashan would, most likely, have me put in prison for attempted kidnapping. And he would be given custody of Lilah. That would work out conveniently for everyone. His family, his bride-to-be, along with her parents, would all be relieved to finally be rid of the "infidel." And the law would be on their side.

I thought of my Russian friend, Katya, who I met when I was in Amman previously. She had been sent to prison for successfully getting her little boy out of the country with the help of her parents, who were visiting. And I remembered the stories she told me of the torture she endured during her incarceration in Jordan. I was certain I would be separated from Lilah permanently and severely punished. It could possibly even cost me my life.

I looked straight ahead and waited for the cab driver's response to whatever Lilah had said to him. To my relief, he laughed.

Surprising myself again, with my own utterance, I let out an anxious laugh. "Ha-ha—what did she say?" I asked, acting as chill as possible under the circumstances.

He replied, "She asked how much this taxi ride will cost because you only have five JD."

"Oh, ha-ha," I forced another awkward laugh.

The driver turned around to look first at me and then at Lilah. He smiled and said, "Don't worry, that will be enough."

A faint smile came over my face, although my cheeks twitched with nervousness. I felt nauseous. I closed my eyes to avoid seeing the city lights whiz by as we sped past them on our way to the Embassy.

When I felt the car slow to a roll, I opened my eyes and realized we were already approaching the compound. I pulled the five JD from my pocket and handed them to the driver. As soon as the vehicle came to a stop, I clutched my bag and adjusted its strap on my shoulder. I took Lilah's hand, pulled her out to step onto the pavement with me, and closed the door behind us.

"Help!" "I'm an American citizen and I need help!" I cried out, remembering the specific instructions Issam had given me.

The cab driver didn't waste any time getting away from the rapidly escalating scene.

"Help! I need help." "I'm an American citizen and I need help!" I continued to yell loudly.

"Mommy!" Lilah began to cry.

"It's okay, honey," I embraced her with one arm as she wrapped both of hers around my waist. "Mommy must yell like this, or they won't let us in. I promise you—everything is okay. Do you hear me?"

She nodded and held onto me as I walked toward the Arab Jordanian security guard who was on duty.

"I'm an American citizen and I need help!" I repeated.

He motioned for me to settle down, then picked up his radio and began speaking into it. He spoke in English, although I couldn't hear what he was saying over my continuous screaming.

"Help! Please help me! I'm an Ameri—"

"Someone will come," he interrupted. "Be quiet now," he said apathetically while placing his radio back into its harness.

It was nearly 11:00 pm already. Besides the commotion I was making, the grounds of the U.S. Embassy in Amman were otherwise quiet that night. I hadn't given much thought to the fact that we would be showing up after regular business hours.

Finally, I heard a U.S. English dialect. "What is it?" asked a young American man as he approached.

"I'm an American and I'm in trouble." "I need help," I said again.

The security guard rolled his eyes and backed away from us.

"I understand," the American said in a tone I felt lacked the warranted response. "Come with me," he said without emotion.

I clasped Lilah's hand tightly to reassure her. "It's alright, honey. Come on."

Without proper introduction, the man led us down a walkway toward the dimly lit building. Not even turning his head to look at us, he asked, "What's going on?"

"My daughter was kidnapped from the States two years ago and brought here by her father. I just managed to escape with her tonight, so we came here for help."

He didn't act surprised—or even concerned, for that matter. I got the impression that it wasn't the first time he had heard that story.

"Okay." "There's no one here to speak with you right now, though, since the Embassy is closed at this hour," he informed me.

Just then, I realized he wasn't wearing work clothes. He had on jogging shorts, a sweaty T-shirt, and running shoes. His hair was buzzed short, military style. Our unexpected arrival had obviously interrupted his evening run around the compound. By his demeanor, I understood he would not be sticking around to console me. But that was fine with me. We had made it inside. That was all that mattered.

"Thank you," I said as he brought us into a rather elegant reception area. It had a vaulted ceiling, neoclassical-style sofas, and highly polished side tables.

"Would you like some water?" he asked.

"Oh, yes," I said, appreciative of the gesture. "Thank you."

"Don't mention it," he said with a more relaxed expression. He returned shortly with two bottles of water. "Now, there won't be anyone here to see you for quite some time," he looked at me directly, making his point very clear.

"I understand." "We're fine," I smiled. "Thank you."

"Yes, ma'am," he nodded. Then he retreated into the dimly lit hallway.

I took a seat on one of the sofas, then pulled Lilah up beside me. It wasn't my first visit to the American Embassy in Amman. I had been there in '93 after Kashan and I were married. But I had never waited in an area quite that nice before.

As Lilah and I settled in, I looked around the softly lit lobby that would serve as our long-awaited refuge. Two huge pictures loomed over us on the wall. They were framed portraits of President George W. Bush and Secretary of State Colin Powell. I felt comforted by the two Americans who appeared to be watching over us that night. Lilah was exhausted, so I patted my lap, indicating that she should rest her head on it. She stretched her legs out on the sofa. I stroked her hair and began to cry.

"Why are you crying, Mommy?" she asked sweetly.

"I'm just so grateful, honey." "I'm so grateful that God helped us get away," I said through my tears.

"It's okay, Mommy. Don't cry. It's okay."

"I know, baby. I'm alright. These are just happy tears, honey. You get some sleep now."

"Okay, Mommy. I love you."

"I love you too, honey. Goodnight."

"Goodnight, Mommy."

Lilah fell asleep within 15 minutes. Her day had been eventful and traumatic. How she would process what was happening to her, or how she could possibly comprehend what had happened to her over the past two years, I hadn't a clue.

My head fell back onto the couch as I considered these things. My breathing began to slow down. I knew there was no way I could sleep. But believing the worst was finally over, I stroked Lilah's hair and closed my eyes. A final tear rolled down my cheek as a familiar peace came over me.

"Thank you, Lord," I whispered gratefully.

I heard no response, but I knew he was there with us as I settled into the warm, heaven-sent solace.

God is our refuge and strength, an ever-present
help in trouble. Therefore we will not fear, though
the earth give way and the mountains fall into the
heart of the sea, though its waters roar and foam
and the mountains quake with their surging.
There is a river whose streams make glad the city of God,
the holy place where the Most High dwells. God is within
her, she will not fall; God will help her at break of day.
Psalm 46:1-5 NIV

He says, "Be still, and know that I am God; I will be exalted
among the nations, I will be exalted in the Earth."
Psalm 46:10 NIV

Chapter 29

BREAK OF DAY

At around 5:30 a.m. I heard footsteps and turned to see a man dressed in a business suit. I stood as he approached. He extended his hand and introduced himself as Consular Officer William Hilsoner.

"I hope you were able to get some sleep," he said cordially. "I got here as quickly as I was able to."

"Oh, I appreciate you coming to greet us so early," I smiled.

"Of course," he said with a nod. "Will you follow me, please?"

"Wake up, sweetheart," I said to Lilah as I brushed my hand softly over her arm to wake her.

She slowly opened her eyes. It took her a minute to remember where she was.

"Come on, honey. We're going into another room to speak with this man."

He led us into an office and motioned for us to sit. Noticing the bench by the wall, I suggested Lilah lie down on it, since she was not fully awake. I sat in a wooden chair in front of Mr. Hilsoner's desk and scooted forward.

"Can I get you some coffee?" he asked.

His offer caught me off guard. I was glad to accept.

"Yes, please."

He came back holding a cup of coffee, two Coffee Mate creamers, and some packets of sugar. In the other hand he carried a small container of orange juice for Lilah.

After opening the juice and handing it to Lilah, I quickly explained our situation. Mr. Hilsoner listened intently. He acted as if he was totally unaware of our presence in Amman. However, I was under the impression that Jev had spoken with someone from the State Department who, in turn, contacted the U.S. Embassy in Amman on our behalf.

Since Lilah's abduction, I'd come to understand that the U.S. wasn't able to help me get my daughter back from Amman. Yet here I was at the U.S. Embassy asking them to do that very thing. I couldn't tell by his demeanor if our story was unique or if he had heard it many times before from other American mothers. He didn't promise they'd help us—but he didn't say they wouldn't either.

"Would you like to make a call to the States to let your family know you're safe?" he gestured toward the phone.

"Oh… yes, please. Thank you so much!"

He asked for the number, then dialed it for me.

"We are seven hours ahead of them, so it's around 11:00 PM on the East Coast," he stated, while handing me the phone.

I nodded that I was aware. "I don't think they'll mind the late call," I added.

He smiled.

Gina picked up on the second ring. I had been looking forward to the moment when I could tell Gina we made it to the Embassy. But when the moment finally came, I got choked up with emotion.

"G… Gina," was all I managed to say.

"Mary!" Gina exclaimed when she realized it was me.

"Gina, we made it!" I said, finally managing to form a full sentence.

"Oh, Mary, thank the Lord! We've been waiting and praying that you made it there safely. Was it difficult to get inside?"

"No, not really—not if you know what to say," I smiled.

"Oh yeah, right. That was crucial advice Issam gave you."

"Yes, it was," I agreed.

"Are they going to get you two home now?" she asked excitedly.

"I'm not sure what happens next. They let me call you right away, so we haven't really discussed anything yet. I'll keep in touch with you guys to let you know our status, as I'm able." "And Gina... will you please call my dad for me?" I began to choke up again.

"Of course. I'll do that right now." "Boy, is he going to be happy," she added. "Okay, Mary, keep us posted, please."

"I will. And Gina, I may need some money for airline tickets."

"Mary, don't you worry about that. Just let us know what you need. We're here for you. And your client Katherine promised to help with funds, too. Remember? Don't worry about money. We got you covered."

"Thank you, Gina. That's such a relief."

"We love you guys, Mary. We can't wait to see you!"

"Love you too, Gina. Talk to you soon. Bye."

"Bye, Mary."

I hung up the phone, hoping that it wouldn't be too long before we would see Gina and Breanna in person. For over an hour, Mr. Hilsoner asked me questions in order to get a better idea of our situation. He left us periodically only to return a few minutes later with more questions. Finally satisfied that he had obtained all the pertinent information, he wrapped up our initial meeting.

"Are you two hungry?" he inquired. "Let's get you something to eat."

"Oh, that would be great!" I admitted. "Thanks, Mr. Hilsoner."

"Call me William, please."

I nodded as Lilah smiled up at him. We followed William through some hallways toward the back of the building and outside to what appeared to be the employee parking area. He led us to a late-model black BMW. Lilah's father had taught her how to distinguish between the earlier model BMWs and the newer ones, so her eyes brightened with excitement when she saw his car. Once we got inside the vehicle and buckled up, we drove through the gate of the compound and out onto the city street.

He took us to a shopping mall not too far from the Embassy. It had an open eating area and benches with tan Formica tabletops. As we sat there consuming the Amman version of a hamburger, I looked around nervously. Eating out in the open like that made me extremely uncomfortable. I expected to see PSD Officers show up at any minute. Paranoia started to kick in. I began to question William's judgment and whether I could trust him. I wondered if the U.S. Embassy wanted us to be caught, just to be rid of us.

"Mary, is there something wrong?" he asked.

I was straightforward and looked him square in the eyes, "I'm afraid that Lilah's father has discovered us missing by now and has the Jordanian PSD looking for us," I answered.

"Well, then," he responded unemotionally, "let's finish up here and get you two checked into a hotel for the night." "Do you need anything else right now?"

"No, we're fine," I answered with a shaky voice. "I think we have everything we need."

After a short drive, William pulled into the Shady Palms Hotel parking lot. He turned around and looked at us. "I'll be right back—stay in the car."

He didn't have to tell me twice. I reached out and squeezed Lilah's hand to reassure both of us. We waited in the car while he secured a room. From the outside, the place appeared to be mediocre, at best. Within ten minutes, he came back to the car to retrieve us.

As we approached the hotel, I noticed the dingy, broken-down brick wall on either side of the cement entryway. The hand-painted wooden sign over the door was faded, frayed, and noticeably crooked. William held open the glass door for us. It was covered with smudges as if it had never been properly introduced to Windex.

A musty, dusty smell met us as we entered the reception area. I stole a quick glance at the man behind the cluttered reception desk long enough to see he was leering at me.

Shady is an accurate name for this place. I hope to God we won't be here very long.

After walking us up to our door on the second floor, William handed me the key to the room along with his business card. "If you need anything, call me."

"Okay, thanks." Then, somewhat apprehensively, I asked, "What's next?"

"I'll be in touch," he said with a firm, staunch look.

"Okay," I answered without questioning further.

He walked back towards the reception area, leaving us alone at the hotel. I closed the door and turned the deadbolt lock until I heard it engage.

I wish he could have been more informative and reassuring. This place is creepy. But at least we are free of our former prison. At least we are now in the care of the U.S. Embassy. At least... I hope we are.

"Mommy, why are we here at this hotel?" Lilah's little nose wrinkled as she asked. I could tell she was just as grossed out by the place as I was.

"Honey, we won't be here long." I hoped my statement was accurate.

Her brow wrinkled in concern as she asked, "Are we going to America, Mommy?"

"Yes, we are, sweetheart. We are going home to America."

Wanting to distract her from a worried state of mind, I pulled a chair out from the table by the window and pointed to a small notepad that was lying there.

"Would you like to draw something for Mommy? How about drawing a picture of the big party we are going to have when we get home?" I handed her a pen from my purse and added, "Sit right here, honey."

She complied with a half-hearted smile. The quilt on the bed looked as if it had never been washed. I looked around the room for a clean space to pray. There wasn't one, so I knelt on the dusty floor and clasped my hands together.

"Mommy is going to talk to Jesus now," I informed Lilah.

Without looking up from her paper, she responded, "Okay, Mommy."

I closed my eyes, pressed my lips together, and lifted my head toward heaven. Being so grateful and yet anxious at the same time, I was simply at a loss for words. I let out a sigh. Sitting there in silence, I eventually felt my spirit settle. A warm peace came over me, producing tears of gratitude. I sniffed and wiped my face with my hands.

"Mommy, are you going to talk to Jesus?" Lilah asked.

"Yes, honey. I am. I'm talking to Jesus."

"I can't hear you, Mommy."

"He can, honey." "He's in my heart," I attempted to explain. "I'm talking to Jesus in my heart."

"Father, thank you," I began to pray aloud. "Thank you, Lord, for getting us out safely. Thank you for making a way. Please protect us, Lord, I pray. Thank you for your provision of everything we need. I am so, so grateful for… everything you've done. Thank you, Jesus. I just… thank you, Jesus." I began to sob quietly.

Lilah came over and touched my shoulder softly. I opened my eyes to see her kneeling on the floor beside me. Tears ran down her soft cheeks.

"Mommy," she said through her tears, "can Jesus hear us?"

"Honey, yes—he hears us."

"Okay, Mommy."

She tried to smile, but instead began sobbing even more. I grabbed her and held her close.

"Honey, it's going to be okay," I promised. "God is helping us now—he's taking us home."

"He is helping us now, isn't he, Mommy?" she rallied. "He's helping us go back to America. Right, Mommy?" she said enthusiastically, as if asking about a superhero.

"That's right, honey," I smiled.

"Now we should be happy and celebrate," I insisted.

Lilah's eyes got wide with excitement. "Can we go get some knafeh?" she asked.

"Well... no," I answered, then took a moment to consider. "But we can sing and dance."

"Huh," Lilah gasped in excitement. "Okay!" she jumped up and began dancing around the room. Then, realizing there was no singing, she returned to me and asked, "What song should we sing?"

"I know a perfect one. We used to sing it when you were little, but you probably forgot it by now." "It's okay," I assured her. "I can teach it to you again." I began singing the song, hoping that she would remember.

"You shall go out with joy, and be led forth with peace.
The mountains and the hills will break forth before you.
They'll be shouts of joy and all the trees of the field will clap their hands.
And you'll go out with joy!"

> For you will go out with joy and be led in peace; The mountains and the hills will break into shouts of joy before you. And all the trees of the field will clap their hands.
> Isaiah 55:12 NASB

I sang it a couple times over before she caught on well enough to sing with me. We sang and danced until we were exhausted, then fell onto the bed together laughing. After a few minutes, Lilah regained her composure.

Still smiling in excitement, she asked, "Okay, Mommy... what's going to happen now?"

"Well, honey, now we just wait for God to show us what's next. He'll show us how he's going to get us home to the States."

Just then, a hard knock on the door startled us. "I need to see your identification!" a man's voice with a heavy Arabic accent demanded.

Lilah and I gasped. I extended my arm out to my side, motioning for Lilah to stay right where she was on the bed. Then I held my finger up to my lips, indicating that she should remain silent as I considered how to respond.

Not convinced that there weren't PSD Officers outside the door waiting to apprehend us, I didn't move a muscle. I had no way of knowing what danger stood on the other side of that door. But what I did know was that men, here in Amman, were rarely prosecuted for rape.

Then it occurred to me: for so many years I had been instructed by my controlling husband to never open the door to a man. It was something I had been trained to do.

Surely the Arab man on the other side of the door will understand why a woman wouldn't open the door to him. How would he know I hadn't been instructed by a man—my husband, perhaps—to keep the door locked and open it to no one? And, if that were the case, it would be disobedient, even brazen, for me to open the door to a man. Yes, I know the rules. I know how to play this part.

"I need to see your passport!" he yelled while continually banging loudly on the door.

Chapter 30

NICE TRY

I understood that the Shady Palms Hotel may adhere to a policy that required all guests to provide identification, but I wasn't about to give him mine. Instead, I ran to the table and grabbed Mr. Hilsoner's business card. It had the U.S. Embassy's official emblem on it, along with William's credentials and contact number. I crept silently across the floor and slid the card underneath the door.

"If you have any questions about me and my identity, you can call this number. Mr. Hilsoner will answer your questions." "Ask him!" I said sharply.

I ran back over to the bed and wrapped my arms around Lilah, holding her close. We didn't make a sound, but listened for his response. After a few moments of silence, the man grumbled and moved back from the door. The sound of his footsteps in the hallway gradually faded away. I breathed a sigh of relief.

"Mommy, is the man gone?" Lilah whispered.

"Yes, I think he's gone, honey."

"Is he going to come back again, Mommy?"

"I don't know, honey," I answered honestly. "I hope not. We can pray that he doesn't."

For the next couple of hours, I paced the room and prayed, occasionally looking out the window for any sign of the PSD or even William coming to check on us. I was extremely uneasy. The longer we stayed there, the more likely it was that someone would come busting through the door to harm us and take Lilah back to her father.

"Oh, Father God, please keep us safe," I prayed continuously.

My stomach was in knots. I was trying my best to trust God, but this dark, dingy hotel room gave me a feeling of impending doom. It was like we were in a formidable holding cell, fashioned to precede unfathomable torture and punishment. The walls intended to protect us seemed plastered with evil intent. I knew we weren't safe there. We needed to check out ASAP.

Lilah went out like a light at around 10:30 that night. She appeared to be totally unaffected by the wretched environment—at least while she slept. But it was nearly impossible for me to sleep. The lights from the street outside constantly shone through the cracks in the filthy, vinyl curtains. When I woke up every hour or so, my nostrils were immediately assaulted by the stench in the room, reminding me where we were. By early morning, it became clear to me that I wasn't going to get adequate rest.

The phone rang at 8:37 a.m., and I nearly jumped out of my skin. Lilah's eyes opened robotically in response. By the second ring, she placed her feet on the dirty floor and started toward the phone as if she were expecting an important call.

"Don't touch the phone, honey!" I grabbed her arm.

Alarmed by my reprimand, Lilah jumped back up on the bed and hugged her legs to her chest.

"It's okay, sweetheart—I'm not mad at you," I smiled to reassure her. After the third ring, I held the dirty receiver to my ear but refrained from speaking.

"Hello, Mary? It's William Hilsoner."

"Oh, hello. Yes, I'm here." "I'm glad it's you," I breathed a sigh of relief.

"Is everything okay?" he inquired.

"I—I guess so, but we had a scare earlier. Someone came banging at the door. They insisted on seeing my passport. I didn't open the door, though. I slid your business card under the door for them." I paused a moment, waiting for his response. When he didn't say anything, I asked, "Did they contact you?"

"No," he answered flatly, seemingly unconcerned. "No one called."

"Oh. Well, that's weird. Maybe they just wanted to harass me. This place is kind of scary."

There was another brief silence.

"I'm going to come by to drop off food for you." "What would you like?" he asked.

"Oh... anything is fine. Thank you."

"Shawarma okay, then?"

"Yes, that's fine." "I appreciate it," I said gratefully. "And coffee, if you don't mind."

"Of course," he answered. "I'll let you know when I get there."

"Well... I'm not walking outside. Will you bring it up to our room, please?" "I just don't feel safe walking outside," I insisted.

"Yes, of course." "Did anything else happen to make you feel unsafe?" he asked, as if a strange man banging at the door wasn't enough.

"No, nothing else. That was it."

"Oh, okay. Yeah, I'll bring it up to you. I'll call the room before I walk up."

"Thank you," I answered.

"No problem. See you soon." Then he hung up abruptly.

Within the hour, William delivered the shawarmas along with some additional snacks.

"I'll be back to pick you up in the morning at 9:00." "We'll get Lilah's passport processed and talk about what's next," he informed.

That sounded promising. I hoped and prayed it would be our final night there at the shady and questionable hotel.

"Okay, thank you!" "We'll be ready to go when you get here," I assured him.

"Okay, then. See you at 9:00." With that, he was gone.

Lilah and I ate our meal of shawarma and soggy fries at the wobbly table provided by the unsavory establishment. Thankfully, my cup of coffee was still lukewarm. Once I finished eating as much as I could under the circumstances, I attempted to lighten the mood.

"When we get home, you will see Ms. Gina and Breanna, Aunt Sharon, Uncle Tieger, Ms. Janis, River, and Stone. How about that!"

Lilah's expression was one of faint but pleasant recollection. It was understandable that she couldn't clearly recall everyone I mentioned. She was barely five years old when her father took her.

"Well, you'll just have to get to know everyone all over again," I told her. "What fun that will be!"

Even though our conversation was lighthearted, the seriousness of our situation made it impossible for me to relax. But I faked it the best I could for Lilah's sake.

"Mommy, can I have the rest of your shawarma?" She looked at me with tilted head and lifted brows.

"Ha-ha," I laughed at her animated expression. "Sure, hun. Go right ahead. I don't want it."

"Are you sure, Mommy? Are you sure you don't want it? Maybe you will want it after—" she searched for the correct word. "—later, I mean."

"Lilah, honey, I won't want it later." "I'm done, really," I waved my hand toward her. "Go ahead, yallah, take it."

"Okay, Mommy. Shukran."

"You're welcome, hun."

Lilah and I spent the day drawing, singing, and playing games. We played a family game we called "Riddle-riddle-riddle-ree—I see something you don't see." Unfortunately, that game got old quickly since everything around us looked so dismal.

Another long night was upon us. Lilah tossed and turned as she slept, assaulting me with her arms and legs in the process. Day or night, I never heard a sound from any other guests in the hotel. It seemed like we were the only ones there. That made it even more creepy.

Finally, morning came, and William showed up to take us to breakfast. Unfortunately, once again, we ate in a public area, exposed for all to see. Once we were back inside the Embassy, I was able to relax, not having to look over my shoulder every second.

"We'll make a passport for Lilah today." "You say Lilah previously had a passport issued before?" William asked.

"Yes, but I don't have it in my possession."

"I understand. That's alright. We will have a new one made for her here at the Embassy. We will need a certified copy of her birth certificate, though." "Can you get that for us?" he inquired.

"Yes, I can get that," I wasted no time confirming.

"Do you need to call the States to implement that process?" William asked.

"Yes, I do," I nodded.

William looked directly in my eyes. "Mary, we don't know if you will be successful in obtaining permission from the police department to leave the country with your daughter. The PSD agencies here in Jordan uphold Islamic family law, which states that a wife or a daughter may not leave the country without permission from a husband or father."

"Yes, I understand. But isn't there a way we can get around that? I mean, I could disguise myself and go by a different name in case the PSD has an APB out on me, couldn't I? How would they even know if I have a husband in this country?" "I'm not even sure I have a husband in this country," I shrugged.

William looked at me with wrinkled brows. He didn't speak but waited for me to continue.

"Kashan said he divorced me, but I have no verification of that," I informed him.

"Not that it would matter, especially when your documents still bear the last name Shehadeh," he explained. "You still must obtain permission to leave with Lilah."

"How would they know that I'm not simply a single American woman traveling alone with her child? I could be a widow for all they know." I rolled my eyes, considering how, in my opinion, Sharia law was unreasonable and downright archaic.

"Mary," William continued without acknowledging my question, "we are hoping that you can gain permission to leave the country by saying Lilah has a health concern that requires attention from a physician." He paused to give me a minute for that to sink in.

Then he inquired, "Is there a doctor in the States who would send a letter stating they are willing to see her in the States for some sort of treatment?"

I put my hand to my chin and thought for a minute. Lilah had been complaining of pain in her chest. When I examined it, I found a small lump there. I planned to have it checked out as soon as we got back to the States.

"I'll ask my friend Gina to call Lilah's pediatrician and explain the situation," I proposed. "I think we have a legitimate need, so… I'm pretty sure Lilah's doctor will agree to it."

"Okay, that's great." "Let's give that a try then," he replied.

Once I placed the call to Gina, it was simply a matter of waiting out the time difference for the doctor's office in Nahaven to open up. Gina must have been at the practice when the staff arrived, because within a couple of hours, the Embassy received a fax bearing the needed medical correspondence from Dr. Bill Victor.

I was hoping that meant we didn't have to spend another night at the scary hotel. It was beginning to feel to me like the Middle Eastern version of The Hotel California—the one you can never check out of.

As it turned out, we would spend another night at The Shady. But by the grace of God, we survived it. Bright and early the next morning, we were back at the Embassy going over our next move.

Lilah and I would be driven to the law enforcement agency that grants permission for a wife, unaccompanied by her husband, to leave Jordan. The odds weren't good, and I knew it. But since I had a letter from a physician in the States, there was a chance my request would be approved.

"Now, Mary, I want you to understand that you may not be successful in obtaining permission to leave the country. We think there's a reasonable chance, though. That's why we're suggesting you attempt this." "Do you understand?" William asked, waiting for my acknowledgment.

I nodded and placed my hand on the handle of the car door. Then I stopped and turned back toward William. "But what if they arrest me?" I asked, suddenly overwhelmed with fear. "What if Kashan has called for them to be on the lookout for us?"

"Well, we don't believe you are on their radar at this point. But again, we can't guarantee anything. We do think it's worth a try, though." "I will be right outside waiting in the vehicle for you," he said with a resolute expression. Then he nodded, indicating for us to go.

The same daunting feeling I felt at the hotel room—times one thousand—rushed through my veins. I trembled and held tightly onto Lilah's hand as we walked across the parking lot toward the building.

Earlier that morning, I'd applied my makeup with steady strokes and meticulous detail. It was my intention that my face convey purpose and legitimacy. And if that failed, I figured I would at least take a decent mugshot.

Once we entered the building, I attempted to appear relaxed. My head moved slowly from side to side as if I were casually scoping out the room. At the same time, I was careful not to make unnecessary eye contact with the men working inside the office. I purposely reined in the natural sway of my hips so I wouldn't be perceived as a female who "walked like that," as Kashan had put it. My sandals echoed throughout the austere establishment as I approached the counter. In as few words as possible, I explained that I would be traveling to the U.S. with my child.

"What is your purpose of travel to America?" the man behind the counter asked.

He supported his chin with a short, stubby thumb. His index finger pointed up against his cheek, conveying both arrogance and the improbability of granting my request. He blinked a few times and raised his bushy eyebrows as he waited for my answer.

My stomach muscles began to spasm. I realized this was not the time to avoid direct eye contact, even at the risk of appearing presumptuous. With my head raised, I looked straight into the man's eyes and articulately explained the seriousness of Lilah's health condition. However, I refrained from pleading. I realized that exhibiting desperation in my demeanor was more likely to accelerate an official stamp of rejection.

"My daughter requires medical attention," I informed the gentleman, "and I will be taking her to America to receive the necessary procedure."

In an attempt to come across as sincere, unperturbed, and confident, I refused to look away from the man. I reasoned that if I conducted myself as though I fully expected to be granted permission, maybe somehow he would be convinced right along with me, so much so that he would ultimately comply.

His small, round eyes moved back and forth as he looked into mine. I couldn't tell if he was in thought or just enjoying the moment. After engaging in eye contact for what seemed like an eternity, he dropped his hand down casually on the counter and looked over the document I'd presented. I suspected he wasn't actually reading it, though, and wondered if written English might be a challenge for him.

He looked back up at me with a faint but notable smirk, as if he'd read my mind. I smiled. He grabbed the document, walked over to an office behind him, and tapped lightly on the door. Then he disappeared inside, closing the door behind him.

When the door opened again, his hairy fingers motioned for me and Lilah to come back into the office. As I approached the door, he leered at me. He took his time before stepping aside for us to enter the small room, then returned to his station.

The man behind the desk didn't bother to stand. He looked first at me, then at Lilah, then back at me again. Without wasting time on pleasantries, he abruptly asked, "Where is your husband—" he glanced down at the paper to read my name, and continued, "—Mary Shehadeh?"

"He's working right now," I answered. "He won't be able to travel with us because of his work. But he will be joining us there later, once the procedure is complete."

"Ah, I understand." He then extended the paper out toward me and said, "Let your husband bring you back here tomorrow." "Then I will give you the permission."

"Ugh," I sighed, purposely portraying annoyance.

"Of course." "Shukran!" I said curtly, as I snatched the paper from his hands.

I reached down and patted Lilah's back and directed her toward the door. My palms were so sweaty I had a hard time holding on to her small hand. It was all I could do not to run out of there. But I took my time, determined to stay in character all the way out the door and across the parking lot.

"No go," I said as I got into the vehicle and pulled Lilah in beside me. "They want me to come back tomorrow and bring my husband," I added indignantly.

William sighed. "I'm not surprised."

I looked at him, questioning why he would send me in there on a fool's task if he wasn't surprised at the outcome.

"Mary, unfortunately, we are limited in what we can do for you. The U.S. Embassy must abide by the laws of this country so that we can have a presence here in Jordan. We cannot override the sovereign authority here. And because of this, it can be very difficult for American women and children to leave this country of their own free will. Islamic family law is the law of the land."

More angry than scared, I was silent as we drove back to the hotel. I wasn't angry at William necessarily, but at the situation in general. Having my hopes completely dashed to pieces left me regretting the effort I'd wasted pursuing it. But at the same time, I realized that any halfway reasonable attempt was worth a try. When we pulled into the parking lot of the hotel, I thanked William for his efforts.

"Try to get some rest." "We'll talk more tomorrow," he said in parting.

Chapter 31

THE HILLS ARE ALIVE - JABAL LINUM

That night, I paced back and forth and prayed. My hope that the Embassy would somehow make an exception to the rule and get us out of Jordan was seriously waning, along with my confidence in their ability to do so.

I thought about all the chances they had taken with our lives already: allowing us to be seen eating in public places, putting us up in the scary hotel, and sending us in alone to ask for permission to leave the country. It was almost like they wanted us to get caught. Increasingly, I began to feel that they would soon put us out on the streets saying, "Too bad, too sad—we tried to help, but oh well, good luck to you!"

"Oh Lord, please don't let them put us out on the streets, of Amman," I whispered, not wanting Lilah to hear.

Then something rose up in me, compelling me to switch my prayers from defense to offense. With obstinate intention, I changed my prayer strategy, refusing to allow the enemy of my soul to gain a foothold of fear in my mind.

In unwavering faith, I declared, "Thank you, Lord, ahead of time, for getting us out of here and bringing us safely home!"

> Do not be anxious about anything, but in every situation, by prayer and petition, with thanksgiving, present your requests to God. And the peace of God, which transcends all understanding, will guard your hearts and your minds in Christ Jesus.
> Philippians 4:6-7 NIV

If this is a wager, I'm placing my bet on the one I know will be victorious, rather than trembling all the way through this terrifying process and then thanking God after the fact.

> "I, even I, am he who comforts you. Who are you that you fear mere mortals, human beings who are but grass, that you forget the Lord your maker, who stretches out the heavens and who lays the foundations of the earth, that you live in constant terror every day because of the wrath of the oppressor, who is bent on destruction? For where is the wrath of the oppressor?"
> Isaiah 51:12-13 NIV

"Mommy, I don't like it here," Lilah whimpered, half asleep. "When are we going to America?"

"Soon, Lilah," I assured her. "Hey, honey, do you want me to sing you that song I taught you? The one about how God is getting us out of Jordan and taking us home?"

"The one with the trees clapping their hands?" she smiled, her eyes heavy with sleepiness.

"That's the one," I answered.

She nodded. I sang the song to her softly, over and over again, until she drifted off to sleep. William came again the following day to take us to the Embassy.

"May I call Gina and let her know what's going on?" I asked when we got there in the morning.

"Sure," he replied, handing me the phone.

Then he left Lilah and me alone in his office so I could make the call in privacy. Although I assumed that all phone conversations made inside the Embassy were monitored for security purposes. But that didn't matter to me. I had nothing to hide.

"Hey, Gina." "Things didn't go well yesterday," I revealed. "The doctor's note didn't make a difference. They told me to come back with my husband." I let that sink in, then continued. "Listen, Gina, I think they're getting ready to tell me they can't help us. I have a feeling they are going to put us out on the street. Remember, the FBI told me back in the States that the U.S. is unable to help get kidnapped children out of countries that adhere to Islamic-based Sharia law? I think the U.S. has already done as much as they can do. Please pray that they won't put us out on the street."

"Mary, Jev and I were talking," Gina interjected. "If we can bring your situation to the attention of more government officials, the U.S. may feel pressured to do something. I believe your father has already been in contact with our State Senator's office."

"Oh, that's good." "Who knows, maybe that will help," I suggested.

"There's an American mother currently trying to get her children out of Saudi." "It's all over the news," she informed me. "I don't think the administration wants the press to gain awareness of your story, especially right now," she suggested.

"I don't understand why not. Shouldn't the American public be made aware of how atrociously unfair things are for women in these Muslim countries?" I shook my head.

"You hang in there, Mary. God's not done." "He has the final say in this," she reassured me.

"I know." "I'm just getting tired," I admitted. "Every second I'm on high alert, not knowing what's going to happen next."

"But God knows," she reminded me.

"Yes, he knows." And then, before we ended the call, I again said, "Please be praying they don't put us out on the street."

"We will." "Now try not to worry," she said, knowing that was impossible.

"Yeah, you too," I answered, knowing that was impossible.

A few minutes later, William came through the doorway with bottles of water for Lilah and me.

"Shukran," I instinctively responded in Arabic.

"Afwan," William replied as he took his chair on the other side of the desk. Then he got straight to the point.

"Mary, we are not going to be able to continue to pay for your hotel room."

Oh no—here it comes.

My body tensed up, bracing for what he would say next. "Oh, I see," I waited for him to continue.

"There is another place you and Lilah can go to, though. It's a bed-and-breakfast type accommodation." "Except... without breakfast," he explained. "It's at a convent here in Amman. I met one of the sisters on a city bus. She resides there and told me about it."

"You mean a convent with nuns?" "That type of convent?" I asked for clarity.

"Yes, with nuns. But you'll have to pay for it yourself. It's pretty reasonable, though, and I think you'll feel safe there."

"Okay, I can pay for it," I responded immediately. I didn't need time to consider. I was praying for God to get us out of that scary place, and as far as I was concerned, this was the answer to my prayer.

"You are able to pay for it then?" he sounded a bit surprised.

"Yes, I can. I just need to make a quick call and get to an ATM to withdraw some cash."

When I called Gina back, she was elated to learn we weren't being put out on the street. She promised to deposit some money in my bank account right away.

"Okay... let's get you back to the hotel to gather your things then," William smiled.

"Thank you," I said, relieved that we weren't being totally abandoned.

When we arrived at the convent, William explained that a reservation had already been made for us. We were instructed to simply go inside and check in. He promised to call the next day to check on us. He then waited in the small parking area to make sure everything was settled with the sisters.

Lilah and I stood outside the door, clutching our belongings. I knocked firmly three times. Footsteps approached. The door opened, and there stood a petite elderly nun in a navy-blue habit and veiled headpiece.

"Wha...?" Lilah gasped in excitement. "Like Maria! She's like Maria in *The Sound of Music*, Mommy!"

"Yes, Lilah, she is!" I agreed, matching her enthusiasm.

"Mary and Lilah? We have been expecting you." "Welcome," Sister Grace smiled as she introduced herself and showed us in.

"Can I wear your um... hat, please?" Lilah asked Sister Grace.

"No, Lilah," I reprimanded. "Honey, you can't wear that. That belongs to Sister Grace."

"Yes, she can wear it," Sister Grace said sweetly as she removed her headpiece and placed it gently on Lilah's head.

"Mommy, look at me!" "I'm like Maria now!" Lilah said, holding her head still so that the oversized veil wouldn't slip off.

"Well, you must sing for us a song then, Lilah," Sister Grace said, joining in on the fun.

Lilah looked stumped for a moment. Then a big smile came over her face. "Raindrops on flowers and sweet little kitties," she sang.

"That's pretty good, Lilah. I laughed. "Now give it back to Sister Grace." I turned to the sister. "Thank you, that was very sweet of you to let her try it on."

I gave William a wave from the window that looked out onto the back parking lot, to let him know all was well. Sister Grace explained that we had access to the kitchen and the common sitting area as well. We also had a private bathroom and use of a laundry room, which was to the left of the kitchen. And if there was anything else we needed, there was a small grocery store on the corner.

Once we were settled in our room, I lay on the bed and expelled a deep sigh of relief. The room was so fresh and clean. Lilah and I even had our own beds! Compared to where we had been, it was like heaven. Peace seemed to permeate throughout the hallways and corridors. We slept wonderfully that night.

In the morning, I received a call from William asking how we were doing and if we needed anything. I requested a Bible since I had left mine behind at Kashan's house.

"Oh, sure," he confirmed. "I think we can get our hands on a Bible for you. I'll have someone drop it off to you later this afternoon."

There were four nuns who lived at the convent. They called the head nun Mother Superior, although her name was actually Sister Sarah. Sister Grace was the one who greeted us at the door. There was another sister named Sister Teresa. She seemed busier than the others, so we didn't have a chance to speak with her much. And Sister Eleanor made four. They were all very kind to us and made us feel welcome.

At lunchtime, we were invited to join the sisters as they sat around the dining table in the kitchen area. During the meal, Sister Grace asked how I heard about the rooms they had for rent. I told them William Hilsoner from the Embassy told me.

"He was told about the rooms you have for rent when he met one of you on a city bus," I explained.

Sister Grace said, "I don't remember meeting a man from the American Embassy, do you, Sisters?"

The other sisters responded that they did not recall meeting anyone on a bus who was from the American Embassy.

"I don't know, but that's what he told me," I shrugged my shoulders and shook my head.

"Well, we are so happy you are here," Sister Grace said with a smile. "And how long are you going to be in Amman?" she inquired.

How I wish I knew the answer to that question.

"Well, the U.S. Embassy is trying to help Lilah and me get back to the States. So, I'm not sure exactly how long it's going to take."

The nuns nodded silently as they consumed the meager portion of food on their plates.

Sister Grace asked, "How long have you been in Amman?"

"Lilah has been here for over two years. But I didn't give her father permission to bring her here. So now, I'm trying to get her back home."

Hearing this, all four sisters paused eating and looked up at me. "Well... we will light a candle for you at mass today," Sister Sarah promised. "Don't worry, my dear, everything will be okay."

"Thank you so much." "I appreciate that," I answered with moist eyes. And I did appreciate it.

I was holding onto my faith the best I could. And being surrounded by these God-loving, faith-filled women was like being shirred in spiritually and protected on all sides.

"Oh, and I was wondering... where is the nearby store so I can purchase some groceries for Lilah and me?"

"Yes, of course," replied Sister Sarah. "The store is across the street and to the left, on the corner. You will find everything you need there."

"Okay, but, um... I'm not sure it's safe for me to walk there." "I'm afraid Lilah's father will be looking for us," I admitted.

"Don't be afraid, he won't find you here in Jabal Linum," Mother Superior guaranteed.

"But... he may have the police, the... PSD looking for us," I protested respectfully.

She considered what I was saying. Then realizing I needed some extra assurance, she offered, "Sister Eleanor will walk with you to make sure you are safe."

"But... I'm afraid they will be looking for an American woman with a child. If I go out with Sister Eleanor, they might see me. Is there a place I can go to purchase a long robe and scarf so I will look like a Muslim woman? That way, no one will recognize me."

The sisters spoke among themselves in Arabic. Then Sister Sarah responded, "Yes, Sister Eleanor will take you there now."

"Oh, thank you!" I said gratefully. "Thank you so much!"

"You're welcome, my child. No need for worry." "God will keep you safe," she said with a smile that conveyed her faith.

Sister Eleanor, the youngest, seemed somewhat out of place at the convent. She was big, burly, and somewhat rough around the edges. On our first walk together, she confided in me that her family had insisted she become a nun because she had gotten into some trouble. She appeared to be a bit simple-minded. I could see how she may be prone to making wrong choices, or how she may easily fall victim to men with evil intentions. Her family, I imagined, had probably put her there at the convent for her own protection. I could also imagine much worse places for her to be in Amman, other than there with the kind-hearted sisters.

From then on, I wore my new black robe and headscarf anytime I left the convent to go to the corner store. And Sister Eleanor always accompanied me.

Sister Grace was the oldest, and her memory was failing. This caused her to repeatedly ask how I found out about their rooms for rent.

"The man from the U.S. Embassy," I reminded her. "He met one of you and was informed that you had rooms for rent."

"Oh, I see." And then after a couple moments of searching her memory, she would add, "I don't remember meeting any man from the U.S. Embassy."

"It's okay," Mother Superior patiently reassured her. "Do not trouble your mind, Sister. All is well. Mary and little Lilah are here with us now, and that is a blessing." "A double blessing," she looked at Lilah and me and smiled.

"Yes," Sister Grace concurred, "a double blessing."

We all agreed that it was divine intervention that brought us together. And the sisters constantly assured me that divine intervention would continue to keep Lilah and me safe.

We spent more time around Sister Grace than the others. Besides her cognitive issues, she suffered from arthritis as well, which kept her homebound. She stayed busy with her knitting but often complained of the pain it caused in both her neck and hands.

Sister Grace was in the stage of life when some people tend to become nostalgic about their younger years. She often mentioned that the sisters were teachers who taught the young Princes and Princesses of the Royal family. I wasn't quite convinced until I saw some old yearbooks from her religious order's Catholic school.

But forgetting that we had already seen them, Sister Grace would pull them out again and again. She was so sweet that I didn't mind looking at the pictures anytime she wanted to show them. I always acted as if it was my very first time seeing them. If Lilah tried to tell Sister Grace we had already seen the pictures, I would hush her up and encourage her to follow my lead by looking interested. She was a sport about it.

Faith in God was something the sisters and I had in common. God had provided a safe place for us to stay: a place where I was free to read the Word, proclaim God's goodness, and say the name of Jesus out loud. My daily routine of spending time with God was by no means encumbered in the convent. It was an environment where I felt very comfortable fighting the spiritual battle that must be won in order to get us home. So, every day, as I was accustomed to in the States, I put on the full armor of God and fought the enemy through prayer.

> For we are not fighting against flesh and blood enemies, but against evil rulers and authorities of the unseen world, against mighty powers in this dark world, and against evil spirits in the heavenly places.
> Ephesians 6:12 NLT

> It is not by force nor by strength, but by my Spirit, says the Lord of heavens armies.
> Zachariah 4:6 NLT

On more than one occasion, after explaining the challenging details of my situation to the sisters, I would inform them that the Lord prepares a table for me in the presence of my enemies. In doing so, I reminded myself of that promise as well. Always supportive, they would nod in agreement.

> You prepare a table before me in the presence of my enemies.
> Psalm 23:5 NIV

But I wasn't always full of faith. There were moments when fear tried to sabotage my trust in God. When this happened, I would often seek out Mother Superior for reassurance.

"If the PSD Officers come knocking at the door asking for me, what will you tell them?" I asked Mother Superior.

"I will tell them you are not here," she promised.

"But that would be a lie, Sister," I challenged her.

"Yes, but it would be a white lie," she stated resolutely.

"Yes, it would be," I conceded. "Thank you, Sister," I said, satisfied that she had my back.

Periodically, I would ask her again, just to be sure her answer had not changed. She was consistent with her promise to protect us from the police if they ever showed up at the door.

Our days there soon became a week, and then approached the two-week mark. Sometimes William or one of his assistants checked in on us to see how we were doing. But the phone conversations between us were always kept to a minimum. I figured if they had something important to tell me, they would. Until then, I waited and continued to pray.

Back in the States, Gina began communicating with an American international attorney on my behalf. He worked in Kuwait during the Gulf War and was taken to Iraq and held as a war prisoner. He made it clear to Gina that there was nothing he could do for us from a legal standpoint. But he was glad to answer any questions she had about the dictates of Sharia law. He also insisted that she not reveal to him where we were hiding in Jordan. He believed the fewer people who knew our specific location, the safer it would be for everyone.

Chapter 32

WORD

At times, when Lilah was otherwise engaged in activities like playing the card game "Go Fish" with Sister Grace, I took the opportunity to be alone with God. Inevitably, I would gravitate toward a room located down the abbey's main hallway. The door to that room was always open, as if beckoning me to enter. It typically served as a private setting for when Father Thomas came to discuss convent matters with Mother Superior.

The walls had been painted a dusty blue color, but they took on a periwinkle hue later in the day. The room was plain with minimal furnishings. It was the same décor theme that flowed consistently throughout the Abbey. The air in the room held a faint woods-and-spice undertone. If it weren't for the tell-tale ashes of Father Thomas's cigar left behind in the ashtray, I might have mistaken the aroma for incense, like that burned during a Catholic liturgy.

There was a small rectangular table placed along the right wall as you entered. It had three metal fold-out chairs pulled up to it. I suppose a former guest might have used the table for making notes in a journal or writing on a postcard to send home. Or perhaps it was used to spread out a map of Jordan while planning a fun-filled Middle Eastern adventure. I should be so lucky!

The room's solitary window looked out onto a sandy path adorned with some stones, a few sprigs of grass, and a cluster of yellow wildflowers. There was a small olive tree right off the walkway. Its branches had grown up against the side of a weathered exterior wall, as if graciously offering some needed support.

Inside the room, beneath the window, was a modest wooden bench. It lacked a cushion, in solid commitment to the convent's poverty vow. There was a single picture on the left wall. It was a printed painting of Saint Joseph, who I assumed to be the Patron Saint of the nunnery. Opposite the window, on the other wall, hung a small wooden crucifix with tarnished metal edges. The room was void of distractions, an ideal place for me to be alone with the Lord.

While in the room often prayed, "Lord, guide me by your Spirit in the Word." I scoured through scriptures, eagerly waiting and fully expecting God to speak to me in and through them.

Psalms offered me encouragement in the face of danger. Proverbs shed light and wisdom on any and all circumstances imaginable. The Gospels revealed Jesus to be the Messiah, Emmanuel, God with us. And the book of Acts portrayed the power of Holy Spirit. But the book of Isaiah seemed to encompass all of those things. I spent hours reading the book of Isaiah.

And that's where I found the promise I desperately needed. That's where I discovered the word God was speaking to me in real time, directly into my present circumstances. When I read it, my spirit leapt within me! My mind was blown by the powerful truth I found there. My heart became engaged. Hope surged: it began rushing through my veins.

It wasn't the first time the Lord had given me a personal revelation of his word. But this was a now word. It was new to me, yet ages old at the same time. It was a spoken, active word that never stopped performing according to God's divine will, one that never stopped accomplishing its mission. It was a heavenly gift and a priceless treasure. But it was even more than that. It was a loving guarantee, a beautiful assurance.

> "You will not leave in a hurry, running for your lives. For the Lord will go ahead of you; yes, the God of Israel will protect you from behind.
> Isaiah 52:12 NLT

When I read it, I knew beyond a shadow of a doubt that it was the passage I desperately needed. It was a personal word from my Heavenly Father that would see us through and out of there. I truly believed that particular scripture was God's amazing pledge that would take us home. I began to recall the promises he'd given me during the past two years. They were promises that directed me. They propelled me and helped me to get that far. They provided the hope I needed to continuously hold on.

"Thank you, Lord, that I don't have to be afraid that some plan conceived behind closed doors will be the end of me, because I know that you will keep me safe." "Thank you, Lord," I declared, "that you prepare a table for me in the very presence of my enemy." "Thank you, Lord, that we shall go out with joy and be led forth with peace." "And thank you, Heavenly Father," I proclaimed, "that we will not leave in a hurry, running for our lives, because you will go ahead of us and you will protect us from behind!"

Those scriptures—those divine compilations of written words—rang throughout my spirit like bells in a church tower clanging in celebration. My faith was elevated to the point of truly believing things would go in our favor. Somehow, I just knew it! So much so that I was overwhelmed with gratitude for what God was getting ready to do, as if it were already done.

> Now faith is confidence in what we hope for and
> assurance about what we do not see.
> Hebrews 11:1 NIV

"Just think, Lord," I said excitedly, "everyone who witnesses what you've done will have to acknowledge you." "Those who don't believe in you yet will begin to believe. When they see what you have done, they will no longer be able to deny your existence."

Tears of sheer joy and intense gratitude streamed down my face. Then, my heart began to burn in his presence.

NOT EVERYONE WILL BELIEVE.

I heard him loud and clear. My heart began to break as I perceived his words. The realization came over me that not everyone who heard my story would believe it was an act of God.

"But how could they not believe, Lord?" I asked, shaking my head. "How sad that anyone would fail to see how amazing you are when it's so... evident."

The thought of it wrecked me. To me, it was the saddest story I'd ever heard. I could only imagine how deeply it must grieve God's heart to love humanity so much that he would do anything for us, yet be largely unloved, unacknowledged, and even denied. Those who consistently refused to believe would be separated from God for eternity—their choice, not his. They were those who have eyes but cannot see, and ears but cannot hear.

> This is why I speak to them in parables: "Though seeing, they do not see; though hearing, they do not hear or understand. In them is fulfilled the prophecy of Isaiah: "'You will be ever hearing but never understanding; you will be ever seeing but never perceiving. For this people's heart has become calloused; they hardly hear with their ears, and they have closed their eyes. Otherwise they might see with their eyes, hear with their ears, understand with their hearts and turn, and I would heal them.'
> Matthew 13:13-15 NIV

> He was in the world, and though the world was made through him, the world did not recognize him. He came to that which was his own, but his own did not receive him.
> John 1:10-11 NIV

Eventually, disappointment and anguish lifted. Then contentment came and covered me like a warm blanket. Not wanting to part with it, I stayed a little longer. A spontaneous song of praise came from my lips. The song was slow and sweet, but I knew it packed a powerful blow against the enemy in the spiritual realm.

Filled with peace and mantled with confidence, I finally left the solace of the prayer room. Lilah was in the living room with Sister Grace. The smile on her face told me she had won her fair share of the card games.

"Lilah, why don't you come lie down with me in our room for a bit? I'm sure Sister Grace has something else to do today besides play cards."

"Do I have to?" Lilah asked, disappointed.

"You go with your mother now, little one. I will do some knitting while you and Mommy take a rest." "God bless you, child," Sister Grace said as she placed her wrinkled hand on Lilah's head and walked to the cabinet to get her yarn.

I thought about how precious the blessing was that came from those tiny, arthritic-knobbled hands—those diligent hands that had been used for a lifetime in service to the Lord.

Soon after Lilah and I lay down, her breathing became slow and steady. I hoped she was dreaming of the trip to Disney she would take with her friend Breanna when we got back to the land that remained just beyond her reach.

Lilah was becoming increasingly anxious to leave the abbey and move on to her next adventure. She was tired of being told it wasn't safe for her to go outside to play. It was difficult for her to comprehend all that she'd been through over the last couple of years.

Whenever Lilah pleaded with me to tell her when we would leave for America, I tried my best to console her. But I couldn't give her an answer I didn't have. One afternoon, seeing how restless Lilah was, Mother Superior came up with an idea. She called for Sadiq, the handyman who took care of the place. When he arrived, Sister Sarah placed some money in his hands.

"Please go purchase a kite for Lilah. You can take her up on the rooftop and fly it with her."

"Oh, thank you, Sister, but you don't have to do that," I insisted.

"It's my pleasure," Mother Superior stated. "She is just a child, and she needs to have some playtime outdoors. Being inside the abbey all the time isn't healthy for her. She must have something besides card games and an occasional ice cream to make her happy while she is here with us."

"Well... is it safe?" I asked with concern. "Couldn't she fall off the rooftop?"

"No, it is perfectly safe," answered Sister Sarah. "There are walls on top to protect her from falling. The children who live in this area often fly kites from the roofs. Don't worry."

"Well... okay," I relented.

When Sadiq returned with a brightly colored kite, Lilah and I followed him up the cement stairway to the top of the building. With his help, we assembled the blue diamond-shaped kite and attached its bright yellow tail. After many attempts, we finally managed to get the kite up and flying. Lilah was delighted. As we looked out across the city, we could see other kites soaring from rooftops throughout Jabal Linum. Sister Sarah's gracious gesture proved to be a much-needed reprieve for Lilah.

But even with the occasional distraction of flying a kite, playing a card game, or enjoying an ice cream after dinner, Lilah's patience was wearing thin. It would have been easier for her if I could have pointed to a date on the calendar and told her when we were leaving. But I couldn't.

Her seven-year-old mind couldn't comprehend why it was taking so long for us to get to America. She had her heart set on seeing Gina and Breanna. So many times, we discussed what the big celebration and the trip to Disney would be like. Each time she imagined it with great anticipation. We had left her father's house to begin our journey to the U.S. two weeks prior, but as far as Lilah was concerned, it may as well have been two years.

I constantly encouraged her, saying that God was going to get us out of there and that we just needed to hold on a little longer. But she got to the point where she couldn't hear it anymore. She needed to see it. One day, overcome with discouragement, she totally broke down.

"When are we going to America, Mommy?"

"It's going to be soon, honey. It's going to be soon, I promise."

"You are always saying this, Mommy. But it's not happening. Every day, Mommy." "Every day, it's not happening!" she began to sob, brokenhearted. "When is it going to happen?"

"Honey," I knelt down, grabbed her by her shoulders, and brought her face level to mine, "it's going to be okay." "I promise you, God is not going to let us down."

"I want to see the trees clapping their hands, Mommy!" "When are we going to see the trees clapping their hands?" she fell to the ground and cried.

I could barely understand what she was saying through her tears. Brushing her hair away from her face with my hand, I sat on the floor and held her.

"What, honey? You want to see what?"

"The trees, Mommy, just like in the song." "I want to see the trees clapping their hands when we leave here to go to America," she said more clearly, as her tears began to slow.

She was referring to the song about God's promise from the book of Isaiah. The words of the chorus declared that the trees of the field would clap their hands. Lilah remembered that promise, and she was holding on to it.

"Honey, I promise. You will see the trees clapping their hands. And it will be soon, because God always keeps his promises." "You can bet on that," I assured her.

Her sobbing reached a second crescendo. I lifted her limp, weary body up off the floor and carried her over to the bed. Rocking her back and forth, I held her as she continued to cry.

Gradually, in sheer exhaustion, her sobs turned into soft, intermittent whimpers. Finally, she fell asleep in my arms.

"Oh, Lord, let it be soon," I whispered as I laid her head on the pillow and kissed her damp forehead. "And let it be that she will see the trees clapping their hands, Lord. Somehow, let it be so."

Chapter 33

HIGH-LEVEL TALKS

If God didn't do something to intervene, I knew Lilah and I wouldn't be going home anytime soon. So I began praying that God would make me and Lilah like hot potatoes in the hands of the U.S. Government. I asked him to put the fear of God into those who were handling our situation. I figured if they believed their jobs were threatened and their careers jeopardized for not getting us home safely, they may be more inclined to help us.

From the beginning, I'd been told repeatedly by the FBI, the State Department, and the U.S. Embassy that they couldn't help us get out of Jordan. They clearly understood the way things worked in that country. But what they did not understand was the way things worked in the spiritual realm. And they did not know my God.

It was Thursday, May 23rd. Each hour that came and went brought us closer to getting out of Amman. Every time the minute hand ticked past 12 on the clock, we were ushered into what could potentially be the hour that would bring good news.

The phone at the convent wasn't ringing, so I decided to call William and inquire about possible developments. I was told that no one at the Embassy was available to speak with me. If I couldn't get through to anyone by that afternoon, I would have to wait until Sunday, the beginning of their workweek.

Finally, Sunday came, but again, my efforts were unsuccessful. I did receive a call from Gina, though. She reminded me it was Memorial Day weekend.

"That explains it," I breathed a sigh of relief. "I was beginning to think they were purposely avoiding me."

"Well, they would if they could, but they can't," Gina responded. "God's not going to let that happen." "We're not going to let that happen," she promised.

After talking with Gina, I felt better. But I was still uneasy with the concept of us depending on the U.S. Embassy. So, while Lilah was drawing portraits of all the sisters in the convent, I went to our room to spend time with the one I knew would, and could, do everything we needed him to. And yet another day was in the books.

On Tuesday morning, the phone rang. It wasn't William, though. This time the call came from a man who introduced himself as Ernest Waters. It was a little unsettling to be speaking with someone other than William.

"You can call me Ernie," he said.

Hmm. Why this Ernie guy, all of a sudden?

"Would you and Lilah like to go get a burger or something?" he asked.

"Sure, that would be great." "Thanks," I responded, still skeptical of why he was taking us instead of William.

"Okay. I'll be there to pick you up in an hour from now. I'll be in a black Toyota sedan."

"We'll be ready," I assured him.

Doubts aside, Lilah and I were more than happy to go out and get a burger with this Ernie guy. It wasn't like we had anything else to do. But, for some reason, I had a hard time believing Ernie was the guy's real name. I wasn't sure why.

Lilah, excited to be going somewhere, waited by the window and watched for Ernie. As soon as she saw his vehicle pull into the back parking lot, she scrambled for the door.

"He's here! Ernie is here, Mommy."

"Lilah, don't go out that door by yourself!" I grabbed hold of her arm as she attempted to run past me.

"Let me get this scarf over my hair first." "Then we'll go out together," I instructed her.

Ernie was a tall brunette with a sprinkling of premature white hair at his temples. His eyes were more gray than blue. He wore a black business suit with a white collared dress shirt. I thought he looked a bit overdressed for going to eat burgers. But I could have said the same for myself in my all-consuming black robe and headscarf. I was already hot and regretting that I wore it. Lilah was the only one who looked appropriate in her calf-length blue summer frock and slip-on canvas sneakers. When we got into the back seat, Lilah wasted no time engaging in friendly conversation with the man.

"How long do we get to stay out before we have to go back?" she asked with a genial and optimistic tone.

I patted her hand, indicating that she should sit back and hush up.

"Lilah, get your seat belt on, hun—you got it?" I asked while I slid my hand into the crevice of the seat, feeling for the receiving end of the seat belt.

Once we were buckled in, I inquired, "Are we going to be eating out in public?"

"Yes," he answered. "But there's no need to be concerned about that."

Easy for you to say.

While we were eating, I asked Ernie if anything happened to improve our chances of getting out of Jordan. His response was nothing I hadn't been told before: "Unfortunately, the U. S. Embassy is very limited in what it can do for American women and children in situations such as yours. And since Islamic family law is the law of the land, it must be observed and upheld by the U.S. Embassy."

I already knew all that. What I didn't know was how the Lord would work around it. But I believed that he would, so I continued to hold onto hope and refused to let Ernie's words discourage me. He was simply telling me what they told him to say. I realized that. However, considering that he came to get us and took us to get something to eat, indicated to me that our situation was still under consideration.

After our afternoon outing with Ernie, several days passed with no communication from the Embassy. But I figured, no news was not necessarily bad news. I believed God was busy behind the scenes working things out on our behalf.

One afternoon, Sister Sarah came home with a giant circus coloring book and a box of crayons for Lilah. To experience how the Lord was taking such good care of us amid terrible circumstances warmed my heart. Astonished at his goodness, I felt nothing less than extremely blessed. We were undeniably residing within God's promises. His words were an incredible comfort to me. I would not have survived without them. His promises were all I had to hold onto. But they were all I needed.

> I wait for the Lord, my whole being waits,
> and in his word I put my hope.
> Psalm 130:5 NIV

Later that evening, Lilah and I ate a modest dinner of canned vegetable beef soup over rice. It was within our budget and sufficiently filling. Once I added garlic powder, basil, and a bit of cumin, which I found in the kitchen cabinet, it really wasn't that bad.

After getting Lilah showered and into her bed, I heard the phone ringing in the common area. It was unusual for the abbey to receive a phone call that late. Not wanting the sisters to be disturbed, I quickened my pace and picked up the phone.

"Hello, Mary," I heard a male voice say. "This is Ernie. How are you?"

"I'm fine, thank you," I replied.

"Is there anyone with you right now?" he wasted no time asking.

"No, I've just put Lilah down to sleep, and the sisters have already retired to their rooms for the evening."

"Okay, good," he responded.

I began to speculate why that was good.

"Mary, I want to inform you that there were talks last night concerning your situation."

"Okay..." I said, eager for him to continue.

"Talks at very high levels," he stated flatly.

"Yes," I said, nodding my head in agreement, believing that God was at work on our behalf. I took in a deep breath and waited for him to elaborate.

"You should be ready to go tomorrow morning," he spoke in an authoritative tone.

Did I hear him right?

"Have all your things packed up and ready to go," Ernie instructed. "I'll be there at 7:30 a.m. to get you and Lilah."

Yes, I heard him right!

"Don't tell anyone," he continued. "Don't tell the sisters, don't tell anyone back in the States. Don't even tell Lilah. Just get your things ready."

He spoke in a direct and emphatic manner. His tone conveyed he would offer no further details. I was silent as I processed what was happening.

"Do you understand, Mary?"

Realizing his words were more of an order than a question, I answered appropriately. "Yes. Absolutely. I'll have us both ready to walk out the door by the time you get here."

"Okay, then. I'll see you in the morning. Goodnight." Before I had a chance to reply, he abruptly hung up.

Surrounded by the quiet of the night, I stood there motionless. A soft light from the kitchen filtered into the room, holding the darkness at bay. I squinted my eyes and they adjusted just enough to make out the dimly lit surroundings.

Is this happening? Are we really leaving tomorrow? Yes, we are. Ernie said so. We are definitely leaving, but... where are we going? Are they simply moving us to another place, or are we going home? Will we be safe? They have left us exposed and vulnerable to being caught before. Will this time be any different?

A flashback of William from the Embassy, taking us to ask for permission to leave the country came to mind. I could see the man, snarling at me smugly, and hear him saying, "Let your husband bring you back here tomorrow—then I will give you the permission." Hoping this would not be a repeat of them putting our lives at risk, I returned to the bedroom and fell on my knees before God.

"Oh Lord, please don't let them put our lives at risk," I whispered. "Lord, here we are, a woman and child in a country where we have no rights. We are defenseless without you. Please don't let them place us in a vulnerable and dangerous position. If this is not you, Lord, please don't let it happen! Because if this is man's attempt to get us out, it won't work. The only way this will be successful is if it is your doing. They talk at high levels, but your words, Lord, are far above human words. Your words, and your words alone hold the power to free us and bring us home safely.

"And if it is you making this happen, Lord, please do it according to your promise in Isaiah 52:12. Let it be that we will not leave in fear, running for our lives. Go before us, Lord, and be our rear guard. Show me that this is you. Otherwise, stop this from happening. Because if this is not you, it will fail, and I will end up in jail or dead, and Lilah will be returned to her father." "If this isn't your doing, Lord, shut it down!" I implored. "I do not want to make a move without you."

Satisfied that I had sufficiently placed it in my father's hands, I hurried to get our things together. I didn't know where we were going, but if it was an open door provided by God, I was going to be ready.

> I know your deeds. See, I have placed before you an open door that no one can shut. I know that you have little strength, yet you have kept my word and have
> not denied my name.
> Revelation 3:8 NIV

When morning came, I showered and dressed. I decided against wearing the long robe. But just in case I needed it, I packed it into the old suitcase Sister Sarah had given us when she realized that we had none, just in case I needed it. The common area of the convent was abnormally still that morning.

Usually, I would hear movement coming from various places within the building, but on this morning, it was dead silent.

Perhaps the sisters are at mass, and it's still too early for Sadiq to be working. I suppose that's the reason Ernie chose this time to come get us. He knew everyone would be gone at this hour.

When I considered not being able to properly say goodbye to the sisters, it saddened me. I couldn't even leave a note because I couldn't take the chance that it would be seen prematurely and mess up the entire plan—whatever the plan was.

Once the sisters discovered we had disappeared without a trace, I was sure they would know that God had worked everything out for us. I felt certain they would remember all the candles they lit on our behalf and believe that the U.S. Embassy had taken us safely away.

They would surmise that if the Jordanian PSD had come to take us, we would have left some things behind. If we were taken by force, there would be remnants of breakfast or personal items scattered here and there. But I was careful to pack up all our things and leave the place as immaculate as it was when we arrived. So, I was quite certain the sisters would know we were alright. Still, I deeply regretted not being able to thank them and say goodbye.

Lilah took no notice of my packing and cleaning as she colored in her new coloring book. By 7:00 a.m. I had everything done and ready to go with thirty minutes to spare. I sat with Lilah at the small table where she and Sister Grace had played Go Fish so many times. It was where we would sit in the evenings and enjoy the ice cream that Sister Sarah would occasionally surprise us with. I would never forget them. They would forever hold a special place in my heart.

Chapter 34

THE GOD OF PROMISE

Whispering words only heaven could comprehend, I waited for the clock on the wall to reach 7:30. Then the sound of tires rolling over pebbles in the parking area out back indicated that the time had come to tell Lilah we were leaving.

"Honey, come on. Ernie from the Embassy is here to pick us up. Bring your coloring book and crayons with you."

I remained calm and moved intentionally as I grabbed our packed bag from the bedroom and motioned for Lilah to follow me to the back door.

"Where are we going, Mommy?" Her eyes brightened with expectancy.

"I don't know yet, honey, but everything is going to be okay," I said, reassuring her and myself at the same time.

"Are we coming back to see the sisters, Mommy?"

"I don't think so, Lilah. It will be okay, though. They will know that God is taking care of us." "Maybe we can write to them later," I suggested.

"Okay, Mommy," Lilah said, her voice a little shaky with uncertainty.

As Lilah and I approached the vehicle, I saw that Ernie had arrived in a black SUV. And he wasn't alone. A dark-skinned man wearing black canvas work pants and a form-fitting shirt stood near the back of the vehicle. The small leather case attached to his belt and his tactical boots gave me the impression he could handle any situation that may arise. His presence was both reassuring and unsettling at the same time.

With a neutral expression, he reached out to grab our suitcase as we got closer. I got into the back seat of the vehicle with Lilah. Ernie sat in the passenger seat while the other man got behind the wheel to drive us.

"What kind of chance are we taking here?" I asked as we pulled away from the convent and onto the street.

"Should go like clockwork," Ernie said definitively.

Free of any assumptions, I asked, "Where are we going?"

"We're going to the airport," he answered. "You have a little over an hour before your flight leaves. You're going home."

Hopeful, but not entirely confident, I pressed my lips together. Tears of gratitude welled up in my eyes. I nodded and looked out the window in an attempt to rein in emotions that could render me unsteady.

"Lord, is this you?" I whispered. "Please show me this is you."

> Then Peter called to him, "Lord, if it's really you, tell me to come to you, walking on the water."
> Matthew 14:28 NLT

I was encouraged that Ernie said things should go smoothly, but I still wanted to know for sure that what we were attempting was God's doing. My confidence was in God only. And until I knew for sure it was him, I could not be sure of anything. Everything in my spirit told me we were going home, but it appeared that my physical body hadn't gotten the memo.

Visibly trembling, I crossed my legs and squeezed my hands together, trying to check my nerves.

"Mommy, are we going to America now?" Lilah patted my arm, gently interrupting my thoughts. Her sweet face was full of hope.

Ernie caught my gaze and held it, waiting to hear my response. Before replying to Lilah, I searched Ernie's face for any sign of uncertainty. He nodded, indicating that I should give my daughter an affirmative answer. I mimicked his gesture and nodded as I turned to look at Lilah.

"Yes, Lilah," I said, giving her a hug and sealing it with a kiss on her cheek. "We're going home, sweetheart."

"Yay, Mommy, yaaaay!" "We are going to America!" she cheered.

As we drove along the highway leading into the airport, I noticed tall palm trees on either side of the road. They were leaning over with their crowns pointing toward the airport. I thought perhaps a windstorm had come through and left them in that peculiar position. If I didn't know better, I would have thought they were bowing down to us bid us adieu [goodbye] as we passed by. I took a mental note and filed it in a folder in my mind for future reference. I labeled it: *Signs That God Had His Hand In This.*

We approached the terminal, and I saw two Jordanian PSD Officers standing at the curb alongside yellow road barricades. I tensed up, hoping they were not on the lookout for a brunette American woman with a seven-year-old girl.

When we got close enough for them to recognize our vehicle, to my astonishment, they moved the barriers aside. Our driver slowed down and pulled toward them. They were expecting us! I looked at Ernie for confirmation. Seeing the question in my eyes, he offered another reassuring nod.

Obviously, this is what Ernie meant by "Should go like clockwork." I just never expected the Jordanian PSD—the ones we've been hiding from for the past several weeks—to be involved in the process.

When the vehicle came to a stop, our driver jumped out and approached the officers. I stayed put. Ernie exited the vehicle and came around to my door. He opened it and extended his hand toward me. Still a bit shaky, I clasped his hand firmly and stepped down from the vehicle. Next, I helped Lilah out and held onto her soft hand.

The warm summer air embraced my legs under the long, flowy dress I wore. Sand from the street somehow managed to get into my sandals. I tapped my shoes against the pavement to shake the grains out, but like stowaways insistent on going to another land, they lodged themselves securely between my toes. The feeling of having sand in my shoes would normally drive me crazy, but not on that day. I had Lilah beside me, and we were going home. That's all that mattered.

"Do I go in now to purchase our plane tickets?" I asked, trying to get a grasp on the plan.

"No, no." "You won't go into the ticket area of the terminal at all," Ernie explained.

"But... what about checking our bag?" I asked, a bit confused. Just then, I saw the driver handing our suitcase over to the PSD Officers.

"Your luggage will be checked for you," Ernie replied. "You don't need to do anything. You and Lilah will come with me to wait in a private room until it's time for you to board your flight."

The officers led the way. Ernie motioned for me to follow them into the building while he and his driver walked behind us. I glanced back to confirm that Ernie and the driver were still there. They seemed to be discussing what their itinerary was after leaving the airport. I noticed that their demeanor was businesslike, but relaxed. That was very reassuring to me.

Then it occurred to me what was taking place. It was playing out right before my eyes. God's word was manifesting right then and there. His promise was being fulfilled. He was doing just what I asked him to do, according to his promise in the book of Isaiah!

> You will not leave in a hurry, running for your lives.
> For the Lord will go ahead of you; Yes, the God of
> Israel will protect you from behind.
> Isaiah 52:12 NLT

And not only that, but he lovingly honored my request to give me a sign verifying it was indeed him getting us out of Amman, and not mere humans. Lilah and I were, in no way, leaving in fear or running for our lives. God was going before us. He was leading the way in the form of two Jordanian PSD officers, the ones who I had asked for protection from. They were the ones God was using to escort us out!

I couldn't help but smile as I looked back once again to observe our protection from behind. God was our rear guard by means of Ernie and the driver from the American Embassy, the very organization that claimed they were unable to help us. The Lord was clearly displaying the tangible hedge of protection he provided for Lilah and me. And I saw it play out right before my eyes. It manifested in the physical realm, although I realized it originated by the hand of God.

I knew then, beyond a shadow of doubt, that we were being saved by The Great I Am. To say I was in awe of what God was doing and how he was doing it would be an understatement. I was absolutely elated. My mind was blown away by the magnitude of it.

How amazing this is, Lord!

Above all, I felt grateful—grateful beyond anything human words could begin to express. It was undeniable to me that God, not man, was getting us out of Jordan. And he used friends, strangers, governments, and rulers to get the job done. But it was God who had orchestrated the entire thing. He had moved upon the hearts and minds of men in various positions to do his will on our behalf.

> The King's heart is like a stream of water directed by the Lord; He guides it wherever he pleases.
> Proverbs 21:1 NLT

Ernie caught my joyful expression and paused his conversation long enough to return the smile. He was all business, as usual, but I could see by the glimmer in his eyes that he was happy for us. I sensed that, in some capacity, Ernie must be touched by how things had ultimately come together for Lilah and me. Because, after all, he knew that the U.S. was simply unable to help women and children in situations like ours. I wondered how he was processing it. I wondered if he knew that he had witnessed a mighty move of God, a miracle, a parting of the Red Sea.

Upon entering the terminal, Ernie guided Lilah and me toward an elevator, causing us to part ways with the PSD Officers. We took the elevator to the second floor. Ernie led us into a room which, he explained, was normally reserved for diplomats waiting to board their flights.

The lavish furnishings there reminded me somewhat of my sister-in-law Faisha's home. Across the room on the far wall was a table laid out with scrumptious-looking breakfast items. A glass pitcher of what appeared to be fresh-squeezed orange juice was nestled into a bed of ice inside a hammered silver bowl. An elegant coffee decanter was surrounded by ceramic gold-rimmed mugs bearing the emblem of the Hashemite crown. There was a lovely silver ice bucket stocked with bottles of both Perrier and Evian waters. Bananas, apples, and oranges were displayed on a two-tiered, silver and gold stand. Sesame and coconut macaroon cookies were laid out on a beautiful sterling serving tray.

I lifted the lid on one side of a silver server to find warm falafel. The other side held freshly toasted pita bread. Hummus topped with toasted pine nuts and labneh drizzled with olive oil was graciously provided. A plate of sliced cucumbers and grape tomatoes adorned with sprigs of fresh mint was also part of the spread.

"Help yourselves," Ernie encouraged us. "You still have some time before boarding."

I made Lilah's plate and got her situated at a hand-carved wooden table with a glass overlay. It was positioned underneath a huge crystal chandelier, which hung elegantly from a polished gold medallion.

On the wall behind the table were words written and framed in gold. My Arabic wasn't proficient enough for me to read them. But as far as I was concerned, they may as well have read: You prepare a table for me in the presence of my enemies.

> You prepare a table for me in the presence of my enemies.
> You anoint my head with oil; my cup overflows.
> Psalm 23:5 NLT

Again, further evidence of God's provision.

After filling a plate for myself, I joined Lilah at the table. We engaged happily while enjoying our last meal in the Hashemite Kingdom of Jordan. Meanwhile, Ernie appeared to be going over some work documents on the other side of the room. Once I finished my breakfast, I walked over and sat on an upholstered bench across from him. When I looked up, he was watching me. He wore a warm smile. Then his expression gradually became more serious.

"Mary," he said, then paused for a moment. "I'd like a word with you on a… certain matter."

"Of course, what is it?" I asked.

"We wouldn't want you to tell anyone that the United States was… well… responsible for getting you and your daughter out of Jordan and back to the States. The U.S. Embassy is normally unable to help women—"

"—women who find themselves in a situation like mine," I finished his sentence for him. "I know," I smiled.

And I did know. I was well aware that things didn't normally turn out the way they had for us. Not in that part of the world, anyway. Exactly what my Heavenly Father had done behind the scenes to make it happen, I couldn't say. And I probably would never know. But nonetheless, he had done it. He had made it happen. That I was confident in. That I was sure of.

"It's just that," Ernie continued, "the U.S. asks that you not tell anyone that we were responsible for getting you and Lilah out of Jordan. We wouldn't want other women to think that the

U.S. Embassy can help in this way. That would be misleading. Do you understand?"

"Oh yes, definitely. I understand completely," I reiterated. "You have nothing to worry about, Ernie, because when people ask me how my daughter and I got out of the Middle East, I will tell them it was the Lord who did it." "Because it was, Ernie," I insisted. "It was the Lord who did it." "And if you ever discuss with anyone how Lilah and I got out of here, I would appreciate it if you," I said, pointing at him, "would tell them just that—that it was God who got us out."

His eyes widened slightly, enough to reveal that he hadn't expected me to say that. While I had his attention, I leaned forward and looked intently into his eyes.

"Because Ernie," I continued, "with man this would be impossible, but with God all things are possible."

He said nothing, but looked directly into my eyes. His expression was mindful and intent, as if contemplating whether my explanation of how this went down was even plausible. Then, leaning back in his chair, he looked over toward Lilah. He appeared to be working things out in his mind. He returned his gaze toward me. He wrinkled his brow in thought and squinted slightly. I wasn't sure if he was questioning my sanity or whether a higher power could have actually had a hand in this.

My expression brightened into a smile as if to say: "Yes, it's true. It's all true!"

Ernie's face softened in response. He returned the smile. I exhaled and repositioned myself, casually crossing my legs and extending them out in front of me. I felt totally relaxed, even peaceful.

Finally, Ernie broke his silence. "If you would like to use the facilities, this would probably be a good time," he suggested.

Taking his advice, I took Lilah into the attached restroom. Just after we walked back out into the room, someone knocked at the door. Ernie opened the door and instructed Lilah and me to follow him. A young man dressed in an employee uniform led us down the corridor. Through the glassed half wall, I could see the ticketing area down below. It was filled with travelers waiting in line to check in. I was so glad Lilah and I were not among them.

Lilah looked up at me and said, "Mommy, are we going to America now?"

"Yes, honey, we are. We're going home now."

As I smiled down at her, I couldn't help but get choked up. I had prayed so hard and waited so long for that moment. Lilah began skipping and pulled me ahead with her as she went. We came to a stop when we reached a flight attendant who appeared to be waiting for us.

Ernie turned and handed me two Royal Jordanian Airlines tickets. My eyes widened in surprise when I saw them. I looked up at the woman standing there and saw the Royal Jordanian tag on her uniform.

I don't know what I was expecting—another airline, surely. Air France, perhaps. Anything but Royal Jordanian Airlines. It made sense, though. Ernie said there had been talks at very high levels. So that meant the Jordanian government had granted us permission to leave the country. Without their consent, we would not be leaving. After all, it was the Jordanian PSD Officers who met us at the airport, took our bag, and escorted us inside.

"Wow," I said to Ernie. "I didn't expect to fly out of here on Royal Jordanian Airlines. It's all just... so incredible!"

"Yes, it is," he smiled and nodded.

"Thank you so much," I said, extending my hand and gripping his firmly.

"Thank you, Ernie," said Lilah, jumping in for a hug.

Ernie startled, then leaned forward to give her a quick embrace. "Best of luck to you both," Ernie said with a final goodbye.

"Thank you again." "Goodbye," I offered a final wave. Then I turned toward the flight attendant and indicated that we were now ready to go.

"How long before we take off?" I asked as we continued down the private hallway toward the gate.

"We will leave right away," she responded in a beautiful Middle Eastern accent. "The other passengers are already seated. You and your daughter are the last to board."

"Oh, really?" "I didn't realize," I said, trying to wrap my mind around it.

"Right this way," she said as she walked us to our seats near the front of the aircraft. "Let us know if there is anything we can do to make your flight more comfortable." "Please notify us if you need anything at all," she said warmly.

"Oh, thank you." "Thank you so much," I smiled.

"Yes, of course," she responded before withdrawing to the utility area of the plane.

"Lilah, look at this," I whispered excitedly in her ear. "God is not only taking us home, but we are getting treated like we are in first class!"

"That's nice, right, Mommy?" Lilah asked, not entirely sure what first class meant.

"Yes, sweetheart," I laughed, not quite sure myself what it meant.

Chapter 35

THE TREES OF THE FIELD

At last, we were airborne. For a brief moment, I looked out of the window to watch the barren landscape fall away behind us. Then I turned back toward Lilah, who sat comfortably in the seat beside me. Once I was sure I had her attention, I pursed my lips over to one side, crossed my eyes together and made a silly face. She reciprocated with her own version of goofy.

Before long, we settled into a higher altitude, which allowed us to unfasten our seat belts. A flight attendant asked if we would like some fresh fruit or something to drink. Elegant inen napkins were provided with our drinks.

Afterwards, I reclined our chairs and raised the armrest so that our seats were no longer separated. Lilah stretched out sideways and laid her head on my lap. I grasped her hand in mine. She nodded off occasionally, which helped break up the nine-hour flight to Shannon, Ireland. We would deplane there, go through immigration, then reboard and continue on to JFK International Airport in New York City.

After being processed through immigration in Shannon, we were directed to wait inside the terminal near our gate. The walls there were made of glass and offered a fabulous view of the trees outside. Everything was green just beyond the runways. It seemed lush compared to the arid landscape of the Middle East.

I became lost in thought, remembering the last time I was in Ireland. It was October 2001, right after 9/11. I was on my way back to the U.S. then, without my daughter.

"Mommy, Mommy, look!" Lilah began yelling excitedly and pulling on my arm. "Look over there!" she pointed toward the trees outside.

The wind was gusting strongly, blowing the trees around. But as far as I could see, the day was sunny and fair. There didn't seem to be a storm brewing. Nevertheless, the wind was blowing quite hard.

"I see, Lilah. There seems to be some kind of windstorm in Ireland today."

"But, Mommy," she persisted, "don't you see that?" "Don't you see that, Mommy?" she asked, hardly able to compose herself.

"See what, honey?"

"Mommy, look at the trees! The trees are clapping their hands! Just like God promised. Just like the song, Mommy." "The trees are clapping their hands!" she exclaimed loud enough to cause others to turn and look at us.

Sure enough, gusts of wind were blowing from opposite directions, thrashing against the tree limbs from both sides simultaneously. This caused the evergreen branches to slap against each other as if they were clapping their hands. I'd never seen anything like it.

Had Lilah not pointed it out to me, I may not have noticed. I watched the miraculous occurrence in amazement. Then I looked around to see if anyone else saw what we were seeing. But the other travelers were too preoccupied with their own affairs to take notice. I looked back at Lilah, who still had her mouth open in amazement.

"Yes, honey, just like God promised," I agreed. "Just like the song, Lilah. The trees are clapping their hands for us. See how God keeps his promises?"

She smiled and wrapped her arms around my waist. I held onto her tightly while we continued to watch the performance of the trees. Tears flowed down my cheeks as I considered God's faithfulness to my little girl. Gradually, the wind died down to a gentle breeze.

"Wow, that was really something, wasn't it?" I said to Lilah, clutching her even closer to me.

Her eyes were still wild from the excitement of it all. She didn't say anything but just nodded her head in agreement. It was clear to both Lilah and me that God's divine handprint was all over getting us out of Jordan. It simply would not have happened without him.

Soon we reboarded and settled in for the next leg of our journey. It would take us a little more than six hours to reach New York. I handed Lilah the brochure that was tucked into the back pocket of the seat in front of me. She didn't find it very interesting, so before long she fell asleep again. The hum of the plane's engines began to gradually lull me to sleep as well. Just when I began to drift off, the flight attendant announced our approach to JFK.

We were the last to deplane because I was having a difficult time getting Lilah to wake up. As we exited the aircraft, two airport security personnel were standing there waiting for us.

"Are you Mary Kennedy?" asked one of the officers.

"Yes, I am," I answered, happy to hear myself addressed by my family name. It was like getting a welcome home gift.

"We've been told to stay with you until you board your next flight to Prominence," he informed us.

"Oh, wow," I said with a shocked expression.

I hadn't expected to be escorted, but the blessings continued. It was comforting to have them with us as we maneuvered through the terminal. When we stopped to go into the bathroom, the security officers waited patiently. They also stood nearby as we ate at the small pizzeria close to our gate.

"Ta' alee hona [Come here]," I said to Lilah as I patted the seat beside me.

"No, Mother," Lilah responded and placed her soda on the table.

I looked over at her, surprised that she had called me Mother instead of Mommy.

With her head slightly tilted and a serious expression on her face, she locked eyes with me as if she were the adult giving instructions to a child.

"No more Arabic," she said, while expertly rolling her r's. "We are in America now. We must speak English."

I did my best not to laugh, then regained my composure.

"But I'm afraid you will lose your Arabic, Lilah. I don't want you to forget it."

"I will not forget it, Mother," she assured me while shaking her head.

I shrugged and said, "Okay, then." "If you're sure you won't forget."

She didn't say anything but continued to give me a stern look. I made a funny face and took a bite of mushroom pizza. Lilah laughed and began eating. Within ten minutes, she had consumed her entire slice.

After finishing our first meal together in America for over two years, we made one last stop at the restroom. I wet a paper towel and scrubbed the red sauce from around Lilah's mouth.

"You don't want to show up in Prominence with pizza sauce all over your face, do you?" I teased her.

"Puh." "Nooo," she laughed.

We began the short walk to our gate. Airport security stayed with us until we boarded. We turned around and gave them a final goodbye wave as we entered the corridor.

"Thanks," I said to them.

"Thank you, please," Lilah said to them.

"Thank you, *please?*" I looked at her using the same head-slant expression she had used on me back at the pizza place.

"I mean… thank you!" "Thank you, very, very much!" she said, then looked at me for confirmation.

I nodded and smiled.

Chapter 36

WHO IS THIS COMING UP FROM THE WILDERNESS?

Our flight to Prominence was on a much smaller aircraft than the one that brought us out of the Middle East. I could feel the turbulence as we passed through the outskirts of a summer storm, but it didn't bother me one bit. I knew God had us. We were just minutes away from our 11:00 p.m. arrival time.

Oh wait. What time is it?

I let my head fall back and closed my eyes while I did the math. It was actually 6:00 a.m. for us since Amman was seven hours ahead. I looked down at Lilah.

This prize of mine... this very precious cargo beside me.

She slept soundly with her head on my lap. The dim cabin lights created soft reflections of gold on her silky brown hair. A few moments more and we would be told to put our seats in the upright position and prepare for landing. The enormity of what God had done, combined with being sleep deprived, had me wondering if this was all a dream. I brushed my hand over Lilah's warm arm for confirmation, then closed my eyes again. God had truly done an amazing thing, and we witnessed it.

Memories of the last two years moved through my tired mind like vaporous ribbons of ever-changing color, shape, and sound. All the prayers and petitions, the heartbreak and tears, the promises and declarations, came forward one by one. They delivered their sentiments into my consciousness. Then, like a mist, they dispersed and evaporated only to reassemble into the following presentation. I was exhausted, but my mind refused to stop.

There is just so much to consider... so much to comprehend.

In my weariness, my mind continued to drift.

"Believe God for something so big that it won't happen unless it's God who does it!" I could hear Pastor Carlos saying.

And I thought of Gina, who sacrificed hours of her life, encouraging me, working behind the scenes, managing things stateside, contacting government officials, speaking with the international attorney—all the time and effort she had given on our behalf.

And then, Janis' voice, encouraging my family: "You have to believe that God will bring them back."

Janis never stopped praying for us. She was unwavering and resolute in her declaration of God's faithfulness. An entire community of believers continuously prayed for Lilah and me. Some of them didn't even know us, but they prayed and believed that God could bring us home. I couldn't wait for everyone in Nahaven to hear the good news that we made it back.

Gina's voice broke in again: "Breanna prays for Lilah to come home every night. And sometimes during the day she breaks down and cries, asking, 'When is God going to bring Lilah home?'"

Yes... the prayers of a child. They reach your ears, Lord.

Words that had been preached from the pulpit at my small church echoed in my head: "God loves us. He is true to his word; he is true to his promises. And he is able to do what he says he will do!"

Tears streamed down my face as I realized there were no human words to express my gratitude to him who did all this for my child and me.

What kind of God is this?

My mind was so tired. My face felt numb and tingly from lack of sleep. Still, I continued to consider these marvelous thoughts of how much God loves us.

> Feeling totally enveloped in his love, I considered how God has compassion on everyone he made. It's simply who he is. This realization made my heart skip as I attempted to grasp the fullness of it.

> The Lord is good to everyone. He showers
> compassion on all his creation.
> Psalm 145:9 NLT

Your promises are for everyone, Lord—for everyone who will believe. How amazing you are, God. How incredible!

I couldn't hold my thoughts together anymore, but I was too excited to fall asleep completely.

"Lord, help me find the words to thank you." "Help me find a way to express how wonderful you are," I prayed softly.

"Ma'am, we're preparing to land," the flight attendant said, tapping me on the shoulder.

"Oh, okay," I said, shaking myself out of the half-sleep I was in.

"Lilah, honey," I said, brushing my hand lightly over her face, "wake up." "We're getting ready to land. Let's get your seat up and your seat belt fastened, sweetheart."

"Okay, Mommy. Are we there?" "Are we home?" she asked sleepily.

"We will be in just a few minutes," I smiled.

Hearing that, she began to rally. She repositioned herself and sat tall in her seat. Then she looked up at me with a somewhat sleepy, yet excited, expression.

Once we exited the plane, Lilah and I walked hand in hand through the corridor inside the terminal at Prominence Airport. I wondered who would be there to meet us. It was pretty late, but I was fairly certain Gina would make the two-hour drive from Nahaven.

As we rounded the corner leading into the terminal, I could hear a commotion in the distance. I began to tear up, realizing there was no mistaking the undeniable ruckus of many Kennedy voices.

That has to be my family making all that noise!

The corridor opened up into a room full of welcome-home balloons and small handheld American flags.

"There they are—they're here!" my niece Heather cried out.

And just like that, we were surrounded. All my family had come to greet us, along with Gina, Breanna, and even Janis. There were tears, hugs, kisses, and laughter. But mostly, there was joy.

When we were leaving the airport that night, I climbed into Gina's SUV. Lilah and Breanna chattered happily in the back seat.

After buckling my seat belt, I looked at Gina and said, "Right now, at this moment, I just might have faith the size of a mustard seed."

> "Truly I tell you, if you have faith the size of a mustard seed, you can say to this mountain, 'Move from here to there,' and it will move. Nothing will be impossible for you."
> Matthew 17:20 NIV

Gina's blue eyes welled up with tears. She nodded and smiled but said nothing. We were both grateful. Grateful beyond words. Then Gina put the car in gear and pulled out onto the highway.

≈≈≈

That was early June, more than 20 years ago—a warm, happy summer of sunshine and celebrations. For Lilah, it was a season filled with things like swimming lessons from Janis and becoming acquainted with a dog named Gubby. On the drive to Disney with Gina and Breanna, we sang "Sk8er Boi" over and over until we all knew the words by heart.

Golden images are forever embedded in my memory of the Father's Day family gathering at my dad's house and Lilah's first-ever bike ride outside the school she would attend in the fall—no training wheels required.

I can still see Pastor Carlos' wife, Stacy, doing a double take when she saw Lilah and me pull up in our Altima for Sunday church service. She quickly put down the things she carried in her hands and ran to embrace the little girl she never met—the one she'd been praying for.

Many lives were deeply impacted by our story. Many had cried, and hoped, and prayed for Lilah and me. And when we returned, they rejoiced and marveled at everything God had done.

It is my prayer that many more will be touched by our story. My hope is that countless others will be inspired by what God did for us—by how he showed up. Because what we may see as a hopeless situation, God sees as an opportunity to show his love for us.

Final thoughts and prayers, some of which are drawn from Romans 15:13 NLT and Ephesians 3:17-20 TLB

I pray that God, the source of hope, will fill you completely with joy and peace because you trust in him. Then you will overflow with confident hope through the power of the Holy Spirit.

And I pray that Christ will be more and more at home in your heart as you trust in him. May your roots go down deep into the soil of God's marvelous love. And may you have the power to understand, as all God's people should, how wide, how long, how high, and how deep his love really is. May you experience the love of Christ, though it is so great you will never fully understand it. Then you will be filled with the fullness of life and power that comes from God.

Now glory be to God, who by his mighty power at work within us is able to do far more than we would ever dare to ask or even dream of—infinitely beyond our highest prayers, desires, thoughts, or hopes.

For when we put our hope in him,
we are truly **NEVER LOST**.

www.ingramcontent.com/pod-product-compliance
Ingram Content Group UK Ltd.
Pitfield, Milton Keynes, MK11 3LW, UK
UKHW041952230426
12048UKWH00008B/287